Bound to You
NICHI HODGSON

Nichi is 28, a journalist and lives in London.

NICHI HODGSON

Bound to You

and you and you

HODDER

First published in Great Britain in 2012 by Hodder & Stoughton
An Hachette UK company

I

A CIP catalogue record for this title is available from the British Library

Paperback ISBN 978 1 444 76327 0
Ebook ISBN 978 1 444 76328 7

Typeset by Palimpsest Book Production Ltd, Falkirk, Stirlingshire

Printed and bound in Great Britain by Clays Ltd, St Ives plc

Hodder & Stoughton policy is to use papers that are natural, renewable
and recyclable products and made from wood grown in sustainable forests.
The logging and manufacturing processes are expected to conform
to the environmental regulations of the country of origin.

Hodder & Stoughton Ltd
338 Euston Road
London NW1 3BH

www.hodder.co.uk

'Freedom is what you do with what's been done to you.'
Jean Paul Sartre

Chapter 1

The door slammed behind me. I stepped up on to the pavement, my white dress shining like a lost cloud caught out after dark. In the cool night air, the clarity of mind that had eluded me all day suddenly reappeared. Where could you get a taxi from round here at 3 a.m. on a Monday morning?

I walked up the road towards the train station. My zebra-print heels were as inflexible as pokers and, after the long walk across London, felt as though they were branding the tops of my toes. My phone battery was practically dead and I hoped to God there was a taxi rank at the top of this hill. For the first time that day, somebody answered my prayers.

As the car pulled away from Sebastian's road, the screen on my exhausted phone flashed up. 'I'm sorry I've hurt you. I hope at some point we can talk.' I thought of him lying there in the bed, his cobalt-blue eyes glazed over. He was paralysed, unable to do or say anything that might in any way compensate for showing me what the world looked like when you didn't have a heart. He hadn't even bothered to come after me. That's how little he cared, how inexorable all this was to him.

And then I remembered. In my haste to escape that awful conversation I had left my make-up bag in his bathroom. I couldn't manage without make-up any more, the way I'd begun to feel. I had to get it back. 'Send it to my office. Do it immediately.'

'Of course,' came the reply.

As the car wound its way down to south London, a series of tableaux played out through my mind. Sebastian smiling at me on the corner of Oxford Street, his dimples radiating out of the geometric perfection of his face. Sebastian clutching me to him in an unyielding embrace. Sebastian, naked, his muscular beauty slapping my senses to attention. Sebastian calling me Nichi *mou*. Sebastian pinning me down and pulling me by the hair until my head spun. Sebastian giving me the headiest orgasm of my life.

But Sebastian was an emotional leper. If only I could put a bell round his neck to warn womankind away from him. If only I could undo the ties that bound me to him.

Chapter 2

'*Ela*, Nichi *mou!*'

That's effectively Greek for, 'Honey, I'm home!', and meant that Christos was back. His footfalls echoed up the staircase to our flat, the flat we had recently moved in to together in an unfashionable part of west London. Then there was a light thud and I heard him pause as he reached the door. It sounded as though he was carrying something cumbersome.

'Do you want a hand?' I called to him from our large room, which doubled up as living quarters and boudoir.

'Wait a minute . . . wait!' I could hear the grin in his voice. 'Don't come out!'

I smiled to myself. Usually, 'don't come out' meant that Christos had a present for me. Ever since we first got together at university he had regularly brought me gifts. It could be anything from a picture of a miniature sausage dog (I have a minor obsession with sausage dogs) ripped out of the newspaper, to the *Shorter Oxford Dictionary* in two volumes, to a pair of shoes I had been lusting after but couldn't afford on my media intern's budget. One of the first things he ever gave me was a white lace skirt with a fuchsia underlay. I remember being unsure about it. It seemed almost too stylish and I was unconvinced that it would suit me, much less that it was my size, but it fitted perfectly. 'Is this man for real?' I remember thinking, before kissing him in admiration. 'Beware of Greeks bearing gifts,' he had intoned theatrically. He loved to play up to the idea of the ancient hero.

The truth of the matter was that Christos was pretty

mythical. We met in the kitchen of our final-year university accommodation when we were just twenty years old. He was such a cliché of handsome Mediterranean man that I remember trying to mentally resist him as a matter of principle. He wore blue jeans, and a tight white T-shirt that highlighted his biceps and bronzed skin to ambrosial perfection. He was the model you would actually have lusted over had he featured on one of those tacky 'Love from Greece' postcards. I was so captivated by his chiselled face, dimpled chin and his dark pooling eyes that I let him stand there, hand held out in greeting, for what felt like hours, before I managed to shake it. 'I'm Christos,' he offered, in his inimitable accent, and beamed at me.

If I'd doubted that love at first sight was possible, partnering up with him at the Latin dance class a week later persuaded me otherwise. My skin sang when he brushed against me, and by the time he had carried me over a puddle on a midnight walk a week or two afterwards, I had no doubt whatsoever that this was the man I always wanted to love.

Now the door flung open. Christos heaved a bright white table with folding legs and two plastic chairs into the room. We'd been eating dinner on our laps for the past fortnight, in what was effectively a glorified studio apartment, complete with a mattress you could fold away and a humming fridge.

'Where did you get those from?'

'Heh!' He puffed himself up, stood legs apart, hands on hips, and pulled an imperious face. 'Us Greeks have ways!' he boasted, then paused for a second. 'Ikea.'

I hated moving house, loathed decorating and DIY, but Christos made homemaking a pleasure. Since we'd moved in, he had done his utmost to transform the appallingly decorated chintzy room into a vaguely acceptable twenty-first-century living space. Now we had rugs and a brightly coloured polka-dot duvet, and an electric-blue painting of a souk at midnight, which we had acquired on a trip we had made to Morocco just before my finals.

I went over to kiss him. He wrapped his arms about me and squeezed me until I squealed in satisfaction. Then he took the table and chairs and arranged them by the bay window.

'There!' He elongated the e, as I did. He loved to mimic my Yorkshire accent.

'Are you hungry then? Shall we have the left-over *melitzanes* for dinner?' I asked, trying out one of the new chairs.

'Yes. But first I must clean that table. And find some mats,' Christos said, and disappeared off to fetch a cloth. Like many Mediterraneans, he was exceptionally house-proud. Unlike many Mediterranean men, he was also prepared to do the cleaning himself. He attributed this in part to his no-nonsense mother making him chip in with the household chores as a child, but also to his abortive time spent in the Greek army, 'where we mainly polished our guns, and sat around under fig trees, eating.' The truth of the matter was that Christos had been a unit commander and was skilled in close mortal combat. Only his physical strength gave him away as having been a fighter. Otherwise, he was as gentle as he was genial. But his soldierly skills came in handy when you wanted him to win you a soft toy from the rifle range at the fairground. Or take your weight as you wrapped your legs around him and had sex against a wall.

'So I heard from the university,' he called from the kitchen. 'Looks like I can start my PhD in the autumn.'

'Bravo, Christos *mou*!' I called back.

While my studying was over, Christos's had hardly begun; he now needed an engineering PhD to ensure he could compete at the highest level in his chosen profession. As much as part of me would have liked to begin a PhD myself, in something as arcane as Petrarchan love poetry or gender studies, my career trajectory in the media simply depended on me being able to make decent coffee and begging editors to give me a break. But I was looking forward to supporting him as he had me. I would never have got a First without Christos's endless encouragement in that final year of my degree; not without his humour, not without his cooking a delicious dinner for me during an essay break. But mostly, not without being able to have passionate sex with him every night, sex which always ended in simultaneous orgasm and *S'agapo*s (I love yous). Afterwards we would fall asleep wrapped up like a couple of gratified cats and I would marvel at my ridiculous luck in having met him.

Christos came back into the room carrying a cloth in one hand, plates and cutlery in the other. He was grimacing. 'Yeah, I'm so bored with studying but diamond rings don't come cheap now, do they?'

I shook my head and started to laugh. Christos had been teasing me about marriage and children ever since I'd told him at university that I thought they were a means of patriarchal control. I'd relaxed my radical feminist rules a little since then but I was still pretty sure that marriage and a family weren't really for me. Truth was that I'd never met a more respectful, equality-minded man, but he still loved to rile me by pretending that he was a domineering male who planned to keep me captive, unable to work or read or socialise with the outside world, 'where your only duty is to serve me! Me, your *Kyrios* (master).' He would teasingly push me to the bed and make what he called gorilla fists before grunting in my face. And then I would usually grab a fistful of black curls at the nape of his neck and pull him into a long, deep kiss to stop him monkeying around.

'No diamonds today, thank you!'

'Oh Nichi, when are you going to accept your destiny as my wife and mother to my children?'

'When someone gives me a proper, paying journalism job, perhaps.'

I was happy about Christos's PhD news but it also reminded me how anxious I was about my own professional situation.

'Look, it's going to happen, Nichi *mou*. You're just starting out. Patience, my eager Egg. Now, would the Golden Egg like salad and some rice with those *melitzanes*?' He hovered a serving spoon above my plate the way his grandmother used to do.

'Egg' was another of Christos's affectionate nicknames for me, meant to quell my anxiety about having a round face, a face I had once starved into a brace of angles when I was anorexic as a teenager. Food was central to Greek culture, and the mealtimes I had once dreaded had become a happy daily ritual with Christos. He had shown infinite patience and sensitivity when we first met but at times I still struggled to eat without fear.

'*Ne, efharisto.*' I nodded. He fondled my cheek.

I tried to use Greek with Christos whenever I could. I had wanted to learn it from the moment we met. I loved language, how the words at our disposal shaped not just what we said, but how we thought about the world in the first place. How could I not want to learn Greek, when it promised to mesh me even more tightly with this incredible man? Outside of the flat we mainly spoke it on the tube so we could gossip about people. Or I would use it to talk dirty at him in otherwise inappropriate locations: on the phone during lunchtimes at work, in the Persian carpet room of the Victoria and Albert museum. Standing in the checkout queue in Sainsburys.

'So you haven't forgotten about the wedding this weekend, have you?' I asked him as we ate.

Mouth full, he shook his head.

'Rachel texted me again today. She wanted to know what I was going to wear. I haven't even thought about it.'

'I'll tell you what you're going to wear!' Christos affected his 'Master' voice. 'That dress you wore to my graduation dinner. The cream netted one with the red flowers, the prom dress, silk, shows off your . . . assets.' He said assets in a filthy whisper and added a dirty 'Hehheh.' Christos loved to play at being what he called 'a sleazy Greek'.

I laughed again. 'And what about you? Will you wear that

very expensive, impulse-purchased designer shirt that you only wore ONCE to the charity ball, Christos?'

'No,' he replied. 'I'll ask my sister to send me a new one.'

'But you look like a Jean Paul Gaultier model in that shirt! Please wear it,' I pleaded.

'Ha! You mean I look like a gay underwear model and I'll get hit on by loads of men and you will find it hilarious again!'

'Well, it's not your fault you're so good-looking gay guys fancy you. If society only valued heterosexual male beauty as much as it did female, it wouldn't be a problem. Anyway,' I smirked, 'you mean I'll get off on it again.'

'Nichi!' he growled, pretending to chastise me for being what he would call crude. 'Look, I don't worry about gay men hitting on me; it's a compliment! Besides, I'm getting so old. Soon we are going to be withered and toothless and saggy and hairy and no one will fancy us, Nichi *mou*.'

'I will always fancy you,' I said softly. 'Unless you carry on doing that weird scrunchy thing you do with your feet when you think the floor is dirty.'

'But Nichi *mou*,' he replied in a grave voice, 'if I stop doing that then I will probably die of a terrible disease long before I become withered.'

'Yeah, or hypochondria!'

'It's a Greek word, you know, hypochondria!' he said, triumphantly.

'Yes, Christos, I know,' I said, rolling my eyes.

'And if I stop doing that thing with my feet, my penis will rot off, just to spite you, because you didn't believe me!'

I shook my head and laughed in spite of myself. These ridiculous conversations. Christos had an almost pathological obsession with his own decay.

'Ah!! You don't have an answer to that one, do you! Do you, Nichi *mou*, you want me to KEEP my penis!'

'I want you to shut up talking about your penis and plan this wedding trip with me, please!'

'Feisty. I like you feisty.'

Still laughing, I pressed on. 'So I don't think we need to stay over. Rachel says we can drive back to London that evening. Only that means you can't drink.'

'Oh, I don't care about that.'

'Well, it should be the other way round really, since I don't even like drinking that much.'

'Ha! No, Nichi *mou*, I'm going to get you drunk so I can take advantage of you.'

'Like at your graduation dinner, you mean?'

Christos and I had a habit of slipping off to have sex in the toilets on formal occasions. Usually just before dessert was served. When I mentioned one of these episodes to my friend Gina, she asked me how I managed not to ruin my dress. 'By taking it off. There's usually a peg you can hang it on, somewhere.' I was never sure who instigated this cocktail cottaging, as I called it. We just always seemed to know instinctively when the other was up for it.

'You exploited me that time. You told me I reminded you of the Turkish Delight Man.'

The Turkish Delight Man was a tanned, turbaned nomad who featured in a TV advert I had been utterly obsessed with as a child. He trekked through the desert to bring a tearful princess Turkish Delight to mend her broken heart, before slicing it in front of her with his scimitar. Even at the age of four I suspected the scimitar was meant to represent something else.

'Well, you do remind me of the Turkish Delight Man, Christos *mou*! And any other number of delicious exotic poster boys!'

I'd always been a shameful exoticist. In contrast to my own light-skinned, light-eyed, blonde colouring, I loved dark-haired, olive-skinned men. And when I met Christos it was impossible to admire anyone else.

'Nichi, it's ridiculous that you remember that advert, nearly as ridiculous as you being mesmerised by David Bowie's crotch in *Labyrinth*.'

'But EVERY girl of my generation was obsessed with That Crotch, Christos, you have to understand. And at the end when King Jareth offers himself up as Sarah's slave. Why does she refuse him?'

'Because she knows what's sexy. And it's not that! I'll never understand David Bowie. It's where our cultures clash.'

I laughed. It had always been a source of amazement for both of us that, in fact, we hadn't experienced any real culture clash. We had grown up in such different worlds, and yet it never caused a problem.

I was born and brought up in Wakefield, a former mining town in West Yorkshire that before its brief coal-driven heyday, had last been truly significant during the Wars of the Roses. Still, I was happy growing up there with my younger brother and our various pets, running my parents ragged as they ferried me to my endless dancing and gymnastics classes, Brownies then Guides, and brass band practice, constantly in need of stimulation and a stage on which to perform.

My parents divorced when I was nine and after the usual bout of awkwardness, they were genial enough to attend all our various birthdays or school plays or parents' evenings together. With my dad only ten minutes up the road, life soon settled down into cheerful suburban normality again.

At eleven, I went to a prim, studious girls' school where, when not concerned with getting in to dinner on the first sitting or endlessly redecorating my hymn book, I was mostly obsessed with becoming a Shakespearean actress, and ploughed all my extra-curricular energies into school plays and musical ensembles. Later, I was ferociously independent and hadn't lived at home since I was eighteen years old and went off to university. I felt close to both my parents and Alistair, my brother, but now that my mum lived in Australia, although we spoke often on the phone, meeting up was a once-a-year event.

Despite being based for the most part in Athens, Christos's family were more present in his daily life than mine were. They knew what friends he saw, where we went at weekends, and always what we had for dinner. But I appreciated their involvement for what it was – absolute care. They had welcomed me into their fold, more formally than warmly at first, but they always asked after me. I knew they were touched that I had made the attempt to learn Greek. I would be visiting them for the third time at the end of the summer, just before Christos began his PhD. I was already looking forward to it.

As if on cue, Christos's mother called.

'*Gia sou*, Mama!'

I cleared the plates away and went into our shabby kitchen as they chatted about Christos's day. The more Greek I knew, the more invasive it seemed to listen to their conversations. But I couldn't fail to hear '*Melitzanes*, Mama!', which made me smile.

I noticed that Christos had tried to prettify the windowsill with a pot plant he knew would die at my hands within the next few weeks. He had also bought me a pink elephant watering can as an encouragement to care for it.

Suddenly Christos's voice broke into my thoughts. Was he arguing with his mother? I paused, holding the knife I had been drying, and tried to decode the frantic Greek. I could pick out the odd thing. References to the garage. Work. Helping your father. Christos had spent most of his childhood and teenage years helping with his father's garage. All that tinkering with filthy engines was part of the reason he'd decided to study engineering. I carried on filling up the cutlery drawer. Soon, he said goodbye to her and I wandered back into the room.

'What was all that about?'

'Just Mama being Mama,' he shrugged, smiling, and cracked his shoulders. 'OK, I'm going to take a shower. How am I still wearing these clothes?'

Christos was interning at a shipping company before he

went back to studying, and was dressed in office smarts, white shirt, charcoal trousers. There was little he looked better in. He started to unbutton the shirt. Underneath was a white T-shirt. I'd never figured out why he needed that too.

'It would be shameful not to wear a T-shirt underneath!'

'What, because we could see your nipples?'

'Nichi!' That chastising growl again. 'No, because it would bring shame on my family. Are you going to have a shower with me too, Nichi *mou*?' he asked, advancing to where I stood watching him undress, and sliding his hands over my hips. He pretended to be sleazy again.

'No, I already had one before you came home.' I replied. 'But I might take all my clothes off and get into bed and wait for you.'

Quickly, coyly, I pulled off my jersey dress.

'Yes. That is how I like my woman!'

I rolled my eyes at him once again, and kneeling on the bed in my diaphanous blue underwear, underwear that Christos had bought me, I reached up to plump the pillows. Suddenly, something struck me across my backside.

'Hey! What's going on?' I cried, startled, clutching my stinging right cheek.

Christos stood there in his candy-striped boxers, brandishing the black leather belt. He was laughing uncontrollably. 'Sorry Nichi *mou*, sorry, I guess I just whipped it off too quickly.' He had accidentally caught me with the tail end of it as he pulled it out of the loop on his trousers.

'Well, do you want to watch what you're whipping next time, please!'

'Ha ha. I WHIPPED you. Hilarious!'

When Christos came back he had a question for me. 'So, Nichi, what do you think about people that like being whipped?'

'Doesn't do it for me,' I replied. 'And I suppose you have to wonder why people enjoy it in the first place. Especially women.'

'I don't trust it either,' Christos agreed. 'But what do you think, is it a kind of self-harm for women, Nichi *mou*?'

'Probably,' I said. 'There's just something about that makes me feel uncomfortable. And anyway, why would you need it if you were having perfectly hot sex in the first place?'

'Exactly!' Christos grinned and pulled me into him.

Early the next morning Christos's phone rang. 'Mama!' he murmured, barely forming the word with his lips. As she spoke and he listened, I watched his forehead solidify into creases, until he looked like a pained classical statue.

'What's wrong?'

'I've really got to go help at the garage this weekend. I'll just fly over on Friday evening after work and come back Monday morning.'

I felt a prickle of annoyance. It was already Wednesday. 'Isn't it a bit of a long way to go just for the weekend? Are they that desperate?' Christos's parents worked so hard and I knew that they struggled without him, but something about this summoning of him, and his readiness to go, set a faint alarm bell ringing.

'They need me, Nichi *mou*. it's not like it happens all the time.' He pulled me to him and stroked my cheek. 'I'll miss you, Golden Egg, but you'll be all right. It'll only be a couple of nights.'

"OK, well, if they need you," I sighed.

"But it means I can't go to the wedding, Nichi *mou*."

Oh. The wedding.

Chapter 3

Later that day, following Christos's announcement, I decided that I had to try and find a way to attend the wedding alone. I wasn't looking forward to the inevitable 'where's your perfect Christos?' remarks when I turned up without the Greek hero, but it mattered far more that I was there for Rachel.

Since I didn't have a driving licence, I had been depending on Christos driving us up from London to rural Oxfordshire and back on the day to attend the wedding. I made a new travel plan which involved taking a train, a bus and then a cab to reach the venue. But it would also require me to stay over at a local hotel. I rang around some of them that afternoon, but with just two days' notice, they were all fully booked.

On Thursday, I had no choice but to call Rachel and tell her I couldn't make it. It was a slap in the face of our friendship to let Rachel down at this stage, and it had sickened me to explain why I could no longer be there. But the fact of the matter was that without Christos, there was just no way that I could get to the wedding.

That evening when I met Christos at our local pub for a drink, I told him that I'd phoned Rachel to officially excuse us. Christos didn't seem to understand the significance of what I'd just had to do and instead made blithe chat about Rachel and her fiancé Craig.

'So the happy couple have been together since they were sixteen, eh? Aww, that's lovely!'

Christos had a sentimental streak to rival a Latin soap opera. From time to time we listened to a late-night Greek radio show over the internet, which mainly consisted of septuagenarian men and women ringing in to read poetry about their lost loves. The presenter, with her smoke-and-silk voice, would lament with them and Christos would wistfully imagine the day he too would join their ranks.

'Yep, since sixteen. I remember when they first got it on. And where. It was in our friend's nightclub in Leeds.'

'Sixteen and you were clubbing, Nichi *mou*!'

'Thirteen and I was clubbing, actually!' I laughed, correcting him.

'So – Nichi . . .' Christos affected the sleazy Greek. 'Does that mean they've only ever had sex with each other? Imagine! One person! How would you even know if you were doing it right?'

'Erm, I think you'd know, Christos!'

'Like the first time we tried to have sex and we failed, you mean?'

This memory still made me wince. Apparently, the first time we ended up in bed together I was too anxious to make love and Christos had had to stop. I say 'apparently' because I have absolutely no recollection of this, and Christos had to tell me. I presume my amnesia related to my guilt, because the fact of the matter was that Christos and I had started out as an affair. Technically, when I met Christos, I was already boyfriended, to a beautiful serious man who had very admirably gone off to do aid work in South America while I completed my final year.

I remember the first time Christos knocked on my bedroom door in the college accommodation block we shared. When I saw who it was, I discreetly dropped the picture of my boyfriend and me into a drawer. A few weeks later, when Christos found his way into my bed, my guilt acted as a kind of chastity device and clamped me shut to Christos's cock. 'Only until the next night though, heh heh!' Christos would always point out.

Now that night I definitely remembered, and the rest. My friend Lizzie renamed Christos 'the Greek dildo'. We had so much sex in that first term that I actually ripped his frenulum,

that piece of skin that joins the foreskin to the penis, and he
had to go to the campus nurse for a special salve. I think we
managed to hold off for all of about another week. Then we
had a desperate, silent shag in a reading cubicle in the library.

'Hey, we have to get you home, Christos. You've got a bag
to pack if you're going to make that flight tomorrow evening.
You won't have time in the morning.'

Christos hated packing, and tonight was no exception. 'First,
let's have a hug,' he said, when we got back to our flat. He said
hug like I did, with a pronounced northern vowel.

We clambered on to the bed. Christos was wearing Kenzo
Pour Homme. I nuzzled his neck, appreciating how delicious
he always smelled. He loved fragrances, to the extent that he
had even done a *parfumerie* course in his spare time. At airport
duty-free shops he knew immediately what scent would suit
me and birthdays always brought a new bottle of something
unique-smelling. 'Because you are secretly high maintenance,
Nichi,' he told me now. 'But don't worry. Your little secret is
safe with your Master.'

'All right, Master, don't you have a bag to pack?'

'I do, I do.'

I got up to go to the bathroom and brush my teeth. Christos
followed. He kissed the crown of my head with soft deliberation,
met my gaze in the mirror and smiled. 'Such a beautiful woman.'

I scrunched up my nose and shook my head, toothpaste
dribbling down my chin. 'Even when you are brushing your
tushy pegs!' It was another Yorkshire phrase he'd appropriated,
and it sounded even more ridiculous with a Greek twang.

He reached for his own toothbrush and we jostled one
another for space until we were both gummy with toothpaste
and giggling conspiratorially into the sink.

Back in our bedroom, Christos frowned at the open suitcase.

'What do you want bringing back from home, Nichi *mou*?'

'Some fruit off the tree, please!' I replied. 'And some of
Giagia's biscuits.' *Giagia* meant grandmother.

'Mmmm,' Christos nodded. 'Home! Food! I'm going to eat so well.' Christos ate for five back in Greece. How he managed to retain his featherweight boxer's body was a mystery known only to the Sibyl. 'It's going to be great when you come with me in August.'

I nodded. I could already smell the hot red leather of the seats in his beaten-up Mercedes, and the fragrant basil bushes by the front door of his parents' house. I remembered how their vegetable incense hit you as the car pulled up the drive. Suddenly, I was the sentimental one.

'Christos? If we ever did get married, could we get married in Greece?'

He stopped packing for a moment and looked right at me. 'Of course.'

On Saturday morning, as I wandered through an overcast Hyde Park, there was a text from Christos, delayed from the previous evening. It said that he'd arrived safely, that he had already been fed four pork chops plus rice plus salad plus potatoes plus cake and apricots and coffee by Giagia and was now enjoying a cigarette under the jasmine trees that shaded the porch. I could see and smell it more vividly than the ashen water sloshing about the Serpentine.

I thought again about Rachel's wedding. At least I'd sent her a decent present. I'd stretched to more than I could afford in guilty compensation but it didn't really make me feel better. I hoped this wasn't going to damage our friendship in the long term. Suddenly it started to rain. I decided that I had better head back and get on with my job application. It was for the one position in recent weeks I thought I might actually have a chance of getting, working as a medical PA to a team of surgeons at a London hospital. Despite my journalistic ambitions, I'd temped before for the NHS and always found it far more stimulating than typing up reports for some two-bit ad agency. Besides, it was the best training for life in a harried newsroom.

There were few things more stressful than having to arrange a bed transfer for a patient with surgical complications. Whatever an editor might tell you, getting copy to print is never a matter of life or death.

That evening, Christos called me. '*Ela* Nichi *mou*, how's my golden egg?'

'Yeah, I'm fine. I went for a walk but came back to do a job application when it rained and I'd got sodden. Now I'm reading. How's the garage?'

'Busy. They really did need me. I got wet, too.'

'Got wet? What kind of wet?'

'I jumped into a swimming pool with my clothes on.'

'*Thee mou!*' I cursed in Greek. 'Why?'

'Because while I was at lunch a little girl fell in so I jumped in after her.'

Classic Christos. He wasn't named after the Saviour for nothing.

'Was she OK?'

'Yes. She just cried a bit. Wanted her mum. Luckily my phone still works.'

'You jumped in with that, too?'

'Well, yes, with everything. Even my shoes. There was no time to think about it. And then I ate lunch with Maria, in my wet T-shirt, heh heh. And Nichi – there were women watching!'

'I bet they wanted to jump you after seeing that,' I laughed.

'They did. The way they clapped their hands afterwards gave them away.'

I'd seen this reaction many times. When women saw charming, delectable Christos cooing at a baby, their eyes would widen in desperate lust. Then they would look accusingly at me as if to say, 'Why aren't you fully utilising those fine Greek genes?'

Sometimes I wished I felt the same, but ever since I was a tiny child I had been adamant that I would never be a mother. In recent years I had told my friends that I'd rather go to prison than have a child. They would laugh nervously and tell me it was only a matter of time before my biological clock rang its alarm, but I didn't think so. I had terrible nightmares about giving birth in a Greek hospital in 40-degree heat, the sweat of my labour pains dripping off the walls. But even I had to admit that the thought of Christos saving a little girl from drowning was pretty enticing.

'Oh, Christos. Forced to play hero when all you wanted was a nice lunch with an old friend!'

'I practically ate half a pig after that. I had earned it. Anyway, Nichi *mou*, I need to go, Mama is calling me. I'll see you on Monday afternoon, can't wait! *S'agapo*! I love you!'

On Monday, the agency called me about the hospital job. I could start that week if I liked. Finally, income! Christos's family had lent us some money to help us set up in London. Without it, there was no way I could have afforded to move down with him and no way I could be trying to pursue my chosen career now. But I felt ashamed at having to borrow from them in the first place, what with the thousands of pounds of debt I had already accrued, including a loan, two creaking overdrafts and an unpaid credit card bill. Not that I had been frivolous with money as a student, but I had elected not to work while I studied to give myself the utmost chance of earning the best possible degree. It had paid off.

I thought back to the day I found out I'd got my First. I ran to the English department office but when I arrived there was still a whole twenty-seven minutes before it opened and I could get my result. I tried to practise my newly acquired yogic breathing techniques as I contemplated my future. I wanted to carry on using my mind, but I was drawn to journalism rather than more study. I had created a literary radio show in my second year at university and felt sure that was the kind of work that would really excite me. I loved learning, but now I wanted to work in a colourful, creative office and live in the capital.

I was so absorbed in my plans that when Christos arrived, panting, having run from the other side of campus, he had to say my name three times before I noticed him.

'Shall we get your result, Nichi *mou*?'

'I'm scared!' I wailed. But I was so relieved he was with me.

'No! Nothing to be scared of, Golden Egg.' He pulled me to him, kissing first one cheek and then the other.

I sidled into the poky department office, which was not too dissimilar to the desk at a police station.

'Name?' enquired the departmental secretary.

'Nichi Hodgson. Nicola,' I managed, in a whisper. I fully expected my heart to beat up and out of my mouth until it lay there quivering on the cheaply carpeted floor.

'Very well done, Nicola. You've got a First.'

I yelped. Christos squeezed my arms, squeezed my cheeks, squeezed me to him, and we laughed in each other's faces over and over again. I owed so much of this to Christos and his absolute faith in me, his unbending support.

I grinned at the memory. Christos had loved me not because of my achievements but in spite of my failures. And I wanted so much to offer that to him now as he undertook this PhD.

The door rattled downstairs. '*Ela*, Nichi *mou*!'

He was back. Thank God. I jumped up from the table and checked my lip gloss in the mirror, grabbed frantically at a perfume on the mantelpiece. I had changed into a skirt that Christos had bought for me, a black flippy thing with multi-coloured 3-D polka dots stitched around the hem, and a low-cut vest.

I went to open the bedroom door in greeting. There he was: white T-shirt, sunglasses, and his tan two shades deeper after one weekend. He looked as if he'd just stepped off the main *dromos* in Athens.

'Eeeeeeeee!' he exclaimed, beaming. It was a noise I made in excitement and now he made it too. 'Egg, Egg, Egg, Egg, how's my beautiful *kali mou*?' He smothered me in his embrace.

He smelled of Kenzo, but also rosewater, mint, and the uniquely Greek scent of mastic chewing gum.

'Happy to have you back,' I murmured.

He dragged his suitcase into the room and dropped to his knees. 'Wait a minute, wait . . . Now, let's see what we have here for Nichi.'

Out of the suitcase he produced an unusual beaded necklace, a new perfume and, finally, a pair of pretty cork-soled wedges. 'To replace those awful white ones you refuse to get rid of.' His thoughtfulness never failed to make me swoon. But he'd never bought me shoes before and I was a little sceptical.

'Do you even know what size I am, Christos?'

'Well of course! I showed the assistant the shape and the length of your foot with my hand, like this.' He closed his eyes and mimed how he had groped through the air, trying to envision my feet, then blinked his eyes open once he had settled on the size. 'Like Lazarus in a shoe mart. And then she helped me pick them out.'

I shook my head incredulously, and then again when I realised that they did indeed fit.

'*Efharisto para poli*, Christos; I love them! Oh, I got a job by the way,' I told him, as I slipped the shoes off. 'Only medical temping again but the money is good. Well, it'll cover our bills at least. Thank God our rent is so cheap. I don't know how anyone affords to rent a double room on their own down here.'

'Excellent news! See! It's all panning out just fine, Nichi *mou*. Let's go and have a little dinner out to celebrate tonight, eh? What would you like? A nice Turkish? Some fatoush?'

I nodded happily. 'Let's.'

'OK, great. Let me wash my hands and then we can go. I'm hungry again already!'

I started to laugh. 'But you've been fed so much at home!'

'Exactly! I've got my Greek appetite back! Anyway, I've got some news for you, too.'

★   ★   ★

'What's your news then?'

Christos finished chewing, swallowed, then took a drink of water, cleared his throat, and let his hand rest against the table, still holding his knife.

'So I was talking to my parents about the PhD. They're very happy about it but they have one or two concerns about . . .'

He broke off.

'About how we are living here in London.'

'Oh? How so?'

'Well . . .' He paused again. It was not like Christos to struggle to find the right words. As well as speaking French and Italian, he was more fluent and expressive in English than half the native speakers I knew.

'Because they think you and me living together is not such a good idea. They think it would be better if I lived with other students.'

The tears welled instantaneously as my throat tightened. Was I hearing this right? Was Christos telling me he was moving out?

'What are you talking about, Christos? We've only just moved in together. We moved down here together! We're setting up together.' Then, 'We're going to get married!'

I had never stated it like that before and now it sounded like a declaration, not of love, but of desperation.

'"You can be a husband or a student, Christos. But not both." That's what my dad said to me.' Christos repeated the cold words almost as impassively.

'What, are you just going to go along with it?' Now I was angry. How dare Christos's family interfere in our future? I was twenty-three, for Christ's sake, not thirteen. How dare they undermine our relationship by not taking it seriously?

'But Nichi *mou*, they're paying for me! I have to consider their wishes. It's no comment on you.'

I didn't see how it could be anything else. 'But Christos, I really don't understand. How can they think I'll be a distraction? I worked so hard for my degree, I know how important it is to have a stable, tranquil environment to study in. And it's not as though I'll be around all day, I'll be at work. You'll have loads of time to get things done. And when I come home from work we can have dinner and spend some time together.'

'You know it doesn't work like that for me, Nichi.' Christos was rigid, ritualistic even about how he got things done. 'I can only work at night. Otherwise I feel like I'm wasting my life, sitting in the library all day and reading some poor man's thesis, who probably lost his penis to underuse, he spent so many hours studying.'

I ignored his half-attempt at humour. 'What, so you mean you wouldn't even *try* to study in the day so that we could spend time together in the evening?'

'It's going to be very hard, this PhD, Nichi. I need to feel that I can study whenever suits me.'

So this wasn't just about his parents. This was about Christos's life with me and the fact that somehow he saw me as a distraction or a burden, possibly both.

And then another thing dawned on me. 'But what am I going to do? Where will I live if you move out?' How was I ever going to be able to afford to live in London without cohabiting with Christos?

'My sister says someone at her workplace has a room going spare from September. We can call for you.'

What?! So this had already been thoroughly discussed among his entire family? Any other time I would have been livid. But right now, I was just too upset that Christos was effectively abandoning me.

'OK,' I replied, tears blurring my vision. 'I just can't believe you told me, rather than asking me about it.'

'Look, it's going to be fine. There's ages yet until we have to sort things out. Anyway, I might not even do the PhD. Let's just wait and see.'

Chapter 4

The next few weeks dragged as though June were on a loop. I started my job at the hospital and Christos continued at the shipping company, all the while making provisional arrangements for the autumn. The early summer sun seemed to shine just to spite me. We tried not to talk about the housing situation and distracted ourselves with games of badminton, cinema trips and weekend excursions to the coast and picturesque towns and villages; basically anywhere we could play at being blithe tourists in our own increasingly strained lives.

'Christos,' I asked one afternoon, as we were reading the Sunday papers at a pub on the South Bank, 'do you want to go and see the Frida Kahlo exhibition this week? It's our last chance before the show closes.'

Christos frowned over the top of the family section. 'I don't think I can this week, Nichi *mou*. I've got to help Frankie and his girlfriend move in to their new flat tomorrow. I'll be working late on Tuesday. And then Layla is coming to town on Wednesday until the weekend.'

Layla was Christos's ex-girlfriend, one of the sweetest-natured people I had ever met and naturally beautiful in a very Mediterranean way, with delectable curves and a dense cloud of dark, waving hair. We had become friends on my last trip to Greece. Christos and Layla had known each other for years and had had a very brief relationship when he was in the army. But it felt like dating a cousin, he told me, and they had reverted to being friends again soon after.

I was so preoccupied by the PhD debacle that I had forgotten that she was due in town but I cheered up at the thought of it. Layla was something of a confidante. We messaged via Facebook, me in stilted Greek, her in fluent chatty English. I would occasionally relate trivial disagreements I'd had with Christos, while she sympathised. Finally I could get a second opinion on Christos's announcement that he was moving out, maybe even get her to have a word with him for me. Gina or Rachel would always listen, but the fact that Layla was both Greek and an old friend of Christos made her better placed to offer some real insight into what I still considered to be his completely out-of-character decision.

'Why don't you ask someone from your new job to go with you to the exhibition, Nichi *mou*?'

Now I frowned. 'Because I don't know anyone well enough to ask yet, Christos. And it's not very English to ask your workmates to art galleries. Only to the pub.'

'There's really nobody? What about the other girl that types with you? You need more friends in London, you know, Nichi,' Christos continued. 'I mean, when I start the PhD . . .'

He trailed off. He'd mentioned the forbidden issue. Neither of us wanted to get into a discussion about this again on a Sunday.

'Yeah OK, I might, I'll see,' I said, taking charge of the conversation.

The next morning I took my place among London's commuters and went to work. In a hospital, everything and nothing is an emergency, and Monday mornings as a medical PA always highlighted that contradiction.

While I had the weekends off, the surgeons I served would nearly always have been called in. Dumped on my desk would be piles of patient notes and half a dozen Dictaphone tapes containing urgent letters for typing. Sometimes, by the time I came to typing them up, overnight complications meant the patient in question had already passed away. I relied on the surgeon to remember that when he or she came to sign, and for them to instruct me to shred the letter. But once I'd had to p.p. a batch and erroneously sent one to the bereaved family. I was absolutely horrified when I found out. Journalism was going to be easy by comparison.

This Monday though, there was nothing on my desk but my own filing and a copy of the *Lancet* medical journal. A long day lay ahead. I remembered what Christos had said about trying to make some more friends, but I was feeling too fretful about our ongoing stand-off over living arrangements, and the prospect felt daunting. The women I worked with were nice enough but they were utterly absorbed with either their partners or their hectic single-girl social lives.

That evening, Christos and I set off to meet Layla for dinner in one of those tired-looking Lebanese restaurants on Edgware Road. Layla had texted Christos to say she was running fifteen minutes late, so I suggested that we sit outside and smoke until she arrived.

Christos asked the waiter for a hookah and two glasses of tap water. He blew on the hookah's coals and took the first long inhalation, forcing the water to bubble up. Refracted through the blue marbled glass, it reminded me of the waves that frothed around the double kayak we had taken out in Greece last summer. We planned to take the canoe out again when I joined Christos there in August, which was fast approaching.

I had been thinking about how I was going to broach the subject of Christos's living arrangements, the details of which I still had no idea about. Emboldened by the fact that Layla would soon be here to distract us if we got into a fight, I dared to ask him if he'd made any further arrangements.

'Well, I haven't found a flat. But I think I've found a flatmate.'
'Oh?'
'Yes. It looks as though I'll be living with Markos.'

With Markos? With that irresponsible, Peter Pan, party-boy advertiser? The guy who spent as much money on champagne as he did on designer furniture?

'With Markos? Are you kidding me? If your parents wouldn't let you live with me then they certainly aren't going to let you live with Markos!'

'Well, it was their suggestion actually,' Christos replied quietly.

'But WHY?' If I'd been angry when Christos announced he was moving out, I was apoplectic now.

'Because we went to school together. Because they know him.'

'But they know me!'

Christos sighed, looked wan with desperation. 'I know they do, Nichi *mou*.' He took my hand across the table.

'I'm going to the bathroom,' I announced, and hurried inside. I didn't want to cry, I wanted to compose myself before Layla arrived. I wanted us all to have a nice evening.

I scrutinised myself in the mirror. Indignation did not suit me; it made my cheeks look even puffier. My eyes were molten with unshed tears. I dabbed gingerly along my lash line with a corner of toilet roll to avoid smudging my eyeliner. There was a flush from the other cubicle. Out came Layla.

'Nichi *mou*, how are you, *kali*?'

Layla embraced me and covered my face with kisses. She was casually dressed in jeans and a scoop-neck T-shirt, her hair swept up in a messy knot, caramel skin gleaming under the flattering bathroom light.

'I'm well, Layla. Well, no, actually, I'm *etsi-getsi*.' That was Greek for so-so and Layla touched my arm in affection and laughed.

'You learned *etsi-getsi*! You're adorable! Why, Nichi *mou*, what's wrong?'

I hadn't planned on telling Layla like this, but better than spilling it in front of Christos and potentially starting another argument in the restaurant. So out came the story, out came my woes and fears and anger. Layla listened intently, smiling. Even when I told her about Markos, she carried on smiling.

'Can't you have a word with him, Layla? Make him understand why I'm so upset that he would let his parents effectively make a decision about our life together?'

Layla's smile began to shrink. 'I'm not taking his side, Nichi, but maybe he has a point about the stress of studying and not wanting that to affect your relationship. When I started my Master's I argued with Constantine all the time.' Constantine was Layla's boyfriend. They were still together after seven years of studying and living across the continent from one another. 'I can totally understand where you're coming from, but it is a cultural thing, unfortunately. Christos is rebellious, but knowing him, he must have thought about this long and hard.'

My throat tightened again. Oh God, Layla, not you too. I couldn't believe she was citing culture clash as the problem here. Wasn't she effectively saying that I was Christos's way of rebelling against his family? That to do the right thing by them meant rejecting me?

'I know the way Greek parents can come across,' she continued, 'they're bloody annoying and ridiculously protective, but what can you do?'

So that was it. Layla didn't really understand either. Or if she did, her answer was effectively 'deal with it'. This was my problem. Christos was going to move out and I would have to deal with it.

Layla could see the raw hurt in my face. 'He loves you, Nichi *mou.*'

'Then why is he leaving me?' I felt like screaming. The idea that this might be about more than Christos's family, that it might be something he himself wanted, was too agonising to contemplate.

There was now just one more month before Christos moved out. At the end of July he would be flying back to Greece for the summer, mainly to help at the garage, and then I would join him at the end of August for a holiday in Greece on the island of Rhodes, where his family were originally from and still had a home. We were both working so much there was little time for us to do anything together beyond having dinner and watching TV.

And we were having less sex than we'd ever had, generally only three times a week. That might sound like plenty to many people, but as time-rich students we had made love once or twice a day, every day. This had continued even after moving to London together. I couldn't tell whether the diminished activity was just because we were finally both working full-time and city-fatigued, or because something was shifting between us.

Christos loved to analyse our relationship. 'How are we doing, Nichi *mou*, do we think? Is our relationship going well? Do you have any complaints with me? How can I improve myself?' He would ask this in a pretend therapist fashion, often when I was reading the newspaper and he was polishing our shoes or folding the laundry. But I couldn't remember him asking the question in recent weeks. I certainly wouldn't have wanted to answer it if he had.

When Christos left for Greece, I cried. I cried because it was the last time he would leave our home together to go back to his. I stood by the bay window and watched him walk towards the tube station, rucksack strapped across his straight strong shoulders, suitcase in tow. He turned back to wave at me. He was crying a little too.

Three weeks of dreary job and slightly tense late-night phone calls to Christos later and I was finally bound for Greece. Waiting in the airport lounge for my flight, I began to feel more at ease than I had done in weeks. I was dressed in low-rise, white linen trousers that hugged my bottom in a way Christos loved (he had urged me to buy them, after all), a green lace-trimmed top with a plunging neckline, and the shoes that Christos had brought me back from his recent trip to Athens. Around my neck was a knotted pearl and silver necklace that Christos had also given me. It nestled in my cleavage suggestively. As I waited for my flight to be called, I stroked it meditatively, as if it were a rosary.

Then Christos rang. 'We're all ready for you, Nichi *mou*. I've washed the car, Mimi has made up your bed, and Tolkien has even had a bath in your honour.' Mimi was the cleaning lady, Tolkien the family cat. 'Are you ready for it, little Egg?'

I was. I couldn't wait to be back with Christos. There was no one like him, and no one better for me.

Chapter 5

As the plane touched down in Greece, my heart heaved with relief. I liked to think that my parents named me Nicola because they somehow knew I was destined to spend time in the land of its origin. I had been taught that my name meant 'leader of the people', which, given my bossy nature, made a lot of sense. But the first time I met Christos's father he called me 'Niki – the goddess of victory!' My real victory, I felt, was in having harpooned Christos. The same Christos who was now waiting for me at the airport.

The double doors of the arrival gate parted and there he was, clad in khaki pants and a white patterned T-shirt, running a nervous hand through his black curls. His skin was now the colour of burnt toffee, shading his muscular body into sharper definition, the sleeves of his T-shirt straining against his deep, bronzed biceps. He flashed me a devoted smile from across the barriers. Christos *mou*.

Christos couldn't wait for me to file out after the other passengers and instead bounded towards me, lifted me up in his arms and swirled me about. In England, witnesses to such a nauseating romantic display would have scowled and tutted, but in Greece, people smiled and nodded in approval. There was something about Christos that could make clichéd romantic gestures seem as though he had invented them.

Christos took my case in one hand and steered me protectively out of the arrivals lounge into the breath-binding heat. Greece was infernal in high summer, but meeting that temperature for the first time again made my skin prickle with delight.

'Ah, *Thee mou, Thee mou!*' Christos cursed. He sweated like an Englishman. 'Why isn't it raining like lovely, grim London?'

'Because Egg needs a hot holiday!'

'Egg's going to get a hot holiday, don't you worry!' He smirked at the double entendre. 'Now, Nichi *mou*, we have two options. Either we head towards home, calling at Giagia's first to get fed, or we go to Paradisos beach. Which is it to be?'

'Beach, please! I need to feel the sea!'

Christos led me to the impractical vintage red Mercedes. I loved it so because its bench-like front seats meant I could sneakily unfasten my belt and slide across right next to Christos.

We took first the motorway and then a coastal path. The beach was craggy, a sepia wilderness that felt as though it was in South Africa rather than Greece. It was nearly always deserted. I wondered if Christos had in mind the same thing I did.

He pulled up under the shade of some olive trees. I was still in my travelling clothes. 'Christos, will you open the boot? Can I get a little sundress and my bikini out of my suitcase please?'

'No, no, you don't need them, Nichi.'

I turned to him. He gave a knowing smile from behind his sunglasses, teeth gleaming against his tanned face.

We were still in sync.

I smiled slyly. 'But what if I get sunburned?' Christos was always poised to douse me in suncream as soon as I stepped into the Greek sun.

'We'll be quick. And you can hide in the sea afterwards. I won't let you get burned, *kali mou*.'

The beach was indeed empty, apart from a lone frappé seller who sat further up the bank, totally absorbed in a newspaper. We wandered across the sugar-soft sand, down towards the water. It was far windier than I remembered it being in past years.

'*Kemathothis!*' I shouted above the wind, pointing at the waves.

'Bravo, Nichi *mou*, you remembered the word for choppy! Isn't it?'

He pulled me in towards him and placed his hands around my face, locking us into an infatuated kiss. I felt a surge of lust swell up from the pit of my stomach. In haste we peeled off our clothes, which Christos weighted down with a rock, and ran to the denser, wetter sand.

I fixed my gaze on the provocative, upward swell of his top lip for a moment, sliding my hands over his body. Then my eyes followed my fingers along the helix of dark hair that ran down his chest, between his nipples and past his stomach to the top of his now swollen cock. He reminded me of the perfectly proportioned illustrations of ancient Olympians I had marvelled over in Classics lessons. I wanted him. I would always want this exquisite man.

I dropped down to the sand and pulled him on to me. For a minute, he kissed me very deliberately. He touched my cheek, then traced a long path down my neck to my collarbone, out along the curve of my shoulder, down the outside of my arm, before resting his hand on the swell of my hip. There, he gripped me, and as he gripped me, I felt a throbbing between my legs. I was already wet.

He placed his hands on my breasts, using first his palms and then his fingers to slowly tease my nipples round in feathery circles. I moaned appreciatively and rose up to kiss him. He pushed back with his mouth, and placed lingering, light kisses down along my throat, before dragging his mouth, then his hands, more roughly down the front of my body. Involuntarily I thrust my groin up to meet first his chest, then his face, then kicked my left leg over his shoulder. Grabbing my thigh with his right hand and sliding his left underneath to grip my bottom, he held me there for a moment, then looked up at me, his face serious with desire.

Christos's skill as a lover came from knowing intuitively when and how to ravish me. Right now, he knew I wanted it hard and fast. He rose up on to his knees, guided my leg from around him and back onto the sand, then parted my thighs. As he slid his cock into me we both moaned and I gripped onto his taut backside, urging him in deeper.

Hard and hot, our bodies jarred against each other over and over. I was so focused on the sensation of Christos thrusting up into me that I could no longer tell what was grit or sand or the wind whipping us with foam from the sea, or Christos's fingers bracing my hips so that he could drive up deeper inside me. This was barely going to last another minute, we were so desperate for one another. Christos wove his hands into my sand-whipped hair and guided my mouth up to his. Three weeks without a kiss and here we were, craving one another like it was the first time. Then with rapid intensity I began to climax and so did he, his orgasm chasing mine, until I, and then Christos 'Ohhhd' with pleasure, his fiercer cries carrying further across the sand.

Afterwards we lay there a while, stuck together with sand and a sense of deep peace. Christos untangled my hair from his fingers, touched them to my lips. It felt so good to remember the raw passion that had drawn us together in the first place.

Suddenly, Christos looked askance. 'Nichi *mou*,' he said, jerking his head towards the frappé seller, 'he was watching us.'

I threw my head back into the sand, and laughed with glee. 'Our first public show! Or was it private?'

'Poor guy. Bet it's the closest he's come to a shag in years!'

'But Christos, everyone knows Greeks get *loads* of sex.'

'Not when they have stomachs and beards like that! You know that's what I'm going to become one day, don't you?'

'I know,' I said. 'I can't *wait*. Then you'll stop going on about it!'

Christos got up, and looked out at the sea.

'*Ela*, Nichi *mou*, let's wash ourselves off and make our way to Giagia's. She's going to be waiting there with her infamous feast.'

I skipped after him into the water. 'It's so choppy!' I shouted again. I'd never seen waves like this in the usually tranquil Mediterranean.

Christos dived into the waves. 'Come on little *fokia mou*, come on, seal!' he called to me.

I tumbled up into the foam, exhilarated to feel the surf on my skin where just moments before Christos had caressed me. I floated on my back for a few seconds, revelling in the sensation of air and water gliding over me, and succumbed to a sensation of post-coital bliss.

Suddenly, a violent wave engulfed me and as I swallowed two lungfuls of seawater, the wave swallowed me, dragging me twenty feet away from the shore. I didn't struggle against it, I couldn't. All I remember thinking was, 'Oh, this is it; I came and now I'm going.' *La petite mort* was what the poets I had studied called orgasm. Surely it was only poetic justice to drown in the sea we'd just made love next to.

To be honest, I'd probably have surfaced in another five seconds or so, but Christos was already there, heaving me out of the current and swimming back to the shore with me clutching and spluttering about his neck, vaguely laughing with relief.

'Egg, please do not drown at the beginning of the holiday! At least not before Giagia has got to feed you, OK?'

'OK!' I agreed. Now safe, I felt suddenly panicked. Christos stroked my head and took me by the hand. 'Come on. Clothes then food.'

We made our way back up the sandbank. I stood there, naked, for a moment, fastening the straps of my cork-soled sandals. The frappé seller tipped his sunhat at Christos.

About an hour or so later, we pulled up under Giagia's vine-draped porch. As we got out of the car, Giagia appeared at the door to greet us.

Christos's grandmother had very light darting eyes, cropped

white hair and had only worn black or occasionally navy blue since his grandfather died a few years before. She looked, for the most part, nervous, but I had learnt that her skittish gestures were a sign of her eagerness to care.

'Nichi *mou, kopiase!*' I knew that meant for me to come in. Giagia placed her hands gingerly on my shoulders and kissed me primly on either cheek. There was a glimmer of a smile about her lips.

Christos draped one arm about her small, stooped frame and kissed her warmly, knocking her ever so slightly off balance.

The conversation now switched to full-on Greek. 'Christos *mou*, now what will you have to eat? It's late, you must be famished, you shouldn't leave it so long to have lunch, you know. Poor Nichi must be starving! How was her flight?' Giagia directed such questions at Christos, in part because she was never sure how much Greek I could now speak, in part because it was a show of politeness.

The table was heaving with homemade food. A dozen kinds of salad, fresh bread, hummus, cheese, rice, potatoes, olives, almonds and apples from the family orchard and grapes from Giagia's own vines. Out of the oven came a whole chicken for Christos and vegetarian dolmades for me. Periodically Giagia would disappear into her huge fridge and fetch something else.

The anxious eater in me always balked the first time I was reacquainted with a real Greek meal. But I had learned over time to eat slowly and state politely but firmly, 'No, I have plenty, thank you.' Saying it five times meant I might only be given two more helpings, if I was lucky.

'So you know your cousin Eleni is getting married, Christos?'

Christos nodded. Contrary to cultural stereotype, Giagia was actually too polite to urge us to marry. But she could hint at what she hoped for us by mentioning other people's forthcoming nuptials.

'Eleni and Matthaios won't be getting married in church. It's their choice, of course. So I went to St Giorgos's anyway, prayed that God will bless their marriage, make them as happy as I was with your grandfather.'

Christos patted Giagia's hand.

I had often asked Christos what a Greek Orthodox wedding entailed, and lingered on the details in my mind as he described it. Christos would have taken some persuading, but my inclination towards flamboyant displays of affection meant I loved to fantasise about a church wedding; how the family priest would join our hands in front of the *iconostasis*, how Christos and I would be crowned with *stefana* and walked three times around the altar, how Christos would throw back the heavy veil from my radiant face once we were husband and wife.

Christos interrupted my reverie. 'Nichi nearly drowned today, Giagia.'

Giagia coughed in alarm.

'Christos!' I scolded. What the hell was he telling Giagia that for?

'So she's not feeling like eating too much.'

He gave me a solemn smile. I made a mental note to kiss him extra hard when we got home.

Giagia nodded sympathetically. 'Well, Nichi can eat as much or as little as she likes. Do you want some more chicken, Christos? Have some more rice.'

'No, no, Giagia.' Christos stood up, patted his muscular stomach. 'I'm creaking, I'm so full. We'd better be on our way. We'll call in again soon.'

As we stepped out on to the driveway, Giagia shouted after Christos, 'Look after her, *leventi mou*, eh?'

Leventi. It was impossible to translate. All I knew was that it was what you called an upstanding man.

As we parked up outside Christos's family house, the familiar fragrances overwhelmed me: first, the sweet basil and almond scents, then the hypnotic night-flowering jasmine. Spontaneously, I started to cry a little. Christos was alarmed. 'Don't worry,' I laughed to reassure him, 'I'm just so happy to be back!'

Christos's parents were not at home. They were at the family beach house; we would be seeing them later in the week. I was glad. Although I could be nothing but gracious to their faces, I was unsure how I would react emotionally to seeing them again, what with my feelings about the PhD still so raw. I entered the kitchen. Everything was as it always was: the biscuit barrel filled with Giagia's delicacies, the cupboard covered in family snapshots, the strawberry napkin ring on the table, reserved for the little English girl.

Also pinned to the cupboard was a card I had made for Christos's parents last year to thank them for having me. It featured a cut-out cat, meant to be Tolkien, shaded in charcoal pencil. Amazing what you could pull off when you wanted to win the affections of someone's family. Tolkien himself languished in the shade by the sink in a bid to keep cool, and refused to come and greet me.

'So Mimi made your bed up, Nichi *mou*.'

Christos and I slept in separate beds in Greece. It wasn't like his parents didn't know we shared a bed back in London, nor even that they were particularly conservative; but old-fashioned house rules still applied. Christos's dad had once told him that it was fine to sleep with me upstairs, just as long as he came back down to his own room before Mimi, their housekeeper, arrived. He didn't want her to feel awkward, he said.

I wandered into Christos's bedroom, ran my fingers over the national youth sports trophies stacked on the bookcase, across Christos's face at six, eight, ten years in the school photos stuck above the bed. I went over to his fragrance collection. Among the glass bottles was a rosary box with a cartoon Virgin Mary painted on the lid. Oh God, I knew what this was! I screwed off the top, and smiled effusively.

Christos came into the room. He took the box from me. 'Our wedding rings – ha ha!'

Inside the box were two cheap silver rings that we had bought for a trip to Morocco we had made just before my finals.

Somebody had told us that finding places to stay as an unmarried couple could prove tricky, so Christos had the idea of buying the rings. When we'd got there, it was clear nobody could have cared less. But we'd kept the rings on for the duration of the trip all the same.

'So, Nichi *mou*, I've got a surprise for you, an early birthday present.' I was still looking at the rings as Christos leant his chin on my shoulder, repeatedly kissing my cheek.

'Oh?' I turned around.

'I won a competition last week on the radio – yes, that radio programme with the nostalgic old people. It's a room at the Fengari resort. It's only for a night but there's a spa, an infinity pool, jacuzzi, a luxurious bed . . .'

His hands came around my waist, strayed up over my ribs to cup my breasts. I turned my head back to kiss him. 'That sounds glorious!'

Out of the corner of my eye I noticed his guitar. 'Oh! Christos, since there's no one else in the house, let's sing!'

Christos frowned for a moment. Then he kissed me again. 'Excellent idea.'

All the way through my childhood and teens, I had sung – in choirs, musical productions, solo to raise money for charity, at karaoke. I loved singing like nothing else, and, right up until becoming anorexic, took it as a matter of course that I would apply to drama school and see if I could make a living out of performing. But once I was ill, I lost my nerve. Along with a lot of other things.

Anorexia felt like the solution, at the time, to the terrifying chaos of my life. When I became ill I was preparing for four A levels, had the lead part in the school production of *Kiss Me Kate* and was absolutely obsessed with the idea that I had to get to Oxford where I could study and act, and make a success of myself. The pressure was inordinate. At first, starving myself gave me an intoxicating sense of being superhuman, as if I didn't need food to survive. Soon, I was ill beyond sense.

Halfway though my final school year, I weighed just five and a half stone and was wearing clothes for ten-year-olds. I knew I needed help. And so began the Sisyphean task of learning to eat again. My desire to be a professional performer had gone. That particular brazen courage had left me. But I made it to university, to study literature, and within weeks I had acquired wonderful new friends. It took longer to regain a sense of my own physical strength and attractiveness, but I managed it. That paralysing fear of food, and the obsessive need for control of my body were, I was certain, gone for good.

So it felt almost like a healing when in my last year at university, after years of being mute, musical Christos coaxed the voice out of me, persuading me to sing along to deeply unfashionable Greek love songs with him, as he played guitar. Tonight I wanted to sing with him again.

'*Ela*, Nichi *mou*, you choose.' He handed me his sheet music file. We ran through a few of my favourites. '*Matia Palatia*'. Palace eyes. '*Louloudakia Mou*'. My little flower.

'I'm feeling sentimental. I'm going to sing this one to you, Nichi *mou*,' Christos said suddenly.

'*Kokkina Heeli Mou*'. The title translated as 'my red lips'. It was one of Christos's favourites because my lips, he always said, had given him the excuse he needed to attempt the come-on that got us together.

One night, barely a week after we had first met, he knocked on my door. 'Come in!' I called.

I was in bed reading a Renaissance seduction manual for men. I was wearing a tiny mint nightie. When he put his head round my door, Christos was embarrassed.

'No, it's fine, enter!' Inappropriate, I thought to myself.

My heart raced. Christos had been working out and his curls dampened about his tanned forehead. As he shut the door, I stole a lustful look at his gym-pumped body, admired how taut his chest was underneath his close-fitting black T-shirt, then flickered my eyes back to the page.

'I just wondered if you were planning on going to salsa class next week,' he said, 'and if so, might you like to practise beforehand?'

'Oh. Well, sure!'

'OK. Great. Well, I'll leave you to it.' He backed out, but for a foot, which remained firmly planted across the threshold, propping open the door.

'You have very red lips.'

It hung between us like a sin. I remembered it now. I had loved it.

I looked up at his handsome face, Christos concentrating on the chord sequences. This hotel trip was going to be just what we needed.

Chapter 6

The next morning we set off for the resort. We took the Kia, not the Mercedes, which wasn't practical for a long drive along the clifftops.

I was still thinking about what Giagia had called Christos as we left her house the other morning. *Leventi mou.* He was indeed my *leventi,* and surely there was nothing that could get in the way of our love, not even this stupid business of him moving out. I had never believed in the One but if there was such a thing, Christos was it. Everything would work itself out.

Christos turned on the radio. '*Louloudaki mou*' was playing. We started to sing along. It was harder to fondle one another in this car but I could still stroke my hand up and down his thigh.

'Nichi *mou*, you're going to have to do the gears if you're going to distract me like that, you know!'

'Ha ha. I can probably just about manage that. Just as long as it doesn't involve roundabouts.'

'One day you'll learn to drive, Nichi *mou*, when the time is right.'

'No.' I shook my head. 'I've decided I don't want to. I think I'm one of those women who is destined to be driven.'

Christos laughed. 'To be driven, eh? See, you with your shoe fetish and taste in luxury perfumes. I've always known you were high maintenance. Born to be served.'

My hand was still stroking up along his thigh. I let it stray further up to his crotch.

'Mmmm, Nichi, be careful!'

'You're a good driver,' I teased. 'You can concentrate. Besides,' I continued, 'if a police car catches up with us they'll let us off. Remember that time when you and Stavros got pulled over sharing a bottle of whisky and the officer just told you to make sure you were on your way home to bed?'

'That was because Stavros knew the officer, Nichi *mou*!'

'Chances are you chat to anyone in Greece for five minutes and you'll find a friend in common.'

'You and your cultural stereotypes of my people!'

'Well, Christos, you shouldn't do such a good impersonation of an Olympian now, should you? An exceedingly priapic Olympian . . .'

Even through his jeans, his erection was blatant.

I flickered my fingers along his fly then slid them up under his belt buckle, teasing open the stiff top button.

Christos kept his eyes fixed on the road.

'Christos,' I wheedled. 'You're not trying to resist me, are you?'

He shook his head, smiling. 'I don't need to.'

'What, you mean you're not the slightest bit aroused right now, Christos *mou*?'

Suddenly, he smacked down the indicator, biceps bracing as he yanked the steering wheel towards me and pulled off the highway.

'Where are we going?'

'To an underground car park I know. I drop off cars for customers who live at the coast there sometimes. It'll be empty. And if it's not, there are pillars we can park behind.'

I loved Christos's decisiveness. It turned me on.

It was stupendously hot and the heat rippled up off the asphalt in waves. I flicked my right leg up on to the dashboard, touching my scarlet-manicured toes to the toasted leather, then jerked my foot upwards. 'Fuck! It's burning!'

Without looking at me, Christos wrapped his hand around my toes, then traced up along the arch of my instep with his fingers, before closing them around my ankle. I lifted my other leg up on to the dashboard, allowing my denim miniskirt to crease right up around the top of my thighs. My skirt had ridden so high that I was now exposing my lacy, lilac crotch.

He looked down at me and gripped a fist around my leg.

'We're here,' he said, easing his foot off the accelerator and turning to the left again. Then, in a rare act of recklessness, he pressed his foot to the floor and plunged us down into the darkness.

'Jesus, Christos!'

'You know you're safe, Nichi.'

Christos eased the car into a bay at the top of the garage, our headlights casting the only light on our surroundings. I could just about make out the bodies of two other vehicles, but it was essentially as he had promised, a dark, discreet space. It was perfect for daytime sex.

He barely had a chance to slam on the handbrake before I lunged at him. We kissed so hard my mouth ached from the off. Christos grappled with his belt, freeing the buckle, and I pulled at the corner of his fly, rapidly releasing the other three buttons. His cock sprang at my fingers and I started to masturbate him over the fabric of his boxer shorts. Christos, meanwhile, clamped his right hand over the lilac knickers, running the thumb of his left under the lacy rim. My knickers were askew, partly exposing my already swollen pussy. He prised away the fabric, sliding the tip of his index finger up in between my lips and towards my clitoris.

I took a sharp intake of breath and stopped my own hand for a few seconds, unable to concentrate on touching him at the same time. Then I slid my fingers behind the fabric of his boxer shorts and began to masturbate him again.

Christos rolled up my top with the palm of his hand, arranged it so that it rested across the swell of my cleavage. Then he inched up the bra, pushing at the underwiring to expose the bottom half of my breasts, and licked along the freed white skin. My nipples prickled against the fabric, desperate for him to flick his tongue over them. But he knew what denying me would do. Christos eased one, then two, then three fingers into my wetness.

When he kissed up along my neck, sinking his mouth into me, I threw my head hard back against the seat. More deliberately now, he worked his fingers in and out of me and I squeezed myself around his hand, clasping my own fingers about his cock.

The tip of it moistened my fingers, and I massaged them along his full length, increasing the speed of my strokes. 'Yes,' he said, leaning in to me. 'Keep going, I'm so close.'

'Me too,' I whispered, and started to moan, the pitch of my utterances climbing higher and higher the closer I got to climax. Christos swelled one final time under my grip. With my free hand I grabbed at his wrist and thrust his fingers full up into me. We shuddered into an electric orgasm, lips caught between broken *s'agapos* and clawing kisses, our heads pressed together.

Afterwards, I laid my head on Christos's shoulder and we stayed there for a moment, looking at one another. In the darkness only the whites of his eyes and the ivory glow of my breasts were visible. Suddenly one of the other cars ground to life, headlights flashing at us accusingly through our rear window.

'Hang on, did we have an audience again? This is getting to be a habit.' Christos grinned at me.

'Time to go, I think, Christos *mou*.'

He was still wearing his seatbelt.

As soon as we arrived at the resort, the receptionist ushered us over to a downy, dove-grey couch, where champagne cocktails had been left for us on a low-level granite table. After a perfectly calculated amount of time, a porter appeared to show us to our room.

'Not bad for a freebie, eh, Nichi *mou*?'

Christos and I admired the room. It was more like a suite, complete with bureau, sofa, mini kitchen, a walk-in wardrobe and separate dressing room. On the bedside tables were finger bowls filled with tiny, blooming jasmine flowers. Despite the room's size, the bed dominated. The sheets were a rich cream, as were the pillowcases and the whisper of valance sheet, which exposed itself from underneath the coverlet.

The bathroom was ginormous. Along the left-hand wall was a whirlpool bath that looked as though it had risen up from a hot spring. Above the sink stood luxury toiletries in oversized bottles. At the far end of the bathroom was a double shower with glass doors. Even if one partner decided to take a bath rather than a shower it meant you were still situated within clear erotic sight of one another. No obstructions.

I went out to the balcony. It was incredible how the infinity pool morphed into the Aegean sea, a sublime aqueous illusion.

'Christos,' I called out. 'Let's swim.'

'Do you like my new bikini?' After some deliberation, I had opted for turquoise plunging cups held together with a bow that would not actually come undone, and skimpy briefs.

'*Very* much! The Master approves! Positively neoclassical.'

Christos was arranging our towels over the choicest poolside chairs. We had the entire place to ourselves.

A waiter appeared and offered us drinks. 'Mmm, I want a cocktail!' The entrée in reception had given me a taste for it. 'Can I have a bellini please?'

'That's so trashy, isn't it,' I giggled at Christos.

Christos laughed back and stroked my hair. 'You can have whatever you want, high-maintenance Egg.'

'I'll have a mojito, please,' he replied to the waiter.

Two minutes later and the drinks arrived. Christos lay back and sighed. For some reason, he had brought down to the pool a mammoth engineering textbook, preparatory reading for the PhD.

'Christos *mou*, no, not that book, not today.'

'*Signomi*, Nichi, I'm sorry, *kali mou*, but I have to. There's so little time now until I start. And once you go back I'll be working in the garage again, then three weeks after that I'm back in London to begin my course.'

I turned my head towards the impassive sun, closed my eyes then reached down for my drink. This was such a treat, to be here with Christos. Nothing else mattered.

After fifteen minutes or so, Christos touched a hand on my thigh. 'Nichi *mou*, you're burning. Do you want me to put some more cream on you?'

'No. Not yet. I'm going to swim.'

I got up and went towards the pool, keeping my sunglasses on. It was early afternoon and the sun was pouring scornful blaze on my white skin. I lowered myself into the water, quickly ducked under. I didn't usually enjoy swimming in pool water in Greece, not when the Mediterranean sea itself was so idyllic. But this was special. Right up until you bumped into the infinity pool's brim, the illusion of being able to float straight out from pool to sea persisted. I wished I could skim out over the sand and glide into it.

Suddenly something shivered up along my leg. I let out a scream. It was Christos, shimmying his hands up along my thigh.

'Christos, DON'T. I thought it was an *octopodia*!' Ever since Christos had described how you catch an octopus, plunging your hand into its mouth and turning it inside out, bashing it to tenderising death on a rock, how sometimes if you weren't quick enough it would wrap its desperate tentacles around your forearms and wrists, I had an almost monomaniacal fear of meeting one in the water. I knew they had to be dragged out of their holes, but still.

Christos laughed and laughed, then started to coo at me, kissing my cheek in comfort when he saw I was actually distressed. 'Nichi *mou*,' he pulled me towards him, 'no octopodia is going to get you while I'm around.'

'But what if one day I meet one alone? It's not impossible that it could have got into the swimming pool.'

'It's pretty impossible. Why do you love to torture yourself with such thoughts? You're like Doubting Thomas with your finger in your own wound!'

I shuddered again. 'Please can we not talk about wounds. They are not a suitable topic of discussion for a romantic swim. Let's talk about . . .' I broke off, letting my legs float up and around him.

'Let's talk about . . . this,' he suggested, pulling me tighter around him. He had a burgeoning erection.

'Do you want to go up to the room?' Christos gave a half-smile.

Suddenly I felt exhausted, as if the adrenaline that had flooded my body in panic over the imaginary octopus had drained me of all my desire. What was wrong with me, why did I feel so out of sorts? 'Yes.' I said. 'I'm tired. I need a nap.'

When I woke up a couple of hours later I was determined to be in a better mood. Even if the whole issue of Christos moving out was still dragging at my mood, we were here now. I needed to appreciate the treat and put the hurt to bed, so to speak. We couldn't afford any more discord.

I decided to wear my new white dress for dinner. It had a gathered peasant-style bodice and full skirt and I knew that Christos would appreciate it.

He came out of the bathroom, a white towel wrapped around his waist. 'Ooh, be careful!' I warned him. 'You're very provocative to me with that tan. That tan against the towel.'

He grinned as he came over to where I stood in front of the mirror, kissed my neck, then murmured, 'Can I watch you do your make-up?'

I patted his backside. 'Of course.'

Christos had a thing about watching me paint my face. I wouldn't have called it a fetish. More a fixation. Mainly, he loved watching me apply mascara. I didn't wear a lot of make-up in Greece, but tonight I applied a lilac mascara Christos had bought me to accentuate my green eyes.

'Why do you like watching?' I asked him.

'I don't know. It's just mesmerising.'

'The French don't call it *maquillage* for nothing.'

'Ha,' said Christos, stroking my neck again. 'Yes. French for deception. Camouflage.'

'Did you wear camouflage paint in the army, Christos?' I was teasing him, but I felt odd. When did this bantering with my boyfriend become so self-conscious?

'No, Nichi. But I wore camouflage pants. And dog tags. And boots. And no shirt. And a nice, wide, well-polished leather belt.'

'Speaking of your belt, why don't you hurry up and put it on, Sergeant? This almost birthday girl wants dinner.'

That evening we dined on the hotel's terrace and chatted about our previous trips to Greece. 'Do you remember the first birthday I spent here, Christos? We had wine that night. You got me drunk, and then the next day we had to have lunch with your grandparents and it was so, so hot, and I was hungover and trying to show your mum and sister I appreciated the dress they had bought me by wearing it over my jeans . . .'

'The dress that was meant for an English autumn, not a Greek summer,' Christos interjected.

'Yes – exactly – and halfway through, your dad leaned across the table, winked at me, and slipped me some paracetamol.'

Even now I buried my head in my hands at the memory, but Christos just laughed, and before long I was giggling, too. This felt better. This was more like the kind of dinner we were used to enjoying before the matter of the PhD had sullied things.

When we got back to our room Christos took his shirt off, then his shoes, then stepped out on to the balcony and lit a cigarette.

I stood at the other side of the glass for a moment, admiring him: his virile physique, the way he blew smoke out artfully across the water between his bounteous lips.

He caught me looking at him and grinned. 'Are you perving on me, Nichi *mou*? Just because I'm smoking with my shirt off?'

'Precisely because you're smoking with your shirt off.' I grinned back.

I went out to join him. He slung his arm around my waist, loosely at first, then winched me in to him until I gasped for breath.

'Ah, now you can't get away from me! You can never escape, Nichi *mou*, I'm going to have you bound up in my grip for ever!'

I started laughing.

'Do you remember the first time we kissed, Nichi *mou*?'

'Of course. It was on one of our midnight walks. It was October. You were wearing gloves. As you came towards me, you slid your hand out of one. Almost sinisterly!'

'Ha! Well, if it was the left one, the *sinistra* one, that would make sense. See, even then you thought I was a sleazy Greek.'

'I thought you were gorgeous. I thought I was in love already.'

'But I was the one who said it first.'

'Well, yes, but what you actually said was, "I think I'm in love with you." Which was somehow more romantic.'

Suddenly, I was agitated again. Talking about how we met, about the first flowering of our love, was upsetting me. Ever since we'd first got together, Christos and I had been inseparable. How could Christos genuinely bear the thought of living apart now?

'What's wrong, Nichi *mou*?'

'I'm too hot,' I complained. 'And too full.'

'Nichi *mou*, that was a very small dinner.'

'But I've barely moved all day. OK, I'm going to have a shower then lie down.'

'Shall I join you?'

Christos still had his arm around me.

'If you like.'

He looked at my face thoughtfully. 'No, you shower alone. I think you need your space.'

When I got out, Christos was undoing his belt. 'I'm going to have a quick shower too.'

In little more than a minute he was back. 'Just a quickie! Heh heh.'

His sleazy-Greek act seemed almost unbearably poignant tonight because . . . because what, I wondered. Then I swallowed hard and confessed it to myself. Because we weren't going to make love. Because here we were in this aphrodisiacal treat of a hotel and I was hiding behind an excuse of fatigue, again. And why was I hiding behind an excuse? Because I didn't want to admit to myself that there was now something heartbreakingly, irrevocably, hope-shatteringly, wrong with Christos and me. And I couldn't make love to him any more.

Christos climbed on to the bed, wrapped up in a white robe. It was nicer than the ones the private patients at the hospital received for convalescence in their thousand-pound-a-night rooms. Christos sat propped up against the luxurious pillows, right leg gently flopping to the side. For the first time ever, I saw him as vulnerable. As forlorn and lonely. Then he turned to me and smiled.

There was no expectation in his smile. Just love.

I went back into the bathroom, and wept.

I lay awake long into the night. Christos soothed me, hugged me, and I clung to him, desperately trying to convince myself that we could get things back on track, but sleep eluded me. My mind turned over and over. I kept switching between determination to do whatever it took to get us through the PhD, even if that meant living apart, and a cold fear that we weren't going to make it.

The next day we had a room service breakfast and a late checkout, as if going through the motions of romance. I went for a proper swim and Christos got stuck in to his textbook.

At around four in the afternoon we set off, back to Christos's parents' house.

We'd been driving about twenty minutes when Christos's phone started to ring. '*Gia sou*, Mama.' Christos's parents were back from the coast.

I was too tired to concentrate on their conversation and started to doze off. I wanted to get home, have a shower, eat out on the terrace, preferably in my nightie, and go to bed. About an hour later I woke abruptly from a fitful nap. Christos had pulled on the brakes hard as we hit the evening traffic. I was in one of those foul, sleep-interrupted moods. And I was getting a migraine.

'Nichi *mou*, so Mama said Giagia and Papous want us to go round for dinner.'

These were Christos's grandparents on his father's side.

'Go round when?'

'Now. We're only half an hour away. Giagia was complaining that you're nearly due back home already and she hasn't seen you.'

I was puzzled. 'But she knows she'll see me on Sunday. We always have the last lunch before I go home with her and Papous.'

'Come on, Nichi. They're old, they want to see their family.'

'Christos, do we have to have dinner with them? I'm getting a migraine. I'm so tired. I don't feel well. Look at what I'm wearing.' I had thrown a cheap, creased sundress over my bikini as we had left, and hadn't bothered to wash my hair after swimming. 'I can't go round like this. It's disrespectful!'

'It's more disrespectful if we don't go when they are expecting us.'

'But they didn't ask! They told us. You told me!'

He was glowering. 'You're being unreasonable. It's no trouble to go round to theirs for dinner, especially not when you're starving. Think about them for once.'

Christos just didn't get it. This wasn't about dinner, it was about decisions being made for me. Again. Last night I had been torn between total commitment to make our relationship work and terror that it might not. But now I felt defiant. What was the point putting the effort in when there was no compromise here?

I couldn't carry on feeling this stifled. Christos had never treated me as a submissive wife-in-waiting and I wasn't about to start now. When I got back to London, I decided, I would be fully utilising my newfound freedom. I loved Christos like nothing else but maybe it was time to build a more independent life for myself. Maybe this was all going to turn out to be a blessing in disguise.

I just couldn't quite feel how yet.

Chapter 7

In the passport queue at Heathrow, I started to shiver. It was already autumn in London. I reached around for my denim jacket, which was knotted around the strap of my bag. It was still damp. All the way back from Greece, I had sobbed into it, sat with it wrapped about my face like a widow's veil. After my emotional parting from Christos, I had wanted to be left alone to cry in peace, and I knew the genial Greek flight attendants would be distressed for me, and only try to offer comfort, comfort that nobody, not even Christos, could bring.

Now, back in Britain, I was feeling fractionally better. Well, perhaps not better, but resolute. I had cried myself into calm and was ready to face the flat again. Originally we had intended to move out at the end of August but there was no way I could move all of our stuff alone, so we had kept it on for a few more weeks. Christos's friend Markos had, in the meantime, bought an apartment in the Docklands. That would be Christos's new home. And my new residence? A room in a shared flat south of the river, where I knew neither the neighbourhood, nor the other tenant.

Back at our flat, I flung my jacket, bag and suitcase on the floor, lay down on the bed and started playing out the last few days' events in my mind.

Dinner with the grandparents had been bearable in the end. Christos's parents and his cousin had also joined us, which saved me from being the sole target of Giagia Georgia's inquisition.

The next morning, Christos and I took a trip to the village where his mother was born.

'There's a small local festival on today,' he told me, 'and the main church will have been decorated by the villagers. It'll be very pretty. I know how you love to get your Orthodox fix, Egg!'

Mama's village was a two-and-a-half-hour drive away from the house and not on any map. I hoped Christos knew the way. In the night, the air conditioning had broken down and neither of us got a decent night's sleep. 'Are you sure you want to drive when you're so tired, Christos *mou*?'

'Yes of course. We need to get out of the house.'

'But we could just check into a hotel if we wanted to do that! Remember? Like that time in Yorkshire at Christmas when we desperately needed some time alone together?'

I was being flippant but Christos failed to catch it.

'*Arketa*, Nichi,' he snapped. 'You're always trying to avoid my parents!'

'Well, you're the one who said we needed to get out of the house!' I snapped back.

Christos's face was thunderous. Then he sighed, and apologised. 'I'm sorry, you're right; I'm tired. Let me have a coffee and a cigarette and I'll be on it. Jesus, this heat!'

On the way to the village we got lost. Four times. 'Nichi *mou*, I'm sorry, but if these *malakas* would only update their fucking stupid maps.'

'Christos, why are we in the car on such a hot day, look, why don't we just call it quits and turn back?'

'No! We've come this far! I refuse to be beaten by these idiots!'

When we finally made it to the village there was little to see. In the church a service was taking place, and as we didn't want to join it, we couldn't exactly go in. Everybody in the village seemed to be at the service. There wasn't even a *periptero* open for us to buy a drink or snack.

'Come on, I'll show you the square where my parents had their wedding reception.'

Christos set off round the back of the church. I trundled off after him then ran up alongside him so that we could hold hands. But it was too hot to hold hands. When we got to the square there was nothing to see. It was just an empty square, bereft of decoration. I don't know what I'd been expecting. 'Imagine – the whole village here at Mama and Papa's wedding reception!'

'The whole village?' I was incredulous. 'Did they know everybody?'

'Probably not,' Christos replied. 'But it's a source of pride to them, especially to Mama. To have your wedding day marked by so many people like that.'

I felt a wave of envy, and then one of resignation. Realistically, we were never going to get married here in Greece. I wasn't part of this culture. I couldn't have had a load of strangers at my reception, pinning money on to my dress and showering me with blessings that I didn't know the meaning of. Not when I couldn't even get the family I would be marrying into to understand me.

For four nights we had eaten dinner with Christos's parents. For four nights I had sat in appetite-snatching trepidation, waiting for the topic of the PhD to come up. But it didn't. I feared, and also slightly longed for, an altercation so I could at least show them how hurt I was by what had happened. But instead, on the afternoon that I left for the airport, they simply kissed me goodbye as pleasantly and as warmly as they ever had. Clearly they felt nothing needed to be said.

Christos, meanwhile, had too much to say. Only he couldn't say it. Before he let me pass through passport control, he clung to me like never before, constantly rearranging my hair, stroking my cheek, fondling the back of my neck like a mother cat about to give up her kitten to new owners.

'*Kali mou*, we had a good holiday, didn't we?'

'We did. I love these holidays. Let's never stop coming to Greece.'

'Ha! Well, I don't think there's much chance of that!'

'I hate leaving. It never gets easier. Always harder. Christos, maybe we should move to Athens?'

'*Arketa*, Nichi *mou*, what rubbish are you talking? I certainly don't want to live in Greece. Why do you think I came to study in Britain? I don't know how you'd manage. I wouldn't!'

'I'd write! You can write from anywhere. Don't you think we could do it?'

'I'd never ask you to do it.'

'But I would do it. I'd do it for you.'

'Nichi *mou* . . .' Tears brimmed in Christos's eyes. Why, I wondered. Because he was touched by my show of dedication? Or because he was feeling guilty about his own lack of sacrifice?

'We're still going to be together at least half the week, *kali mou*, you know that, don't you.'

'I know. I guess that just means half the week sleepless.'

He grinned and pulled the sleazy-Greek face. 'Oh, I hope so. I'll be making up for the nights we are alone.'

'You'll have to. I can't sleep without you any more, Christos. The bed's emptiness, it . . .'

I couldn't get any more words out after that. I think we must have held each other as though our love depended on it, but I don't remember. Amnesia felt preferable to a memory of abject pain. Like the first time we'd tried to make love and failed. Why didn't I remember the first time? Was that some ominous portent for everything we built together afterwards?

An officious attendant waved at me, demanding I clear security.

'Three weeks, Nichi *mou*. Then we'll be back together again.'

I nodded dumbly. 'Together again' had a hollow ring. Together again didn't mean the same thing any more.

The next morning, which was Saturday, I woke up early and cheerfully determined. I was fed up with feeling sorry for myself, of thinking myself abandoned, and decided to reframe the separate-living situation as an opportunity for newfound liberty. I could write and read uninterrupted. I could go to extra yoga classes. I could have dinner whenever I wanted, including in bed if I so chose, with my plate on my lap and my laptop

resting on my lower legs, a practice that Christos absolutely
forbade.

So I began to pack. After all, my new room was ready for
me whenever I wanted it. The sooner I moved in, the sooner
we moved on to the next phase of our relationship. I would
have to wait for Christos to bring a couple of large things over
to the flat in the car when he returned, but I could take a
suitcase, at least, and maybe a rucksack.

I packed what I could and, an hour later, heaved myself up
on to the tube with my belongings, like a determined snail.
When I changed at Victoria, a beautifully mannered young man
with exquisite tattoos covering his arms asked if I'd like a hand
with my suitcase. I said no. I made it a rule to never carry a
bag I couldn't lift myself. I didn't need any help.

At my flat, my new housemate Helen was watching TV in
the living room, laughing raucously at some animal out-takes
programme. I said a polite hi then dragged my bags into my
new room. There was a bookcase, desk and dressing table with
an elegant oval mirror mounted on it. Identikit furniture from
Ikea, I guessed. And a double bed. But that was it. God, it was
like being a student again.

I put a framed photo of me and Christos on the desk so
that I could see it from the bed. Suddenly I didn't want to stay
here tonight after all. I'd move in properly tomorrow.

On Monday morning I made a different commute to work, via
Waterloo Bridge, often voted 'best view of the capital' by its
residents. I thought of the Dr Johnson quote: 'When a man is
tired of London he is tired of life', and marvelled at the thought
that I had barely awakened to the city at all.

This was to be my last week at the hospital. When I got back
from Greece there was a letter waiting for me to say that I had
been successful in my application for an internship at an arts
magazine, and could I start a week on Tuesday. I had applied
for the post months ago. It was the perfect distraction from the

impasse that was currently my relationship with Christos.

When I arrived at work I rang the job agency that contracted me out to the hospital to tell them that I'd no longer be needing my secretarial position, then informed my line manager, Susan. She was a gracious lady in her early forties, richly attractive, with one of those immaculate blonde bobs that always hung just so.

'Come back any time you like, my lovely, if the writing doesn't work out. Hope they're paying you well at this new place?'

'Well, actually, they're not paying me at all.' I don't know why I felt ashamed, but I did. It wasn't my fault the creative industries thought it OK to exploit flaming graduate ambition and translate it into flailing free labour.

'Oh!'

I could tell Susan didn't understand.

'It's just what you have to do, Susan. Eventually you get enough experience to apply for a paying job.' At least I hoped that's how it would pan out. 'I've been trying to save up money so that I can afford to work the next month unpaid. But thank you for saying I'm welcome back.'

She smiled at me like a deputy headmistress dismissing a prefect. 'Well, you always will be. Take care of yourself – and who knows, maybe next time you're back it'll be with a ring on that finger!'

I feigned a smile in reply and muddled my way out of her office.

That evening I called Gina. She had texted me to say she wanted an update on how the holiday had panned out.

Gina was one of those supremely life-enhancing people who combine dry humour with a relentless optimism, and have a rare ability to see the wood for the trees. I had known her almost exactly the same length of time as I'd known Christos. We also met in our final year at university and I knew I wanted to be her friend from the moment I saw her. There was something about Gina's strut that exuded a sense of shrewd mischief and before long we were curled up in each other's rooms discussing

Sylvia Plath, the merits of men in eyeliner and watching episodes of the awful yet addictive US show, *Gilmore Girls*.

These days, Gina was a restaurant manager. She still had the same long, loose black curls; she still loved to dance in cute boots and coloured jeans, and was still impervious to most male attention, despite being jaw-lockingly attractive. Gina prioritised her friends and her family above anything else, often to her own detriment.

Now I tried to put into words how things stood with me and Christos and found myself struggling.

There was a sceptical silence on the other end of the line before she launched into a barrage of questions. 'So, when is Christos coming back? Is he back now? Will he be back for your birthday?'

'Soon. Not yet. Yes. Everything's fine, really.'

But Gina wasn't going to be palmed off that easily.

'So what happened about the living arrangements? Did you manage to convince his parents that you're an excellent study companion?'

'No. But we talked it through,' I lied.

'So does that mean he's going to be staying at yours most of the time? Did he agree to evening study breaks?'

'We didn't get on to discussing the fine details.'

'You know, Nichi, you deserve his time. If he treasures you . . .'

'He gives me his time, Gina,' I snapped. Then I backtracked. 'Sorry, I didn't mean to be rude.' I sighed. 'I'm just a bit on edge, what with the new flat and the upcoming internship. Anyway, tell me how you are . . .'

Thursday was my birthday. Ordinarily I'd have taken the day off but with only three working days left at the hospital before I went wageless, it made no sense to lose a day's pay.

I was late to the office. My mum had called me from Australia and then Christos rang on his way to the university library. He'd arrived back in London yesterday morning and had spent the day moving all of his things out of our old flat, which we had now officially vacated, and into his new one.

'*Hronia polla*, Nichi *mou*! Happy Birthday! Do you have your present?'

'I do! Shall I open it while I'm on the phone to you?'

'No, that makes me nervous! *S'agapo*! Open it when I'm off the line.'

We were meeting for dinner later, but Christos had wanted to make sure I had something to unwrap when I woke up. Before I left Greece, Christos had pressed a tiny blue box on me. 'Not a diamond,' he laughed. I opened it now. Two tiny star-shaped silver earrings twinkled back at me. They were from an exclusive Athenian jewellers. They were beautiful. The man could have written a textbook on how to woo.

As I hurried through A&E to my office, I thought about that phrase, '*hronia polla*'. It basically translated as 'many years' and made me think of the conversation we'd had about times past that night in the resort. I hated waking up on my birthday without Christos beside me. Why hadn't I gone over to stay at his last night? He'd said he was too tired but it wouldn't have been any trouble to him to let me crawl into his bed.

When I got to my desk there was a decorated chocolate caterpillar cake perched on a filing cabinet at the top end of the office. My colleague Emma grinned at me. 'What did the divine Christos get you?'

'These earrings.'

'Let me see?'

I touched the studs protectively. Emma came over.

'Oh my, they're not diamond, are they?'

'No, not diamond.'

'The man's got good taste. Just wait for the big one.'

That night Christos and I met my younger brother, Alistair, for a quiet dinner in Soho. My brother was busy studying for an MA and though we were close, we rarely managed to meet up any more. He was ferociously intelligent, quiet and thoughtful, with a dry sardonic wit. He got on with Christos as if they were already family.

We started reminiscing about the fun we had had together over the years. Alistair began to laugh. 'Do you remember when we made you that Giorgos card, Christos, for your birthday? It had a picture of George Michael on the front during his Wham! days and you thought it was from the guy in the gym you knew who was also called George . . .'

'. . . and that he was cracking on to you, Christos *mou*!' I added. 'Oh God!'

'Yeah, and then I nearly went and confronted him about it because of you two!'

The three of us laughed together, and dinner carried on in this way, punctuated with our shared memories.

As soon as the bill had been paid Alistair had to make a move. 'Don't study too hard, Mog,' I warned him. Mog was our mutual nickname for one another.

'I won't, Mog, don't worry. Good luck with the PhD, Christos,' he said.

I gave Alistair an affectionate kiss on the cheek, and they patted one another on the back, before he slipped off back to his university halls.

Christos and I sat facing each other. I was happy and relaxed. This was the right way to spend a birthday, with two people I liked as much as I loved. 'What do you want to do, Christos *mou*? Shall we stay at mine tonight? Or I can stay at yours? I don't have any clean clothes but I think you have that dress at yours, don't you, the one I left in Greece that Mimi sent over with you?'

Christos gave me a troubled smile then leaned across the table to stroke my head. 'Nichi *mou*, I need to go home tonight.'

'Well, like I said, I can come to you.'

'No, Nichi *mou*. I mean I need to go home alone. I just have so much reading for tomorrow. I need to be up early in the morning. Need to be ready to study.'

I stared at him. Not tonight, Christos. Not on my birthday. 'But Christos, I need to be up too. I'm still at the hospital this week, remember?'

'Well then, all the more reason for us both to stay at our places tonight. I'll come across at the weekend. Sunday, perhaps. I'll make you a nice dinner.'

'But Christos, it's my birthday!'

'But Nichi *mou*, I'm here! We've had a nice dinner with your brother and now we can just go home and prepare for our busy days tomorrow.' I started to put on my jacket. 'Come on, Nichi, you know how difficult this is for me. You saw how Alistair had to rush off there to get back to his books.'

'Christos, it's just one night. My birthday night. Jesus, when are we ever going to have sex any more? We might as well be bloody married!' The waitress looked over at me nervously. I clearly looked as though I were about to make a scene.

'Let's go,' Christos said, and ushered me out of the restaurant.

We walked to the tube together in silence.

'So do I need to make an appointment to sleep with my boyfriend these days or what?'

'Nichi *mou*, things are going to be a little trickier from now on. But come on, this is just one night.'

If he didn't understand why this night wasn't just like every other night then I couldn't explain it to him.

'See you on Sunday, yes, little Egg? Golden Birthday Egg?' He took my face in his hands and kissed me.

I was beginning to lose patience with this.

As the weeks passed it become apparent that my birthday blue-balling, for want of a better expression, was not an exception. I couldn't remember exactly how many times Christos and I had seen each other since that night, but I could probably count them on two, maybe just one hand. Even at the weekends he was holed up studying. I, meanwhile, had started at the magazine, a happy and laid-back assignment, which left me restless for even more stimulation come the weekend.

Late one Wednesday night, Gina texted me. We hadn't been in touch since the night just before my birthday when her inquisition over Christos had cut just a little too close to the bone. 'Lady, I am so sorry I missed your birthday, I'm a terrible, terrible friend. Why don't we arrange a dance night one Saturday soon and I'll make it up to you xxx'.

A dance was just what I needed.

I texted Gina back and asked whether her friends Clara and Jane, who I'd met at her last birthday party, were also free. I needed to get to know more people in London, didn't I? And I needed some fun. 'How about this Saturday? The sooner the better!' 'What are the chances, my lovely! We are all free!' came the reply.

Saturday arrived. At about 6 p.m. I retrieved my outfit from my wardrobe. With Christos's encouragement, I'd bought a black and turquoise body-con dress from a beachfront boutique back in Pefkos. It was far more figure-hugging than I would usually have opted for but it was cleverly moulded and clung in a flattering way. Tonight would be its first outing, and a long overdue one for me.

The plan was to meet in Soho for drinks and then dancing. No fuss, just a bit of cocktail-lubricated fun. 'And nowhere full of sleazy guys please!' I had pre-warned Gina, who was organising our night out. 'Er, Nichi, you're talking to me!' Gina had replied. 'Queen of Anti-Sleaze!'

We met at nine o'clock. Gina's chosen venue was just as she had promised: buoyant with cocktails and the right kind of filthy house music, and free of irritating men. After two pretentious pomegranate martinis, I began to unwind. Clara and Jane, both law trainees, were making me laugh with tales of the unctuous solicitors they had to work for.

'Nichi's going to laugh herself out of the dress, Clara, if you carry on like this!'

Gina tugged up the neckline of my dress playfully and as I turned to face her something skimmed into my peripheral vision. A man with dark, tousled hair, very pale skin and eyes like seascape marbles was staring at me. Those eyes. They were like lasers.

I looked away.

'Do we want more drinks?' Clara asked. Jane and Gina both nodded vigorously.

'Nichi?'

'Yes, please. Although just a V&T this time.'

'I'm helping,' said Jane. 'Double?'

'Sure! I'm well on my way! Might as well carry on!' I was already pretty tipsy but I couldn't remember the last time I'd got so pleasantly drunk with friends.

'I'm going for a fag,' stated Gina. 'Will you be OK with the bags, Nichi?'

'Of course!'

I waited for them to shuffle off then glanced around the room again. The man with the marble eyes was gone.

I thought about texting Christos and then decided against it. I was still irritated with him over his decision to leave me to sleep alone on the night of my birthday. Plus, I didn't text when I was drunk. For a start I made typos that irritated the hell out of me the next day when I read them back. And I really needed to let go of this. I needed to have some fun and forget about it.

I looked over at the bar. Clara and Jane were being ineptly chatted up by two guys who looked barely out of sixth form. Jane, I could see, was even getting her ID out to show them her age in a bid to put them off.

I wanted to dance, but in these shoes and this dress with this much alcohol inside of me it was probably a bad idea. Where was Gina?

Suddenly I had a sense that I was being watched again. I spun round.

'Hi.' It was him. The man with the marble eyes. He had snuck up behind me.

'Lovely earrings you're wearing there.' He was close enough to admire Christos's birthday present. 'Where are they from?'

I opened my mouth to say, 'I don't know, they were a birthday present from my boyfriend,' then changed my mind.

'Greece,' I replied.

'Ah, *akrivos*, I'm half-Greek!'

Oh, God. How is that once you know one Greek you seem to attract a dozen others?

'Are you Greek?' he asked me.

'*Ohi, alla milo ligo*,' I replied. No, I just speak it a little.

I could tell he was impressed. His smiled. He had tight little dimples beneath those tantalising eyes. I was running out of safe places to gaze.

'Would you like to dance?' he asked me.

'Can you?' I asked back. I don't know why. Why did it matter if he could dance? I wasn't entirely sure if a dance was what he was really asking for.

Then I got a grip, gave myself permission. It's your belated birthday night out, I told myself. You like dancing. You can have an innocuous dance with an attractive half-Greek man without it meaning anything.

'Sure,' I said and got up and followed him.

A minute later and it was clear I should have trusted my instincts. Wasting no time, he put his hands on my backside and pulled me in towards him. I should have said something. But I didn't. He smelled good. Some kind of musk aftershave but I didn't recognise it. I looked at his eyes again. His seascape irises had all but receded and been replaced with two black buttons.

'What's your name?' he asked me. Was he slurring? He was drunker than I was. Which, right now, took some doing.

'What's yours?' I threw it back at him.

He smiled. He didn't reply. No names, then. Instead, he slid his hand up my back, underneath my hair. He tugged at it clumsily. I shook my hair out of his grip.

'Don't pull my hair,' I said. 'That's not nice.'

'Oh, sorry,' he smiled. 'You're vanilla, then.'

What did that mean?

He leaned into me. I could sense things were getting out of hand but I was so drunk I felt as though my body and mind had parted company hours ago, that nothing I thought had any bearing on what I did. I could taste the musk and alcohol on him, could feel the beat of his lust. He bore into me with his now-onyx eyes, came so close that I could feel his lashes graze my face, then stopped his lips a centimetre before mine. 'Kiss me,' he murmured.

'I can't,' I said.

'Yes, you can,' he replied. He elongated the 'can' until it sounded like a yogic drone, and slid the hand that had been in my hair up to the nape of my neck, gently swaying the whole of me from side to side.

How can you? I should have asked myself. But I didn't. Right then, in that moment, I knew that I could.

After what felt like two hours, but must only have been thirty minutes, I came to on the cold, damp bathroom floor of the bar. Gina was leaning over me, scooping me up. 'Come on, Nichi, we're going home. We've been looking everywhere for you. What happened?'

I shook my head, touched my fingers to my lips. They felt as though they'd been bitten.

'Well, anyway, it doesn't matter now. Just as long as you're safe. I would not like to be waking up as you tomorrow!'

On Sunday afternoon Christos texted. 'OK if I call you now, Golden Egg?'

'Yes,' I replied. I couldn't manage an X. A traitor's kiss.

The phone rang. My heart thumped in my chest like a drum ripping its skin. I paused before answering it.

'Hi, Nichi *mou.*'

'Hi,' I replied faintly.

'Nichi, are you OK?'

'Christos, I need to tell you something. It's very serious.' I must tell him right now, I thought. I have to tell him right now. 'I cheated on you last night.'

Silence. For each year of our relationship a second passed. 'Did you hear me?' I quavered.

'I heard you,' he replied. His voice was darker and lower than I had ever known it.

'Christos. Christos *mou* . . .'

Down the line came a half-choking, half-wailing sound. Then Christos spoke again. 'How?'

'In a club. I met this random.' I couldn't even bring myself to say man. 'We went somewhere. Christos, I was drunk. Far too drunk. Utterly wasted, in fact . . .'

Christos knew I rarely drank; surely he'd understand that only if I were completely inebriated would I do something so out of character. I swore to him that I would never do anything as stupid ever again as long as he loved me.

'Nichi,' he interrupted. It came out as three vowels, the second one a sob that obliterated the c.

'Christos, I was off my face. It was a mistake, a terrible mistake but it doesn't mean anything, we can forget about it, you can forgive me. It can't touch us.' I gasped for breath, my own sobs sucking the air out of my excuses.

'Nichi. Nichi . . .' Christos released my name as if he were breaking open a bad spell. He was crying uncontrollably now. Why had I thought this was the right thing to do? My confession had crumpled his heart.

'I'm going to go. I have to go,' he sobbed.

'Christos, please . . .'

'I can't. I can't. I can't,' he repeated, as if trying to shake off the awful truth of my transgression. Then he managed to gather himself for a moment, stifling his own sobs. His silence stopped my heart for a second.

Finally, he spoke.

'Nichi *mou* – you've broken us.'

Chapter 8

At the end of October, I still ached. I was settled in my new flat, at least as settled as I could be anywhere without Christos, and although it had never been our joint home, in my wardrobe, my jewellery box, on my iPod and my bookshelves, he lingered. There wasn't a single part of my daily existence he had not slightly rearranged. Life was on mute. I'd torn up then tossed back at him our gift of a relationship. But still, I lived. There were pressing, professional distractions that left with me with little choice.

I had managed to turn my one-month internship into two, and had performed well enough for the magazine to ask me to stay on longer still. As much as I relished the opportunity, and still got a thrill out of knowing that I was working as an editorial assistant, with words and thoughts, and the kind of culture that enriched rather than eroded life, I simply couldn't afford to work for free for a third month. The trouble was, now that I had had a taste of the kind of intellectual and creative stimulation I had prayed hard study would provide, I couldn't bear to go back to the hospital. I had an interview for an entry-level position on a small travel magazine the following week, and I was crossing all possible digits in the hope I would get it. If I didn't, I was going to have to find another way to earn money.

I was also struggling to fit myself to single life again. I suppose it is one of those myths perpetuated as much by those in London as those outside it that metropolitan downtime consists of fusion cuisine dinners, taxidermy art shows and clothes-swapping parties in disused red telephone boxes. Truth is, it's just as easy to stay in on a Saturday night with only a bottle of wine and the television for company if you don't have many people to share your free time with. In the advert breaks between *The X Factor* I would toy with my phone and think about texting Christos. But I knew it was inappropriate, that it would only lead to more stress and confusion for the both of us. I could cope with making myself miserable but not him. What I wanted now, above anything, was to make a circle of depend-able friends, people who would enrich my life.

I wasn't entirely alone. Besides Gina, Jane and Clara, I did have one or two older friends around. Bobby, for example. Bobby and I had met at a Freshers' Week party and bonded over our mutual bafflement at finding his trousers nearly entirely upright in my bathroom sink the next morning, as if he'd just stepped out of them. We both loved the theatre and were simi-larly impecunious so would often go to Shakespeare's Globe together on the £5 standing tickets. Three hours on our feet could be pretty tough going even for a couple of Bard-batty English grads so we had constructed a two-part solution, which involved splashing out a tenner and going to the first half of a weekend matinee, then wandering off to browse the second-hand books in the stall further down the South Bank and then on to somewhere for a cheap dinner, before returning for the second half of the evening performance on another ticket.

'So, when did you last see Christos?' Bobby asked me gingerly as we wove in between the rows of books in the half-time break of a trip to see *Romeo and Juliet*.

'He came to drop off a birthday cake his grandmother had sent to me about two weeks after he returned from Greece. We both started crying as soon as he laid it down on the counter-pane.'

'Oh, Boggle,' Bobby sighed, using his university nickname for me. 'I don't think I really understand what's wrong with you two.'

'Me neither,' I replied, my eyes filling.

These theatre trips were good for me in some ways, but art as a substitute for love had its hazards. Exposing myself to the sonnets woven into *Romeo and Juliet*, for example, just made me pine all the more for Christos.

Christos and I, meanwhile, were in only minimal contact. It was all we could do to stop ourselves entering into tortured circular conversations.

'Nichi *mou*?'

'Christos!' I would exclaim with relief when I answered the phone to him. Maybe this conversation would be the one. I lurched from one day to the next longing for these opportunities.

'How are things?'

That's all it would take for me to start sobbing.

'Christos . . . this is insane, we can't carry on like this. We've got to try again.'

At that point his voice would begin to quaver too.

'Nichi *mou*, we've been through all this,' he would wobble. 'I'm like a wounded animal that has climbed too far into its shell.'

'But Christos, we love each other. We shouldn't be apart!'

But as far as Christos was concerned, there was no other way. The 'cracked vase' of our relationship, as he had allegorised it, and which I had broken, could not be repaired.

About a week after the outing with Bobby I was distracted from my professional, social and romantic conundrums when my mum phoned to tell me that my very elderly aunt had died. She had been 103, and the funeral was the following week. Would I go?

When I was a little girl Auntie Lillian was a figure of baroque intrigue to me. Originally from my home town of Wakefield, she had moved to the twee seaside resort of Minehead in Somerset with her invalid husband Albert, after he suffered a heart attack in his forties. There she ran a bed and breakfast at a time when working-class women didn't officially run much of anything. Growing up, I had spent childhood summers camping in the West Country, and we always spent an afternoon or two at her house, a stuffy bungalow covered in lace soft furnishings that smelled like boiled fish. It had been the 'show home' when she had first acquired it, and there, among Auntie Lillian's clocks and costume jewellery, I admired her wartime women's fitness medals and listened as she regaled me with tales of the 'men friends' who would take her out dancing while Albert rested up at home. She always wore coloured shift dresses with a cardigan draped elegantly over her shoulders, a tissue tucked up the sleeve, and pale pink lipstick, even well into her nineties.

She had been a handsome, rather than a ravishingly beautiful woman, 'always getting her knees out', I remember my late grandma once saying as she tutted over a picture of Lillian that I later ended up with. According to family rumour she was supposed to marry Albert's brother, but he committed suicide shortly before the wedding. Did that mean she'd lost her first true love, I would often wonder. When she died, among her possessions was a jewellery box full of other people's wedding rings, both men's and women's. I had heard vague stories of how she had acquired or been bequeathed them by her dancing partners.

There was never any suggestion that Auntie Lillian had been unfaithful to Uncle Albert, but she clearly had an allure for men that she wasn't afraid to exert. The rest of the family dismissed her air of innate superiority and thirst for adventure as arrogance. But her boldness in an age when women rarely escaped the apron strings of motherhood, let alone secured their own financial future, established her as a subversive figure of admiration to me. Plus, she had encouraged me to write letters to her all the way through my childhood, which meant that I owed her, in part, my love of language. There was no question of me not going.

On the morning of the funeral, I stood in a damp towel and

examined my wardrobe. I dragged out a dark, double-layered dress with an overlay of off-white polka dots. Then the only smart black jacket I possessed, which was chic but cheap, meaning it was cut a little too tightly about the chest. Black stilettos. I examined a pair of black chiffon knickers. Was it disrespectful to wear sexy underwear to my great-great-aunt's funeral? Or commemorative? I decided it was commemorative and put them on.

I took a train from London Paddington to Taunton, and a cab from there to the crematorium.

My mum had warned me that there were unlikely to be many attendees at the funeral but as I pulled up in front of the chapel I was still startled. This couldn't be right. Could it? A distant family friend I had never met but recognised from photographs, and a representative from the care home Auntie Lillian had been living in for the past fifteen years or so, exchanged pleasantries. They were only waiting for me. One hundred and three years old, and only three people at your funeral, not counting the vicar. Already I felt like weeping for her.

The service was short, and the hymns traditional parting psalms that I had learned at school. 'The Lord is My Shepherd', 'Dear Lord and Father of Mankind, forgive our foolish ways'. I sang as loudly and as brightly as if I were leading hymn practice in assembly, as I sometimes did when I was music prefect. I powered through the higher notes, only occasionally quavering. Mine was the only voice filling the airy, sunlit hall.

Though he was sweet enough, the vicar failed to say anything of genuine relevance or poignancy. He hadn't known Auntie Lillian. And neither, really, had the care-home worker, or the family friend. To be honest, I only knew her through distant, distilled memories, passed on to me by others and herself as an old woman. The real Lillian was the energetic girl from St John's dairy who had dreamed of escaping south and running her own B&B, the tease with just the tiniest hint of coquette about her, the dancer, the antiques collector, and the indomitable lady who had only given up driving her precious silver Beetle in her eighties.

As the service came to a close, the vicar announced that we would now hear her favourite song. It was a rendition of the old tune, 'A Nightingale Sang in Berkeley Square'. Sometimes I passed through the real Berkeley Square on my way to my internship. As the muted brass swelled, I cried properly for her, for a life that had once brimmed with verve and fun. With nobody to recollect them, the memories of her life shrank in on themselves.

I looked back around the empty crematorium. 'Don't end up like Auntie Lillian!' was the familiar cry whenever I told a relative that marriage and children were not my priorities. Was this what was going to happen to me now that I had lost Christos? I imagined myself holed up in a poky little flat, with only my yellowing books and a couple of geriatric sausage dogs for company, lingering by the window every weekday afternoon as I watched young mothers shepherd their children home from school, wondering whether I had missed my chance.

Well, if so, there was nothing I could do about it. Even if you had children it didn't mean they would turn up when you died, did it? And Auntie Lillian had been married, after all. No, this was simply what happened when you outlived all those who had loved you, the result of having enjoyed your life so that you weren't entirely run into the ground and only fit to pop your clogs by retirement age.

On the train back home I reflected on my own situation. Funerals should be life-affirming; so how was I to usher in the next positive phase of my life? By focusing on my career, I decided. I have always found salvation in work, not the futile grind (which I've done plenty of) but the creative kind; the work that you would do whether they paid you or not, if you could only magic away the bills. I thought again about Auntie Lillian and the social expectations she faced. There were no such

strictures on me. I was lucky enough to have the opportunities
and liberty to do what I liked. So I had better get on with it.

No sooner had I made my resolution than Lady Fortune's
wheel stopped on an unusual proposition. Life had forked
before my eyes.

I got through to the final round of the travel magazine job
but was rejected in favour of the other graduate applicant. It
would have been a fun and rewarding position but as much as
I admired her writing style, I couldn't honestly claim to want
to be the next Martha Gellhorn.

I rang Susan at the hospital and asked her if there was any
work. 'For you, Nichi, of course. Just let me know when you
want to come back.' That was reassuring news. But it was also
stultifying. It made me feel defiant. There had to be another
way to make money in a city crawling with opportunity.

On Friday, Gina texted to ask if I wanted to go to a Halloween
party that night. Jesus, it was the end of October already.
Christmas would be here before I knew it, and I would have
absolutely no money to buy anybody's Christmas presents. It
looked like I was just going to have to bite on my frustration
and return to temping. Tonight though, I was going to dress
up and dance and forget about it.

I met Gina in Kensington at 8 p.m. Kensington was a pretty
unlikely place for a house party. Well, unlikely considering the
kinds of people we usually hung out with. They certainly
couldn't afford to live in Kensington.

'Don't worry,' she said when I raised it with her. 'We're going
to the seedy part of W-something, not the slick!'

Costume was optional but encouraged, so Gina and I had
struck a compromise and decided to only wear clothes that we
already owned, and not to go for Gothic overkill, lest the
party was dire enough to force us into town instead. Gina was
therefore wearing a black jumpsuit accessorised with flat
leopard-print boots, while I had opted for red heels and a

pinstripe pinafore dress with a plunging neckline and massive tie-behind bow.

For a girl who stands at just five feet and half an inch tall, I have to say, I have inherited a rather generous chest, which the dress certainly enhanced. At my thinnest I had absolutely nothing to fill a bra at all. There is a Van Gogh sketch called *Sorrow* that depicts the artist's mistress, Sien, allegedly a prostitute, hunched over her distended stomach and tiny shrivelled breasts. For a long time I had it stuck above my desk to remind myself of how I must never mutilate my body again. One of the great things about learning to eat once more was getting my boobs back, and whenever I was feeling anxious about my weight, which sometimes did still happen now that I was no longer the size of a ten-year-old child, I made a point of flaunting my cleavage to reassure myself.

We walked for ten minutes past Holland Park. The area didn't seem that sleazy to me. Slightly past-its-best decadent, perhaps? Suddenly, I knew where we were. Wasn't this where sixties seductress Christine Keeler first lived with her West Indian lover, before she moved in on John Profumo? I'd been reading a book about it only the previous week. I told Gina about it.

Gina laughed. 'You and your wayward anti-heroines, Nichi!'

'Well, you should read about her! She's sort of like a proto-feminist! And she didn't care if anyone thought she was a whore, which was pretty impressive for the time.'

'If you say so!' Gina replied. 'But she didn't sell sex, did she?'

'Well, no, I don't think so. But she was an erotic dancer.'

'That's not the same as being a prostitute,' Gina reprimanded me.

'It's still making money out of your sexuality,' I replied. 'And she clearly knew how to get what she wanted out of feckless men.'

I surprised myself. Did I really think that Christine Keeler was admirable? Well, yes, I supposed I did.

Gina and I turned into a neat cul-de-sac.

'Number twenty-three.' Gina pointed. The front door was flaking purple, with William Morris-style panelled glass above the frame. It must once have looked pretty opulent.

Inside, the flat was disappointingly mundane but it had been very well bedevilled for Halloween. Black billowing sheets drowned the walls and the only illumination in the main room came from a few church candles and strings of iridescent paper skulls, which one of the attendant art students had cleverly interwoven with fairy lights.

'Hey, Gina, glad you could make it!' A buxom blonde girl dressed like a bloodied Little Red Riding Hood approached us. Behind her was a rangily handsome wolf, who I took to be her boyfriend.

'Tina, Jamie!'

Red Riding Hood and her wolf came forward. I saw now that he had a realistically gory wound painted on his furry neck and his head was encased in what was effectively a metal bear trap.

'Brilliant!' I said, gesturing at the wolf's neck.

'Isn't it?' Tina cackled back. 'And here's the most brilliant part.' She held up her hand to demonstrate that she was carrying a lead affixed to the trap, which essentially functioned as a collar. Wolfboy, then, was her prey ensnared, rather than the other way round. 'I do like a bit of feminist revisionism,' she said, with a wink. 'Help yourself to drinks, ladies. There's some kind of punch, or else wine and spirits on the table over there.'

As we went over to fetch drinks, Gina and I continued the conversation we'd been having outside.

'I've got a friend who put herself through a Masters by pole dancing. She says she's not a sex worker, but a sexy worker.'

I burst out laughing and shook my head. 'Well, if that makes her feel better! Isn't the cock just on the wrong side of the trousers?'

'Oh, I'd say so,' offered a knowing voice.

The interjection came from a startlingly made-up woman with glorious bright red hair wearing an elegant black halter-neck dress and patent-leather kitten heels. The dress exposed an intricate Japanese tattoo that crept down her back like clematis.

I glanced at Gina. Was this one of her friends? Gina seemed to be shrugging her eyes at me.

The woman immediately sensed our unease, tittered to herself and swept forward, hand outstretched in friendly greeting. 'I'm Sapphire. Lovely to meet you both. Great party! Haven't they fixed it up freakily?'

She had a low, contralto voice and spoke with an odd cadence. I couldn't place the accent. English with a hint of something else. Or maybe that was just her quirky glamour tricking me. I couldn't tell how old she was either. Something told me early thirties. She had a poise rare among women of my and Gina's age.

'I'm Nichi.' I smiled back. 'And this is Gina.' Gina looked at Sapphire warily.

'So,' I pressed on, 'Sapphire . . . that's an unusual name. Siren-like!'

'Oh,' she laughed blithely. 'It's not my real name. It's my domme name.'

Domme name? I could see that she had caught the consternation cross my face. 'Domme. As in dominatrix. I sexually dominate men for a living.'

'Ahhh!' I replied, dropping my intonation so as not to sound too clueless. I knew what dominatrixes, er, no, what was the plural? – dominatrices – I knew what dominatrices did. For a very tidy sum they tied up overweight businessmen who fantasised about being punished for their capitalist sins, didn't they?

'How do you find it?' I asked casually. I wasn't particularly interested in the mechanics. Besides, she must get sick of being asked inane questions by giggling men and women desperate for lascivious detail.

'Beats working in an office all day. And for The Man.' She

gave me another, more effusive smile. It was the smile of a cream-fed cat. I couldn't decide whether I found her pretty or not. I found her something else, but I couldn't put my finger on what.

Gina eyed Sapphire suspiciously. I could tell that she didn't think too much of her. Having seen that I seemed relaxed, she made her excuses and slipped away. But I stayed. I was intrigued.

'I used to work in the spa industry, you see,' she explained. 'In Paris. Serving a lot of very prissy, spoilt women all day long. I'm an excellent service provider so one day I figured there had to be a more lucrative way of making money out of the fact that I enjoy indulging people.'

Service provider. That was an odd way to put it. Weren't dominatrices usually duped man-haters, or women who had been abused by demonic father figures as little girls?

'That's interesting.' I replied. 'I thought you had to enjoy beating up men to be a dominatrix.'

'Oh, well, don't get me wrong – the beating comes later. I'm not a natural sadist, though. It's really more about mind games. I mean, I do tie them up, spank them, use CBT on them . . .'

'CBT?' I asked. The only CBT I knew was cognitive behavioural therapy, the technique the eating disorder clinic had used to try to get me to believe I wasn't fat when I weighed less than six stone.

'Cock and ball torture,' Sapphire said. 'Basically, tying pretty ribbons around their private parts. Or clipping on weights. Just makes the area more sensitive.'

'So you touch them?'

'Only minimally. Usually not with my hands. With a cane or a crop or something. She glanced down. 'Or my shoe. And you? What do you do?' she enquired.

'Oh, I'm a journalist. Well, I'm trying to be a journalist. I've been interning but the magazine I was working for couldn't pay me so I'm probably going to temp again.' I could have lied but she'd only ask me what publication I worked for. And besides, you never knew who you were going to meet at one of these parties, and what contacts they might have. It paid to be honest.

'Where do you temp?'

'At a hospital. As a medical secretary. It's an odd use of my degree, but at least it's helping people.'

She smiled, nodded, lit a cigarette. Then said, 'You have a great figure, you know.' She gestured to my chest.

'Oh, well, no, I don't.' I blushed. 'A decent rack is just one of the perks of not being skinny.' I could see that she was pretty lean herself, with a small bosom. 'But I'm comfortable in my own skin,' I continued. 'Sex appeal doesn't have much to do with dress size. I learned that the hard way.'

She stared at me thoughtfully, as if totting something up to herself. But she didn't ask me any more questions.

'Nice shoes, too. Not that I ever get to wear open-toes myself these days!'

I was puzzled. I looked again at the acute triangular toes of her patent kitten heels. I'd always had a curious contempt for patent leather ever since my mum had bought me some shiny black sandals as a child. I had refused them because I thought they were too tarty. I must only have been six. How could I have known what tarty was? But I did. Then I went to a party where a classmate of mine was wearing the same sandals and I remember feeling regretfully covetous.

This time my curiosity got the better of me. 'Why not?' I asked.

'Oh, I'm just so busy. I can't keep up with the clients, so I'm nearly always dressed for work! And you can't wear open-toed shoes for my job. I've a late booking after this, in fact. He's picking me up. Here, take my business card. Have a look at my website over the weekend. Do you have a card?'

I shook my head regretfully.

'What's your mobile number?'

I reeled it off unthinkingly, then scolded myself. Why hadn't

I asked what she wanted it for? Did she want me to interview her or something? God knows who would take that as a pitch. Domination wasn't unusual enough to elicit a news story but neither was it acceptable enough for a feature on alternative career women, for example. Sapphire was a sex worker. And who ever wanted a piece about sex workers unless it was a report on punter violence or police miscarriages of justice?

'I'm going to call you,' she said. 'How do you fancy being my vanilla girl?'

'Your what?'

'All you have to do is sit there and stare at the clients as I dominate them. Not every session, but two or three times a week, just for an hour. You don't have to wear anything special and you don't have to say a word. And I'll pay you for your time, of course. It'll be a lot more than your hourly rate at the hospital.'

I hesitated. I felt out of my depth. Christine Keeler aside, I knew virtually nothing about the sex industry, past or present, except that it was something proper feminists were supposed to be very anti. But I needed money and the petite demon in me longed for mischief. I was curious. And above all, I needed a distraction. I couldn't keep dwelling on the Greek tragedy that had become mine and Christos's shattered future.

'Well, that sounds great. I'll look at your website.' But I did have one immediate question. 'What's in it for them if I'm, er, vanilla?'

'The thrill of seeing your first-timer's face react spontaneously to their submission. It's such a turn-on for them.'

So it was my vanilla-girl virginity they were after. My first time to be faked again and again. Hmm. I wasn't used to being a faker! But I was a good actress. I wondered how long you could stay vanilla, though.

'You're going to be fabulous,' she told me. 'I can't wait!' And with that she wrapped her red lacquered fingers around my arm, then swept out.

I wandered back over to Gina, who was chatting with the now unleashed Wolf. 'How was your inquisition with the Mistress?' Gina joked. 'Did she try to recruit you to her Dark Arts or something? Jamie says she's always scouting parties in the hope of finding an assistant.'

'Gina, I'm a journalist,' I reminded her.

I reminded myself.

Chapter 9

I looked at Sapphire's website over the weekend, as instructed. It had pictures of Sapphire in queenly pose, shot from the perspective of someone on their knees, and looking as though she could tear a man limb from limb with just her aggressive smile. Sapphire in white jodphurs with a riding crop; Sapphire in an elegant rubber prom dress holding aloft a pair of women's knickers; Sapphire dressed in a power suit and vertiginous stilettos, brandishing an unfastened collar in her beautifully manicured hands.

On Tuesday, Sapphire called me.

'Hi, Nichi, how are you? Had a good weekend? Did you manage to take a look at the website? Nothing too terrifying on there, I hope!'

I had perused a list setting out what Sapphire would do: over-the-knee spanking, tie and tease, public humiliation, feminisation, strap-on worship, foot worship, and CBT – the same CBT that she had explained to me at the party. Underneath the list was an ambiguous statement. 'This is not exhaustive and I am happy to consider your proposal for subservience to me. If you're lucky, I might even satisfy it.' There was also a disclaimer. 'Please note: I do NOT offer intimate body worship, penetrative sex or hard sports. DO NOT ASK FOR THESE SERVICES.'

'No, nothing too alarming,' I replied, mirroring her language.

'Well, like I said, all you have to do is sit there and stare. Now, about the money . . .'

On her website, I had clicked on 'Rates'. Jesus. This woman earned as much in two hours as I did working a full week at the hospital.

'Obviously as you're only my assistant we can't charge for you the same as for me, but how does a hundred pounds an hour sound to start with? We can always raise it once . . . well, let's just see if you enjoy it first.'

One hundred pounds an hour? Lord, this sounded too easy to be true. To sit there and stare? I mean, any idiot could get that from me for free on the tube if I was feeling sod-side out, as we say in Yorkshire.

'So, the client I went to see after the party, well, I was telling him about you. Don't worry, nothing personal, not your name or occupation or anything like that. He'd love to meet you. Are you free on Thursday?'

Yes, I was free on Thursday. Technically, I was free every day. I was unemployed, after all. But . . . No buts, I told myself. It was one hundred pounds.

'Yes, I'm free on Thursday.'

'Oh, that's great. So his name is Robert and he'd like to take us to lunch, which he'll pay for, and then back to my office for a session. I'll be chastising him, all you have to do is watch me. And then you can go home. With one hundred pounds.'

What was there to say, apart from, 'Sounds great.'

'Wonderful! Well, I'll text you the name of the restaurant. It's some Italian place. As for costume, well, you suit dresses, so just remember to look like an everyday girl. Wear what you'd wear if we were having lunch together. Anyway, I'd better run, my eleven o'clock is here. Oh, and one more thing – think of a new name for yourself. We never use our real names.'

Two nights later and I lay in bed wondering what I was letting myself in for. I had hung up my outfit on the wardrobe. It consisted of a dark flared dress decorated with tiny roses, with sleeves and a high neck, and barely heeled Mary Janes. It didn't shout sex; it announced sedately that I had more important things on my mind than flaunting my flesh.

I had been through the safety issues with Sapphire on the phone earlier that afternoon. 'The lady I rent the office from is also an escort. She knows exactly what time I'm meant to be in and what time I'm meant to be out. I text her when I arrive and when I leave, and she comes and checks up on me if she doesn't hear anything. There's a water-based fire extinguisher in the room we work in. If anything was ever to go wrong I'd hose them! But it won't. It never has. There's nothing to worry about.'

I had so many other concerns and questions, though. Would the client wear shirt and braces? Have halitosis? Call us 'my dears'? I mean, what exactly were these men's motivations? Was this just going to be an excuse for them to ogle our young, firm (well, firm-ish) bodies? Or were they after something else altogether? And how would it feel watching someone taunt and tease someone else sexually? Sure, I'd watched porn, but never the domination kind. I knew this was play violence but – was it? Did you have to be a bit unhinged to indulge in it?

I couldn't answer any of these questions. I would just have to wait and see. Just think of it as acting, I told myself. After all, that's what I'd wanted to do all the while I was growing up. And if it's terribly disturbing, you never have to do it again. One for the memoirs. Besides, who knows – it might even turn out to be thrilling. Despite my nerves, I giggled to myself at the thought, before finally sinking into sleep.

'This is Robert.'

Robert, Robert. My, what a ham of a man you are, Robert, I thought. Robert actually looked like a waxy ham, as he glistened damply beneath his striped polo shirt. Mid-height, receding hairline concealed with a crew cut. He was alarmingly normal.

'We'll have one gin and tonic, Robert. And one mineral water. I'm allergic to alcohol,' she confided in a stage whisper. I hadn't noticed that at the party but then I'd been too engrossed in our conversation to observe what Sapphire had been drinking. She'd remembered my usual, though. The Ham wove clumsily between the chairs to the bar.

'So, did you think of a name for yourself?'

'Yes!' I said brightly. 'Athena!' From one goddess to another, I'd decided. I don't know why but I thought giving myself a Greek name would somehow enlist Christos as a kind of invisible protector.

Sapphire winced. 'Hmm, it's a bit – artificial. I think for a vanilla girl you need something simpler. How about . . .' Her eyes scanned the room, then she paused and looked right at me. 'How about Jade? Jade suits you so much better. Draws attention to those gorgeous green eyes!'

Her bleached teeth beamed at me like little pearl-handled knives. The Ham was struggling back from the bar with the drinks. 'Oh, and quickly, while I remember, I've told him you're a student; most of them love thinking they're helping out some poor girl who needs the money to study! Just play along with it!'

'Permission to pass you your drink, Madam?' the Ham said breathlessly to Sapphire.

Sapphire nodded and held out her hand. 'Give Mistress Jade hers too, please.'

Mistress Jade! This was hilarious and bizarre. But it did make me feel pleasingly superior.

'Mistress Sapphire says you're studying politics, Mistress Jade. I've got an MA in political science, myself.' A thin twang of Tyneside seeped out of one side of the Ham's mouth.

'Literature, actually,' I corrected him with a smile. I looked at Sapphire to check this was OK. She winked back at me.

'How's work?' she asked him. It was an innocuous enough question, but also weirdly personal. Did the clients really want to talk about their everyday strains and stresses like this? Apparently so. Over the course of lunch it transpired that the Ham was a self-made man. Not quite a millionaire, but the CEO of a PR agency, all the same. He had a chip on his shoulder about where he'd come from, and how far he'd come since. It was the most unattractive thing about him.

'Would you like dessert, Mistress Jade?' Robert asked.

'No thank you.'

Sapphire's head tilted almost imperceptibly.

Uh oh. I wasn't meant to be polite, was I? It was harder than I thought to be rude and mean. I corrected myself. 'No.' My voice tinkled unpleasantly, like the only coin in a charity tin. I was going to need to master coolly scathing the way Sapphire had.

The bill came and was paid.

Sapphire was hardening before my eyes. She flicked her head towards Robert. 'Go to the bathroom and think about what you've done. Mistress Jade and I will wait outside.'

What had he done, I thought? Apart from telling a couple of truly abysmal jokes. Maybe that's just what she said to all of them.

'Yes, Madam.'

As he left, Sapphire turned to me. 'Forget your manners. It's a turn-off.'

'God, I know, I'm sorry'.

She shot me a look. We both laughed. 'Argh, no more sorries!' I scolded myself. Sapphire was friendly towards me right now but something told me she could ice me out in a second. Correcting myself was better than having her do it.

'So, here's what's going to happen now. We're going to take a cab back to the flat.'

I glanced down at my phone, double-checking that I'd given Gina the address just in case Sapphire was the one I needed to be afraid of.

'When we get there, he'll give us the fake leather pants he's bought for me – he's a leather fetishist, you see, albeit a tight-fisted one, so they're Topshop fakes. Then I'll change in front of him as I verbally humiliate him. All you have to do is sit there and watch. We'll be done in about forty minutes, I'd say. Feel free to pitch in but there's no obligation to actually say, and certainly not to *do*, anything at all.'

As we waited, I realised that my heart was pounding. The feeling was a cross between being on the way to meet your first boyfriend, and being sent to the headmistress's office for your first serious school-rules transgression. At once both terribly exciting, and excitingly terrible.

When the cab arrived, the Ham scuttled towards and then away from the vehicle, an apologetic crab gingerly pincering the door handle. I noticed then how shallow his breathing had become. Sapphire stepped up into the cab, one slim leg after the other disappearing into the back. I hesitated, dared for a moment to look directly at him. His eyes were watering. I got in too.

Inside the cab, the Ham's language became even more ingratiating. 'Goddesses, I've brought you these.' Out of his briefcase he brought a handful of high-end fashion magazines. 'I thought you would like to read them on the way to my *punishment.*' He whispered the last word so as to conceal our intentions from the driver. The fact that he was kneeling on the cab floor did ever so slightly give him away.

Ten minutes later and we had reached the 'office'. It was a grubby white terraced house split into flats, with no garden and no drive, the kind of nondescript property London is full of. Suddenly I realised I had no idea at all what to expect. Would we be entering a cosy living room? A decadent boudoir? A fully kitted-out dungeon? God, I really had just gone along with this without thinking it through properly, hadn't I? Gina, at least, knew where I was, but who knew what was actually going to happen once I was on the other side of this door?

Sapphire's right hand swept in and out of the pocket of her leather jacket, placed the key deftly in the lock, turning it soundlessly as she touched a red-tipped finger to her lips, urging silence. Did that mean there were other people living in the building?

The Ham, who had only moments ago been struggling with our bags and the cab fare, was now close behind me, breathing wine-clotted breath into my hair in a fug of paranoia and lust. It urged me across the threshold, and a moment later I was blinking in the plum light cast by a pale white bulb closeted in a red paper lantern. Thick black drapes framed what must be the windows, and there was a faint smell of mildew, uriney jasmine and something else that I couldn't place.

On one end of the mantelpiece stood a statue of the many-armed Hindu goddess of destruction, Kali. For some reason, the statue comforted me, gave me faith that this really was a thinking woman's endeavour, that this wasn't just about servicing sexist men and their sexual whims.

Then I started to take in the rest of the room. Mounted next to Kali's head were crops, whips, canes, flagellators, chains, a horse brush, hairbrushes, and rubber hairband-like rings. Across the hearth hung smaller straps, some plain leather, some supporting coloured balls, and one with an oversized fake penis projecting from its centre. The strap was as narrow as a neck-brace, and I imagined Sapphire armoured up to the hilt in it.

In the right-hand corner, attached to the wall, was some kind of strange, X-shaped restraining frame, and what looked like a dirtier version of the horse I'd never quite managed to vault over in school gymnastics, its leather skin split like a lip. Next to it was a bookcase on which was displayed an array of ladies' shoes. Although limited to black and red, here was footwear for all occupations: PVC stilettos and low-heeled leather courts, police-woman's lace-ups and embroidered oriental pumps. Slingbacks, kitten heels, brogues, platforms and perspex stripper heels. Even wellingtons. Above them, spare shoelaces suffocated brass hooks.

'So, how do you like my dungeon, Mistress Jade?' Sapphire asked. She was smiling indulgently, not at me but at the Ham. 'This is Mistress Jade's first time at the dungeon, Robert.' He gave an audible groan. 'See,' she laughed. 'I told you it turns him on.'

The Ham fell to his knees. 'Please may I kiss Mistress Jade's feet, Mistress Sapphire? Please. I just want to show her how grateful I am to her for letting a pathetic, ugly, overweight pig like me be in her presence.'

Sapphire smirked. 'No, you may not. Mistress Jade is just here to watch. If you are exceptionally well behaved, I may – I stress MAY – let you kiss mine. But first go to the bathroom and wash. I don't want your filthy piggy self despoiling my lovely office.'

He nodded rapidly, and backed away, head hung in prostration.

When he was safely in the bathroom, Sapphire turned to me. 'You OK?' My heart was thumping a little less ferociously now. This was like being part of some surreal university play where the emotions are so overheightened it leaves you wanting to laugh at every glib action.

'Yes, I'm fine,' I replied.

'OK, good. Now, why don't you sit over there on that throne.' The 'throne' was one of those seventies-style high-backed wicker chairs with a rich damask cover thrown over it, situated at the back of the room. 'I'm going to walk around him a bit and then sit here while I tease him.' She gestured to another giant armchair, with a slightly stained seat cover, nearer to the door.

'I know this all seems far more ridiculous than sublime so don't worry about laughing at him, will you? If you want to laugh, just let it out! The more humiliated he feels, the more it turns him on. And the more he's turned on, the more likelihood of him coming back.'

I really couldn't understand how two women laughing at you could get you off. But I wanted to find out.

There was a timid knock on the bottom of the door.

'Enter!' commanded Sapphire.

Butting the door open with his head, the Ham crawled in on his hands and knees. I giggled involuntarily. He really did look utterly ridiculous. As soon as he saw me laughing he looked into my eyes longingly.

'A-a-a-a!' Sapphire clapped her hands. 'Did I say you could look at her? Did I?'

He hung his head in shame and shivered.

'No, Mistress, you didn't.'

'No, that's right, I didn't.' Then she softened. 'Aww, my poor little pig-toy. You're just so weak when there's someone else around, aren't you? You can't help but show off.' She cooed at him like he really was a scrabbling animal.

He looked up at her like she'd just called him the most handsome man on earth. This was bizarre.

'Now, Robert, I want you to crawl to my feet and bring me your tribute.'

His tribute? What was that? Out of his back pocket, Robert produced a crisp white envelope folded once over, and put it in his mouth. Ah! Our money.

'Now, I want you to present it to me in the way I like.'

Robert rose up on his knees for a moment and began to undo the buttons at the neck of his polo shirt, before pulling it up and over his head awkwardly, so as to avoid dropping the envelope clutched between his teeth. Then he fumbled with his belt and struggled with the zip of his jeans, before yanking them down past his rotund white stomach. With his jeans about his knees, I could now see that he was wearing white Calvin Klein briefs. For some reason that made me laugh again.

Sapphire turned around to face me and smiled gleefully.

'See, she's laughing at you, Robert. She thinks the sight of you in your try-too-hard underwear is funny. And I—' she bent down and pushed her face right up before his '—happen to agree,' and let out a peal of nasty laughter, before knocking him sideways with her knee.

The Ham groaned as if Sapphire had just slid her hand into his briefs.

'Get back into position. But before you do, take these jeans off. And your shoes and socks. And those pathetic pants of yours.'

The Ham scrambled to free himself of his remaining clothes. I felt embarrassed for him and, for a moment, wondered where to look. But my curiosity drew my eyes back to him.

He looked right at me again. He still had the envelope in his mouth. As I glanced at his pasty body, I could tell that he saw the look of mild contempt upon my face. I could also tell that he had a violent erection because of it.

'What did I say?' Sapphire hissed at him. 'You do NOT look at her. She doesn't want to see you! And she certainly doesn't want to see THAT.' Sapphire pointed at his penis, and swooped down towards him. He cowered in fright, dropping the envelope. Sapphire spun around to face me, shaking her head like a she-lion. She was pretty terrifying.

'I give up,' she said, still with her back to him, and went to sit in her chair. She closed her eyes, thrust her chin and chest up towards the ceiling as she arched back into the chair and kicked one long, slim leg up into it, drawing attention to the crotch of her tight black jeans. Then taking a deep dramatic breath, she opened her eyes again in wide accusation. Her red hair seemed to burn in the purplish light.

Meanwhile, the Ham had frantically crammed the envelope back in his mouth. He kept his eyes fixed on the floor now, body quivering. His cock was even harder.

'Bring me that tribute. This charade has already gone on too long. And where are my leather leggings?'

He sneaked a hand up to the envelope, temporarily removed it from his mouth. 'They're waiting for you in the bathroom, Mistress. I thought you would want to change in private.'

Sapphire stared right through him, then turned to me. 'Mistress Jade – before I slap this man's face until it matches the colour of his balls, would you be so kind as to fetch the leggings for me?'

I nodded and got up out of my throne awkwardly, taking care to give the Ham a wide berth as I retrieved the leggings. When I came back into the room he had crawled to rest by Sapphire's feet and she held the envelope in her elegant fingers. She patted him on the head. 'Good piggy. Ah, Mistress Jade, thank you,' she said as I passed her the leggings.

She held them up to the light and scrutinised them.

'Do you like them, Goddess?' the Ham asked overenthusiastically.

'No,' she snapped. 'They're awful. Terribly unflattering.'

'But you have a wonderful figure, Goddess,' came the Ham's reply.

'Shut up. When I want your opinion on my figure, I'll ask for it. Did I ask for it?'

The Ham said nothing. She slapped him across the face with the back of her hand. He whimpered with arousal.

'I asked you if I'd asked for it, you impudent slug.'

I let out a half-gasp, half-laugh. Impudent slug. That was a good one.

'No, Mistress, no, Madam, no, Goddess, I'm so sorry, I shouldn't have spoken out of turn.'

He buried his face into the carpet at her feet.

'Well, anyway, I'm going to put these disgusting things on. Back away.'

He shuffled back along the carpet towards the door. I caught him sneak a glance at me. Sapphire had bent down to undo the zips of her high-heeled boots and didn't see it this time. Should I report him for it? Maybe not. I didn't want to get too involved. I already felt far more involved than I'd anticipated I would do. So sitting and staring wasn't actually entirely passive. But it was certainly more psychologically intriguing than I had bet on it being.

Sapphire placed her boots to one side and sat up.

'Right, now, are you going to watch me while I put these on? Since you've paid so much money for the privilege?'

Wow. She'd actually just mentioned the money outright. Wasn't that a little crass?

He crawled hurriedly towards her.

'Yes, Goddess, oh, please, Goddess, it's such an honour to bring you your tribute.'

She picked up the leatherette leggings and held them up to examine them once more, then placed them on the arm of the chair. Then she began to unbutton her jeans, fingers inching down along the fly teasingly. The Ham was mesmerised. She snapped her fingers at him.

'Look at my face, you fool. Don't stare at my snatch.'

'No, Madam, of course not, Madam.' He looked up ador-
ingly into her eyes.

'That's better.'

Sapphire arched up out of the chair and inched the fabric
of her jeans down around her bottom, stopping them halfway
around her hips to reveal a hint of black lace. Her skin was
even whiter than mine. Hang on a minute, what should I be
doing? Was I allowed to look? I decided to flit my eyes between
the two of them, as if watching a game of tennis. I guess I'd
learn this way just exactly what actions turned the clients on.

Sapphire sat there for a moment, stroked the edge of her
knickers, then said to the Ham, 'Don't even think about what
you can never have. You're not, are you?'

'Of course not,' he whispered thickly. 'But Mistress,' he asked
her, 'may I, can I . . . can I touch myself?'

Sapphire sighed. 'What do you think, Mistress Jade? Do you
think Robert should be allowed to touch himself?'

I looked at the floor. It was too much. She was asking me? I
had no idea what the right answer was. I forced myself to meet
her gaze. Thankfully she could see that I was uncomfortable.
'Robert, I think you might make Mistress Jade uncomfortable if
you do that.'

His face fell.

'And besides,' she said, smiling wickedly, 'I think it's good
for you to go home frustrated sometimes – don't you?'

Robert clearly didn't but he knew what the correct answer
was. 'Of course, Mistress Sapphire, whatever you and Mistress
Jade wish.'

'Well, since I'm so benevolent, how about a compromise.
You can touch yourself. But no cumming. And let's shift around
so Mistress Jade doesn't have to see this.'

She got up out of her chair, jeans still slung down around
her hips, and swiveled her chair. Then she directed him so that
he had his back to me. The strip resumed.

Sapphire continued to ease her jeans down around her small,

pert bottom. Then she stood up and rapidly pulled them down to her ankles, her slim white legs gleaming as she stepped out of them.

'Now, where are the leggings?'

'There, Madam!' He pointed to the edge of the chair. She kicked his hand out of the way.

'I know where they are, you moron, I put them there! It was a rhetorical question!'

She snatched up the leggings, smiled at him, then sat back down. Draping herself seductively over the chair, she pointed the toes of one manicured foot and directed it into the leg hole, inching the fabric up past her heel and around her calf, until her toes thrust forward and out of the bottom. The Ham moaned. She slid the leatherette all the way up her leg, then repeated the motion on the other side. I couldn't see what the Ham was doing, but his movements were becoming increasingly jerky. Sapphire smiled one last wide smile and arched up and eased the leggings up over her bottom. The Ham groaned so loudly I jumped in my throne.

'Oh Mistress, oh Goddess, there is no one who can put on leather like you, Mistress. Oh God, oh God, how I work just to serve you, just to earn money to pay to see you do this. Please may I kiss your feet, Goddess? Just one kiss on each foot, please. I beg you.'

Sapphire held up her left foot and danced it about in front of him. Then she rested her toes on the floor, the rest of her foot held up in an impossible arch. 'Kiss it then!' He did her bidding. His whole body was shaking, shaking so much that I wondered if he wasn't about to break the conditions of the leather show. Then Sapphire held out the other foot in front of his face. This time she didn't bring it to rest on the floor. 'Go on!' she barked, but just before he could go to kiss her hovering foot she playfully kicked him in the face.

'Ha!' she said. 'You're greedy. And greedy little pigs don't always get what they want. Now off with you! Get up, take your clothes into that bathroom, get dressed and disappear!'

*   *   *

After he had gone, Sapphire explained to me.

'They're not usually like that, you know. He's such a creep. Slobbering and sliming himself over the floor and wanting to be treated like an animal. He's the kind of client everyone thinks you have to deal with on a day-to-day basis. But I figured he could be your baptism of fire.'

If that's as creepy as they got, I could handle a few more of them a week, I thought.

Sapphire continued. 'It's usually much more obviously erotic than that. And I'm generally much nicer to the ones I like. Even when they are middle-aged and balding.' She grinned.

I quite liked the very unappealing PR exec crawling about the floor like a, what had she called him, again? Impudent slug, that was it. At least I didn't have to feign any kind of sexy act. It was easy like this. And hardly sex work. I wasn't sure how I felt about 'more erotic'.

As Sapphire rearranged her Titian locks into their chignon, her BlackBerry vibrated. 'Oh, look at that! That's Charles asking if he could see us both on Monday morning. And while we were sessioning, another of my clients got back to me and asked for Wednesday. So much interest in you already, Nichi! And honestly, I can't tell you how pleased I am with you. It's easy just sitting and staring, isn't it?'

I couldn't deny it. It was. A bit too easy. And God, I needed the money.

On the train home I fingered the brushed nylon hem of my dress and wondered if I looked different. I scanned the faces of my fellow passengers. Implacable as lizards. They had no idea what I'd been up to. And why should they? What does a sex worker look like anyway?

Jade. I tried the name out again. What was a jade? A worn-out horse. A wanton woman. An emerald substitute.

It's just because you've got green eyes, I told myself. Don't read so much in to it.

Chapter 10

Over the next few weeks Sapphire and I saw an array of male submissives, thankfully none of them like the Ham. The vanilla-girl ploy was proving irresistible to the clients. Mainly because it wasn't a ploy at all. Each session Sapphire would push the boundaries of my knowledge of BDSM, otherwise known as bondage, domination, sadism and masochism, a little bit further. But I was still frequently visibly startled by what I saw.

I watched my first over-the-knee spanking and my first crop-ping (basically a beating across the backside with a horse crop.) I watched Sapphire tie them to chairs, the horse, or the X-cross, (an upright wooden rack for tying a slave to) and tease them mercilessly with her hands, feet and other implements. The balls on leather straps, I learned, were gags, and I winced the first time I saw Sapphire thrust the ball between a submissive's teeth. 'Don't worry, Nichi, it's all in the control of the hand movement. Right before I hit his teeth I slow it down so that he has time to bite around it.'

Safety, both ours and the clients', was of paramount import-ance to Sapphire. She was a trained first aider and at the start of each session, if she hadn't already done it by email, she would ask the submissive to confirm the intensity required, listening intently to his answer. 'Like I said when we first met, Nichi, I'm not actually a sadist!'

Initially I looked to the clients' erections as proof they were enjoying themselves but I soon learned that this could be misleading. Some of them never got hard at all. 'It's all in their heads,' Sapphire would explain. 'They'll go home and wank over it later.' That, to me, seemed like a complete waste of money. If they didn't even get hard at the sight of us, wouldn't it have been easier and cheaper to sit at home and watch BDSM porn?

'Of course not!' Sapphire had explained. 'You can't put a price on a natural reaction. Or on real women subjecting you to your fantasy humiliation scenario.'

The stereotype of the geriatric former public schoolboy longing for a nostalgic caning only held true occasionally; there were bankers, lawyers, financiers, marketing managers and social workers, all longing to feel the wrath of Sapphire's tongue and the back of her hand while I sat and observed. Their fantasies were as unique as they were – and yet each wanted the same basic thing: they wanted to be subjected to female sexual power. From the moment the submissives handed over that white envelope, Sapphire was in complete control. She was the directrice of their sexual fantasies, and they didn't have to do a thing but let her guide them. I was beginning to under-stand how that could be intoxicating.

About a month after that first session, we were booked by a man with a penchant for verbal humiliation. Sapphire read me his email as we drank tea and did our make-up prior to his arrival. 'Dear Mistress. I hope this missive finds you well. I am a forty-something entrepreneur looking for an intelligent domin-ation session. I have three degrees and several published academic papers to my name. As such, along with a good hand spank and some tie and tease delivered by your strict self, I would love to experience a nasty verbal dressing-down, or perhaps a commentary on my humiliation by a scathing friend of yours?'

'So.' Sapphire elongated the o, as she applied mascara in the mirror. 'How do you feel about playing my assistant today, rather than my vanilla girl?'

'Um . . .'

'It's more money,' she offered immediately. 'I just think with your literary inclinations, you'll be great at this verbal stuff.'

It was true that it was hard for me, with my love of acting

and my university radio experience, to keep my mouth shut. I loved hearing the combinations of insulting adjectives Sapphire would string together, and would often sit there with my own composition scorching the tip of my tongue. And while I was still hunting for a paid journalism job, this was arguably a better use of my creative skills than temping.

'Well, sure, why not. He sounds interesting.'

'Oh, *such* an interesting one. The last time he came here we enacted a fantasy whereby he was a male model, and I was a female artist drawing him in an art class. He wanted me to walk around him and critique his appearance. Basically, to objectify him the way women are objectified. He said he wanted to know what it felt like to be at the mercy of my scrutinising gaze.'

So he wasn't just thinking with his cock. That was actually rather reflective for a male sexual fantasy. I liked the sound of this guy.

'That's very cerebral. Sounds a bit too good to be true! Will he really get off on just being objectified?'

'I think the trick is to make him feel as though you are dissecting him, weighing him up as a sexual possibility, but ultimately rejecting any kind of physical experience with him – which obviously you are because you won't come into any bodily contact with him. You're just trying to take him down a peg or two.'

That made more sense. I thought about all those untouchable beauties who populated Renaissance love poetry. Basically, I had to play with that will-she-won't-she power. And be a bitch with it.

'But don't I need to sex up my outfit a little bit if I'm to get involved in the tease?'

I looked down at my clothes. I was wearing a long embroidered prom skirt and a tight black scoop-neck sweater, tights and flat leather riding boots. December daywear.

'Oh, I don't think so. Like I said, he's cerebral. Not that what you look like doesn't matter at all, but you can still see your shape. That sweater is tight as, Nichi! Maybe just pull your skirt up around the tops of your boots. And anyway, don't worry about anything; I'm the one who's going to test for a "response".' She winked at me as she readjusted her stocking tops and fished around in her make-up bag for her signature dark-red lipstick.

I still felt a little unsure. At that moment, I realised something about myself: I wasn't a natural tease. Despite my feminism, if somebody expressed interest in me in a bar and I was interested too, I would angle myself to best emphasise my curves. Could domming teach me a different kind of seduction? Could I really turn on a man dressed, not in a figure-flaunting outfit and heels, but in my everyday clothes, and with just the power of my words and the odd hard stare? And if so, why did Sapphire wear the outfits she did?

The doorbell rang. 'Would you answer it, Mistress Jade?' Sapphire said, with a smile, reeling us both into character. 'He's called James. Well, that's the name he's given, anyway.'

I got up and went to let him in. The man on the doorstep was handsome with tousled blond-grey hair, ice-blue eyes and a very slightly hooked nose. He gave me a funny little bow, his forehead setting into concentrated creases. 'Hello, James. I'm Jade.' I offered him my hand then remembered what Sapphire had said about not talking in the hallway. I ushered him into the office.

'Well, hello, James dear, how are you?' Sapphire gushed. She was like a business-class air hostess, especially with that suit and stockings combo, and her red hair hoisted up into its trademark chignon. 'Would you like a drink? You know we only have water, but still!' she tinkled.

James smiled gravely. 'Some water would be wonderful, thank you. Oh, but first may I give you this.'

He brought out the requisite white envelope.

'Thank you so much,' Sapphire replied, as if she were a professional fundraiser and he had just donated to her campaign. She tucked the envelope in a jewelled tea caddie kept on a desk in the corner of the room. Always get the money first, was the sex worker mantra. But sometimes, slightly alarmingly, Sapphire forgot with the regulars. I guessed it was because she was so comfortable with them that she trusted them to pay up, regardless. So far, they always had.

'Mistress Jade, some water for James, would you oblige?' I went off to fetch a glass of water. When I returned, Sapphire and James were already in an in-depth conversation about microloans to women in sub-Saharan Africa.

'So that's where I make my business "give back", as it were,' James was explaining to her. 'Ending female poverty is, after all, crucial to enabling female emancipation.'

'Oh, we're all for ending female poverty, aren't we, Mistress Jade!'

'Are you a student?' James asked me.

I nodded.

'Mistress Jade loves literature, James. That's why I invited her along today. I think she has the requisite skills to be able to . . .' she paused '. . . disassemble you.' Sapphire was winding us both into the role play now. An hour did go fast, that I knew, and there was a lot to fit in if this guy was to be spanked and teased to the soundtrack of my cutting observations. I settled into the throne.

'Anyway, James, that's enough of your small talk. I don't want to hear your voice again for a while. Instead, I want to see some humility, please. And you're wearing too many clothes. Lose some. But keep your pants on.'

'You're wearing too many clothes.' It was a line I would come to hear many more times, but its accusatory tone always appealed to the clients. James began to undress obediently, placing his clothes in an exacting pile on the floor. Sometimes, if they were going back to work, the clients would ask for a hanger on which to place their suit jackets. I supposed it was in a bid to avoid the crumpling that they presumed, in their paranoia, would out them as punters.

Sapphire circled James for a moment, trailing her white hands over his body. He was in extremely good shape for a forty-something, with a well-defined chest and burgeoning six-pack.

'Have you lost weight?' she enquired.

'I've got a personal trainer, Mistress. He comes to my office five times a week.'

'Well, I'm glad to see you're getting your money's worth out of him!'

'Yes, Mistress.'

As she danced her fingers across his chest she paused to squeeze his nipples. He flinched and began to breathe more rapidly. Then Sapphire dug her nails in. I looked down at his cock. Hard already.

'Hard already, I see,' I said, witheringly. 'Disappointing.'

Sapphire's eyes widened in approval and she bit her bottom lip excitedly. James looked at me too. God, he really was a handsome older man, wasn't he. My own breath caught in my throat a little. I concealed this with a brusque 'Aherm!'

'Sorry, Mistress,' James breathed, in my direction this time.

Over the past few weeks I had noticed that there was a direct correlation between how handsome the clients were and how intimate Sapphire was with them. Now, I was beginning to understand why. Engaging with him like this was exciting me.

'Well, let's see what we can do about that hard-on, shall we?' Sapphire smirked. 'Otherwise Mistress Jade will be forced to give her devastating opinion on it.'

I spoke again. 'And it will be highly, shall we say . . .' I paused, searching for the right word. 'Belittling,' I pronounced finally. James stared at me silently. His blue eyes were wide in alarm, and full of longing.

Sapphire went over to the desk and brought forward a straight-backed armless office chair. She sat on the chair, making sure to slide her skirt up to reveal her stocking tops, then patted her slim, silky thighs.

'Over you get.'

James shuffled over and lay across her knee, his head hanging.

'I want you to count out loud as I spank you. And don't forget your manners. Mistress Jade, pay close attention to how this . . . object,' she paused for effect, 'reacts to his treatment and feel free to voice any concerns you have either about his physique or his level of arousal.'

Over the course of fifteen minutes or so, I watched Sapphire warm up James's bottom with soft, well-paced and then harder, more frantic smacks.

James counted Sapphire's strokes out loud and said, 'Thank you, Mistress' after each set of ten. Sapphire smoothed her hands over his finely shaped bottom, occasionally digging her red nails into his white flesh, and after each set I would offer an observation, on the tensing of his shoulders, the shape of his biceps or the sight of his ever-straining cock, sometimes complimenting him on his physique, but mainly observing what little control he had over himself. Remembering what Sapphire had said about disassembling him, my aim was to reduce him to a hub of attractive but essentially useless body parts. If he flinched as Sapphire went to strike him, I teased him for being a sissy. If he moaned with arousal, I chastised him for indulging his feeble male desire. Basically whatever was wrong with James, I was there to vocalise.

Once Sapphire had given him a final rapid hand spanking and made him go and examine his flushed, pink cheeks in the mirror – 'Oh my, don't you colour up well for a man!' – she tied him to the X-cross. It was already mounted with wrist and ankle cuffs and as she yanked each of his limbs into place, she pressed her body against each one in turn, to ensure he couldn't get away, looking up at his face as she did so, taunting him sensually. James was silent but there was an incriminating patch of damp on the crotch of his briefs.

'Still got that indulgent erection, I see,' I ventured. 'Mistress Sapphire troubles herself to give you a thorough corrective spanking, and that's how you repay her? Such a rude, vain, undeserving little man.'

Sapphire looked back at me, where I was reclining on the

throne. 'Mistress Jade, I don't suppose you'd like to come and get a closer look at this pathetic specimen, would you.' She trailed one finger over the swell of his cock and looked up into his face. James remained silent but shuddered, involuntarily closing his eyes.

I hesitated for a moment. Sapphire noticed my reluctance, and reassured me, in keeping with the role play. 'I wouldn't suggest that you deign to touch him.'

James opened his eyes and looked at me. Was he really a very notable entrepreneur? There was something distinctly aristocratic about him. His movements, even while he was shackled to a cross in his underwear, were so poised, so gracious. I did want to get a better look at him. 'Oh my, and Mistress Jade, he smells so good. Is that Kenzo Pour Homme you're wearing?' she asked him.

Christos's fragrance. My heart turned over, but this was no time to lose concentration. I got up out of my throne, dropping my skirt as I did so, and sauntered over.

'Now, where were we?' teased Sapphire. 'Oh, I know.' She reached over to the rack of implements above the cross and selected a riding crop. 'I think it's perhaps time to try and beat that erection out of you.'

James took a sharp intake of breath. I knew that didn't mean Sapphire was actually going to beat his balls to a pulp, but he didn't. She brought the crop down to his briefs, and slid the end of it up under the fabric of the left leg, until it was stretching out his waistband. Lunging her body towards him, she peered down into his briefs.

'Are you proud of this?' she asked him. Even just through the fabric I could see that his cock was sizeable, but suggesting otherwise tapped in to that basic male insecurity, and humiliated him.

'No,' he replied weakly. 'I know that I'm arrogant, that I think I'm well hung. But there's also a voice in my head that warns me I could be wrong.'

I was standing to the right of him now, about a foot away.

If I'd reached out my arm I could have taken his erection in hand myself. But I didn't.

'Well, you clearly haven't been listening to it, have you,' I replied sarcastically. 'Else Mistress Sapphire and I wouldn't be wasting our time re-educating you now. Maybe though,' I went on, 'it's just that you're rather deluded.' Sapphire peered into his briefs again. 'Able to kid yourself into thinking that you are not under women's constant surveillance,' I continued. Sapphire let the waistband snap back against his skin. 'Able to forget that women don't always like what they see when they see you.'

'Yes!' he gasped.

Aha. We'd found his trigger.

'Good at deluding yourself into thinking every beautiful, intelligent, sexually awakened woman you meet can't help but fall for a narcissistic fool like you. Good-looking, monied, educated, suave, do-gooding . . . I bet you think you're a walking seduction. What girl wouldn't be impressed by a man who donates money to women in Africa? What woman wouldn't want to suck off such a generous cock?' I pursed my lips, punched the word 'cock' out into the air. I was pleased with that last sentence, with its multiple meanings, its cruel suggestiveness, its bitchy character assassination. I felt powerful, and lustful. I hoped this was what he'd wanted.

I could see James's pulse beating in his throat. His hard-on was raging. It was working. Sapphire held the crop like a spear. Placing it flat against his stomach, she slid it into his waistband and began to inch his briefs down with it, revealing his throbbing cock.

'Do you think,' I paused, placing my hands on my hips, and moving closer in to him, fixing my eyes on his face now, 'that we, for example, having seen what a narcissistic waste of organs you are, would ever fantasise about sliding ourselves on to THAT?'

Sapphire let the waistband smack back on to his cock. He cried out. She simpered up into his face then yanked his briefs down to his ankles. James jumped in lustful panic, rattling the cross. He was fully exposed now and I took a good look at him. Oh my. That was a very appealing cock. I looked at Sapphire. Her eyes were gleaming. I was pretty sure she was thinking the same thing.

'No,' he whispered thickly. 'I would never presume to know anything,' he said apologetically. I could smell the Kenzo on him. How I loved that fragrance.

'Good job,' I said, as Sapphire swung back the crop and smacked his balls with it.

I gasped involuntarily. I thought James would crumple but he didn't. Instead, he arched back against the cross in pleasure. Sapphire smacked him a few more times. Each time, his body tensed and then sank into a luxurious spasm. No matter how much she hit him, he clearly wasn't going to lose his erection.

'Well, James,' Sapphire announced, 'I think it's time for you to have your reward. Or perhaps it's your punishment.' I wasn't exactly sure what Sapphire meant by that, but I presumed she was going to let him orgasm.

She reached back over to the rack and took off a large vibrator. Or rather, a top-selling back massager from the US that had somehow become a cult sex toy, in part from being used widely in online porn videos. I'd watched her use it on clients before. It gave them rapid, shuddering orgasms.

She slid the switch to turn the device on. It started to whirr. She brought it down to the base of James's cock. He jerked in gratitude and started to undulate against it.

'Well, aren't you quite the little whore, thrusting yourself up against the toy like that,' I whispered into his ear. He turned his head sharply towards me and looked up into my eyes, desperately aroused. He was panting frantically now.

Sapphire dragged the vibrator up along the shaft of his cock, lingering over the underside of the head, before running it back down again. Every so often she would remove it completely and let James hang here, his face completely overtaken with anguish as he waited for the next stroke. Any minute now he was going to climax, I could tell. I stepped back away from him. I knew it sometimes happened accidentally, but I wasn't ready to be ejaculated on.

Sapphire, meanwhile, was sliding the vibrator up and down his shaft with one hand and stroking up and down along the insides of his thighs with the other. 'What a good little slut you are, taking my tease like this,' she murmured, clawing at him, groping for his balls.

'I'm coming, I'm coming,' James cried. Just as he was on the brink of climax, Sapphire released her hand from his balls, then yanked the vibrator off his cock, turning what should have been shudders of satisfaction into jerks of incredulous frustration, leaving James ejaculating into thin air.

'That'll teach you,' she breathed fiercely into his face. 'Your first ruined orgasm.'

Jesus! So that was what Sapphire meant by a ruined orgasm! I'd heard her mention it several times but never figured out exactly what it was. That had been cruel. But, God. Denial was intoxicating. He hung there for a few seconds panting, coming out of the role play. Sapphire was rapidly unshackling him. Most of them wanted out of the office as soon as they'd climaxed. It broke the submissive spell and then they just felt stupid. But James didn't seem to be in a rush to move anywhere. Finally, he lifted his head up and heaved a smile at both of us. He really was bloody handsome, I thought to myself yet again.

'Gosh, ladies, that was wonderful. That was the best session I've had for, well, let's just say a very long time.' Then he looked right at me. 'She's quite the asset isn't she, your eloquent assistant.' I turned my head away so that neither Sapphire nor James could see me blush.

'Nichi, you did so well today. James even gave me an extra £50 to give to you as a tip. Look, why don't you become my permanent assistant? You're a natural at this. You never freeze up and you never run out of things to say. And I know that you're not afraid of touching them.'

How did Sapphire know that? It was true that I'd been so close to reaching out for James's cock today that I'd had to dig my own nails into my hand to stop myself, but how could Sapphire have figured that? Maybe she hadn't. Maybe this was just her way of trying to persuade me to join her in the ranks of London's professional Mistresses.

'I can train you up to become a proper domme. And then, when you feel ready, you can take on some of your own clients. Think of how much money you could make. You could just work a couple of times a week and fund your interning. Hell, you wouldn't even need to get a paying journalism job if you got a handful of regulars. You could write for free!'

On the way home I considered Sapphire's proposal properly. The financial crash wasn't exactly going to be turning journalism's economic fortunes around any time soon. On the site where Sapphire and I advertised we had noticed that rates for even conventional escorting were dropping – it was a myth that sex work was recession-proof. But the majority of the clients that came Sapphire's way never quibbled on price. They were ingratiating, and they wanted to serve us.

It never failed to amaze me that submissive men always found money for this kind of sex. They were so desperate for it. That was the part I actually found tragic. The old line 'my wife doesn't understand me' took on a special resonance in the case of our clients. For the vast majority of them, this wasn't about wanting to cheat, or to get off on being intimate with another woman, but about wanting a sexual experience they could never ask their partners for. At home, in their own bedrooms, to ask to relinquish the dominance society had foisted upon them was emasculating and would have diminished them in their wives' and girlfriends' eyes. Coming to Sapphire and me gave them a temporary respite from having to play the conqueror, and liberated all of us from rigid sexual convention that stipulated that men should always be on top. I had no doubt that we were actually saving marriages.

Besides, today, I'd experienced a kind of sexual alchemy. Something I didn't know existed had been invoked in me. I'd actually felt myself getting turned on by James, his adoring gaze and the way his tremulous, pliant body, tied up on the cross for us to tease, responded to my mental manipulation. There were far worse ways to earn a temporary living.

But if I was going to do this I needed to set myself an end date. Hadn't Sapphire once told me she had wanted, ultimately, to get into advertising? I didn't see her making any moves towards it. You could get stuck in sex work. You could get a little too used to the money. I didn't want that to happen to me.

The next morning I texted Sapphire. 'I'm in!'

Immediately, she called me. 'Nichi, this is amazing! I'm so pleased! OK, well, first things first. Costume. Do you have a black pencil skirt? What about stockings? And stilettos? And a black jacket?'

They were office basics; didn't every woman have these in her wardrobe?

'Is that all I need?'

'Well, you've seen what I wear. They never complain! It pains me to think about all my expensive leather and latex, which I never get to show off apart from when I update my pictures. The Executive Bitch look is where it's at. Oh, these men,' she sighed. 'So unimaginative!'

'OK, but what do we do about telling the clients?'

'Well, if they're new ones I'll say I offer sessions with my assistant; if they're old ones, I'll tell them that you've decided to become a vanilla-domme! How does that sound? But we can start your training straight away. Greg again, you remember him, the fully grown schoolboy, he's coming tomorrow morning at eleven o'clock for OTK spanking.'

And so my full initiation into the role of dominatrix began.

Chapter 11

Over the course of the next few weeks, Sapphire taught me everything she knew about domination. Or at least everything you could teach. It was clear that domming at its highest level was an art – the art of psychodrama and mindfuckery, far more cerebral than it was physical, and that it would take years to perfect. A good domme was part perverse sexual therapist, part human puppeteer; her ability to invoke an almost hypnotic devotion in her slave a seemingly superhuman power. But essentially, the secret to being a good domme was to be able to get into the head of your male submissive, to be able to run with his fantasy and then fly with it somewhere even he didn't know he wanted to go.

In the meantime, there were still practical skills to be acquired. Spanking, for starters. Greg, our eleven o'clock, was to be my guinea pig. There was a technique required of good spanking. Unless a submissive was what you called a total pain-slut, you couldn't just start whacking them on the backside. Erotic spanking required a combination of bodily stimulation and the build-up of suspense. The aim was to spank close enough to the genitals so as to excite the nerve endings there, and also around the anus, and to encourage your submissive to slip into what is called 'sub-space'. Depending on the client, this could be anything from a mild calming of their speech to them entering an almost meditative state.

Some of the clients never actually entered sub-space at all – Greg was one of those – but hanging upside down over an attractive young woman's knee, unable to get up unless she let you, while she subjected you to a few sharp swipes across the backside, usually had some kind of chastening effect.

Greg liked to enact schoolroom scenes. Greg was as obsessed with costume as James had been nonplussed by it. Now that I was Sapphire's assistant, this meant that I had to dress up as a prefect in a cropped white shirt, tie and a pinafore, which bulged unobligingly over my 34D breasts. Sapphire played the headmistress in a very tight black power suit, visible stocking tops and glasses perched authoritatively on the end of her nose.

Greg worked for a shipping company and was in his mid-thirties. He had not been educated at public school, but still he turned up to 'class' in cut-off pinstripe trousers and a suit jacket complete with home-made school badge. Really, he just loved to lech at us in our outfits, and to be spanked and then caned repeatedly. He also liked to push his luck.

At the beginning of the session, Sapphire informed him that she was training me up to carry out some of her spanking duties 'since we seem to be inundated with naughty boys this term.' Greg was the first man to ever go over my knee. As I exposed his bare bottom, I could feel his growing erection grazing my thigh. Greg was actually very attractive, with olive skin, black, slightly hooded eyes and a shaved head, which made the sensation erotic. I went to fondle him. That was the great thing about domination. If a client you found physically repulsive asked you to touch him intimately, you could simply refuse him on the basis that he didn't deserve to be indulged. But when he was hot, you could manhandle – or should that be womanhandle – him at your own behest.

Greg had a honed, footballer's body and some nondescript tribal tattoo at the base of his back. 'A filthy little tramp stamp!' Sapphire pronounced. Generally speaking, I loved tattoos on men, but this was tasteless. It made me feel disdainful towards him, and I harnessed that feeling as I gave him a really good spanking, cupping my palm slightly as Sapphire had showed me, to produce the requisite noise.

Caning was more difficult. It required absolute precision and meticulous care. If you struck too low, it would mark them across the tops of the thighs and sting unpleasantly. If you struck too high you could damage their kidneys, although that really was a worst-case scenario. Sapphire didn't let me cane this time, but she talked me through what she was doing as she was doing it. For many of the clients, the sound of the cane whooshing through the air was what turned them on; it heightened the anticipation of being struck. Sapphire would strut about and whip it about their ears first to wind them up.

'The thing about domination is that most of the clients don't want marking because they have partners to take into consideration,' Sapphire explained, placing one consummate hand on Greg's backside and taking a few practice strokes with the other. 'But caning is a bit different – it's all *about* marking. You are aiming to produce half a dozen neat stripes across the backside. A lingering reminder in the days to come, of his deviance.'

After Greg had been caned, he asked if he could quickly go back over my knee. 'Just for a final ten, Mistress.' I suppressed a smile, but was happy to oblige. I needed the practice, didn't I? So back over Greg went. Only this time, when I got to the third stroke, he slid his hand down my navy-stocking-clad leg and clutched at my ankle, and then ran his fingers back up again.

Before I'd even had a chance to strike him for it, Sapphire swooped on him. 'WHO gave you permission to manhandle my prefect like that?'

Sapphire was fanatical about boundaries and had always told me that I could end a session right then and there if a client overstepped the mark.

'No one, Mistress.' Greg smirked into the carpet and wriggled about over my knee. He was such a cheeky bastard but his good looks and charm made it funny rather than sleazy. Even Sapphire was trying not to laugh.

'Right! Up with you!' Greg clutched at his burning backside, boxer shorts around his ankles, tie and shirt askew, grinning up at Sapphire like an extra from *Gossip Girl*. 'Bend over the horse. You've earned four strokes with your own belt.' And just like that she whipped it out of the loopholes of his makeshift short trousers.

Being hit with your own belt was particularly humiliating; it implied that you weren't worthy of being hit with one of Mistress's implements. Suddenly I had a flashback to that time when Christos had accidentally caught me across the backside with his. I smiled. Greg interpreted the smile as a sign of something else.

'Mistress Jade, would you like to be hit with the belt?' ventured Greg.

'No. She would not,' growled Sapphire, grabbing him by the scruff of his neck and pulling him towards her.

'But Mistress Sapphire, something tells me Mistress Jade needs a small punishment, too.'

'Why?' asked Sapphire suspiciously. 'What's she done?' She let go of him, pushed him back.

'Looked provocative in her uniform. Look at the way her tits protrude out of the top!'

Sapphire scoffed. Then she sidled right back up to Greg and asked seductively, 'What sort of punishment were you thinking, Greg, for Mistress Jade? A ten-strokes-across-my-knee sort of punishment?'

'Yes, yes!' he replied, rather too eagerly, rearranging his cock. She smiled indulgently at him, reaching out her arm to pull me towards her. Shit, was she actually going to do it? I felt my bottom tighten in anticipation of being spanked. I'd never been spanked. How hard was Sapphire planning on hitting me? Was I going to be able to take it? At the last moment she brought her arm swiftly back towards Greg instead, and grabbed him by the balls. Greg let out an excited whimper.

'You'll get to kiss her plump little ass before I get to spank it. Neither of which is ever going to happen. Mistress Jade does not get spanked.'

'So do I get punished again for my insolence, Headmistress?'
Whatever the outcome, it was a win-win for Greg.

For many of the clients, domination was a much more conflicted
experience. Some of them were deeply ashamed of their submissive desires, desires which they had often carried around for
years without confessing them to anyone, let alone enacting
them. Sapphire and I worked hard to explore their fantasies
with them in an accepting and compassionate way – providing,
of course, that what they wanted to experience wasn't going
to result in any actual harm.

One day a hirsute, twenty-something builder turned up at
our door. He was quite short, stockily built with a beautiful
cleft chin. He had with him a bag full of chiffon and lace and
needed, he told us, to be transformed into Victoria, a need he'd
harboured since he was barely a teenager. Victoria was a little
girl who deserved a thorough hair-brushing – and by that he
meant two hundred strokes on his backside, rather than a girly
grooming session.

Victoria liked to wear old-school bloomers under her pale
pink petticoats and even had an adorable black wig neatly
arranged with Hello Kitty hairclips. There was something about
Victoria that was impossibly sweet, and Sapphire and I just
wanted to cuddle him, dressed as he was like a nursery rhyme.

But as eager as he was to share his seven-year-old-girl style
with us, he was also clearly deeply troubled by his predilection.
He lived in fear of his friends finding out about his kink and
asked us if we thought he were 'normal', a question we heard
on an alarmingly regular basis. 'Honey, no such thing!' Sapphire
would reassure him, but that didn't seem to be the answer he
was looking for.

Public humiliation was one of the trickier kinds of domination to pull off. Sapphire had one client, Xavier, an incredibly
charming and impeccably groomed Swiss financier with a mop
of dark-blond hair and light hazel eyes. He also had a luscious

French accent and the most inviting dimples I'd ever seen on a client.

Xavier came to London on business every couple of months. He was obsessed with buying women's knickers, which he liked to wear to multi-million-pound deal-making meetings. He loved to fantasise about how shocked his colleagues would be if they found out, and how humiliated this would make him feel. Mostly, he told us, he fantasised about telling them that his Mistresses had 'made' him do it, that he was our sissy slave, and he wrote Sapphire long, exquisitely constructed emails in which he would detail his servitude to us and general abuse suffered at our hands.

One day he asked if we might accompany him on a shopping trip to a lingerie store. Being paid to chaperone someone, especially an affable good-looking guy, around a shop seemed too good to be true. But it was a little more complicated than that. What Xavier actually wanted was to be forced to try on and then buy women's underwear.

Together, the three of us browsed the store. Despite his chic appearance, Xavier had really quite tarty taste in underwear, and Sapphire and I spent a good ten minutes tutting and steering him away from the tiny bordello-style scarlet thongs he gravitated towards. After a few more minutes of 'correctional' styling, Xavier had settled on several pairs of knickers in an array of styles and colourways. He was desperate to try them on over the top of his own midnight blue, microfibre boxer briefs. We knew he was wearing these because Sapphire had demanded he send a picture when he was getting dressed this morning. Back in Geneva he played water polo and trained hard to maintain his six-pack; his scantily clad body was a joy to behold.

The first hurdle was getting him into the changing room. As you've probably noticed, men aren't generally allowed in the women's, and sales assistants are trained to prevent coupling among the coat hangers. We tried a few tactics, claiming that we needed a 'man's opinion' (which amused us greatly – as if we were the approval-seekers), then, that he was just bringing us different sizes, both of which were foiled. Finally, we managed to sneak him in when the sales assistant's head was turned.

Squeezing us all into a tiny boutique ladies' changing room was like piling two wayward monkeys into a phone box with a skittish springbok. We clawed and wrenched at his clothes, fondled his heaving, hairless chest, sporadically sshing at one another through stifled giggles and matching scarlet manicures. When Sapphire clamped her hand over Xavier's mouth to prevent him from complaining and demanded he put on a saucy panty parade for us NOW, Xavier was clearly in some kind of submissive paradise. His chocolate-pot eyes pleaded with the pair of us to push the game even further.

Hang on a minute. 'What's that?' I asked. The bulge beneath his briefs looked too boxy to be merely his penis. 'That's not just his hard-on, surely?'

Sapphire smiled and patted his thigh in approval.

'Oh, he's such a diligent little slave, I'd completely forgotten about that!'

Sapphire peeled back Xavier's briefs to reveal what looked like a grated metal cage around his cock. It prevented him from getting an erection and from masturbating, and had a combination code lock set into it. At Sapphire's touch I could see him start to strain within it. But the cock cage was forbidding. There was no room for manoeuvre.

'Do you need any help in there?' came a voice from outside the cubicle.

'No, thank you!' Sapphire chimed back as if she didn't have a nearly naked slave in a chastity belt hidden behind the curtain. I laughed again, this time in panic.

'Relax!' said Sapphire. 'She's hardly going to waste police time reporting a couple of giggling girls with their hands on a silly man's trussed-up junk, is she?'

When she put it like that, I supposed not.

'Now, Xavier, since we're running out of time, choose the pair of knickers you think Mistress Jade and I would most like to wear.'

Xavier groped desperately towards the dressing room chair and selected some violet silk Brazilian-style briefs. They had a full bottom, then small but not shoestring sides, and were designed for wearing under low-rise jeans. Sapphire had steered him towards them.

'Excellent. You're going to buy us each a pair, plus a matching bra. Then we'll all be knicker-sisters!'

Xavier gulped and nodded as if he were a teenage boy we'd just accosted for a threesome on his way home from swimming practice. Sapphire and I slunk out from behind the curtain and waited for him by the tills.

Xavier already had our measurements noted down in his phone. He selected the underwear and approached the till. He was sweating, his dimples tightening as he tried to affect a polite smile for the pending transaction.

He looked over to us. Sapphire arched her eyebrows and turned her head slightly to the right. It was a signal but for what, I didn't know. Xavier went up to the sales assistant, a pretty young Asian woman, and offered up the two bras and three pairs of knickers.

'Did you find everything you were looking for today?' she asked him as she ran through the garments, her eyes fixed indifferently on the till.

'Yes, thank you.' He was clearly jittery. In her capacity as oblivious sales assistant, she was effectively being used as a free vanilla girl. 'If only the men of the Six Swiss Exchange could see him now!' I whispered to Sapphire. Sapphire giggled with satisfaction. 'And women!' she replied.

Xavier turned around to drink in the image of us laughing at him.

'Sir?' The sales assistant required his credit card. He blushed. In a fluster he dropped his wallet. Sapphire texted him my remark. His phone, which Sapphire had sunk deep into his pocket as we left the changing room, now vibrated too close to his cock cage, causing an involuntary rattle. The assistant looked at him, startled.

'Fuck,' I bit into my scarf to stop myself from laughing and chanced a look at Sapphire. She was staring right at him and licking her painted lips. Xavier read the text message then slid the phone back in his pocket. Sapphire texted him again. I didn't know what this time. Again, the phone vibrated audibly against his cock cage. Was he stupid or something? He'd slid it right back in there. Or was he just a glutton for public humiliation? Again, the assistant looked at him, this time with increasing suspicion, her mouth souring down at the corners slightly.

'He'd better do it, or he's going to be in big fucking trouble with me,' Sapphire murmured. Suddenly Xavier addressed the assistant. 'Do you think those knickers are the right size?'

The assistant stared at him warily. I sensed a hint of scorn. She flicked back her long dark hair over her shoulder. 'Well, it depends who the knickers are for, sir.'

'Right,' Xavier replied weakly, his dimples hardening like rock literally petrified.

'Are they for one of your friends over there?' She gestured towards us. Oh God. I think I knew what Sapphire had texted him now.

'No, no,' he breathed, then gulped again, looked at the floor, then her face, then over again to us, his eyes imploring us simultaneously to end and to prolong his humiliation. Then finally he plucked up the courage. 'They're for me, Mistress.' The sales assistant stilled her hand on the bag she was packing. Sapphire and I held our breath. Then the cashier laughed. 'Very funny!' she said.

Oh God, that was even worse – she didn't believe him! The pleasure of a genuine vanilla reaction had been scuppered, and Xavier looked utterly crestfallen. He took the bag from her lilac-nailed hands and, with his head down, beat a retreat back to us.

Afterwards, Xavier took us for a restorative cocktail in a bar in Covent Garden where the inky blue light bathed drinkers with an incriminating glow. Sapphire informed Xavier that after successfully purchasing the underwear for us, he now had her permission to release himself from the cage and gave him the combination code. 'Go and do what you need to do and report back here in two minutes.' Xavier bolted to the bathroom. Ten minutes later he still wasn't back.

'Do you think he's done a runner?' I asked her.

'No idea,' Sapphire replied, frowning as she sipped on her cocktail. Then a message on her BlackBerry flashed up. 'Sorry, Mistresses, but I'm having some trouble back here.'

Sapphire rolled her eyes and patted her chignon, as if she were a pre-Raphaelite martyr. 'Let's go help him.'

In the disabled toilet, Xavier was desperately but very unsuccessfully trying to bring himself to climax, his dark blue pants shackling his ankles, the cock cage carelessly tossed onto the floor.

'I've been locked up for so long I can't seem to cum,' he explained, his face blank in desolation.

Sapphire cooed at him sardonically.

'Nature can be very cruel sometimes,' he said to her forlornly.

'Well, what do you expect?' I replied. 'Nature's female.'

The next morning, Xavier emailed Sapphire to say thank you very much for our time but our services weren't quite what he was looking for. 'But we gave him everything he asked for! And more!' I cried. 'Do you think it was the sales assistant not believing him that spoiled it?'

Sapphire shrugged. 'Who knows? I think he's spent so many years wanking over that scenario that the reality couldn't possibly live up to the fantasy.'

The shopping trip may have been something of a failed experiment, but we had come away with our fee, free underwear and some amusing anecdotes. We wished Xavier well in his fruitless quest for fantasy fulfilment. Sometimes, whatever you gave them, it still wasn't enough. If we couldn't satisfy Xavier, who could?

Besides being a source of amusing stories, fixing our finances and occasionally turning us on, domming also provided us with genuine friendship. I realised that for the first time since Christos and I had split, I had stopped feeling quite as lonely.

Sapphire was friends with another couple of girls who worked as mistresses in a for-hire dungeon about fifteen minutes away. Angela and Violet had met at university in the female wrestling squad. After graduating and moving to London together, they'd soon discovered that they could wrestle men for money and get paid a lot more for it. After that, domination was a natural progression. Angela was a Valkyrie-like blonde, slim, tall and impossibly haughty. Violet was smaller with a rangier frame and chaotic black hair that made her look beautiful and slightly crazed.

Sometimes we would all meet for lunch and end up shocking the restaurant staff when our competitive Mistresses storytime got out of hand. There was a healthy rivalry between us, and we would often try to outdo one another with tales of the most debauched thing we'd done to a client that week, or the nicest gift we had received. But there was also a special camaraderie between us. On occasion, we would even 'loan' our slaves out to one another.

'Oh God, I've got American David again tomorrow afternoon. He's currently going through a knickerless face-sitting phase, but I've had an argument with Tony about it.' (Tony was Angela's boyfriend). 'He said it made him really uncomfortable. One of you lot wouldn't take him for fifteen minutes at the end, would you?'

Sapphire and I remained silent. We never did anything that constituted 'intimate body worship' as the advert jargon ran.

Violet shrugged. 'Send him to me. I don't have anyone to care what I do! But you have to do me a favour too – lend me your maid one day this week?'

Angela actually had a man who paid to clean her house. That was one kind of slave we could never get enough of punishing.

Violet suddenly had another thought about the face-sitting obsessive. 'He doesn't lick without asking though, does he?'

Angela laughed. 'He doesn't try it with me. Depends how strict you are, Violet! I don't know where you draw your boundaries!'

We may all have had different boundaries, but what we all

agreed on was a single, exacting standard of safety. Sometimes Sapphire and I would perform outcalls, visiting one of the clients at their home or at a hotel, in which case we would ask one of the other dommes to be our security call. This basically involved us giving them the address of where we were going, with instructions to phone us twenty minutes after the session ended. If they called us three times without us responding, they were to call the police.

It was for the same concern about safety that I declined Sapphire's offer to train me in medical play. She told me that she had on occasion practised urethral play – 'you basically stick something long and fine down the end of their cock' or covered their scrotums with needles until their genitals looked like a pincushion – but it made me shudder and I had absolutely no interest in practising it. I drew the line at using the violet wand, an electric shock-box that plugged in to the mains and pulsed out a mild current which you could then direct to whichever part of the client's anatomy you had dominating designs on. You could shock yourself with it if you grabbed the end without the correct fixture mounted, something I had done several times, even under Sapphire's guidance. I was risk averse, and the violet wand was both as sadistic, and as masochistic, as I got.

In the week before Christmas, Sapphire and I were booked up to three or four times a day. I made more money in that week than in the whole of the previous two months put together.

'It's just because everybody wants to get a bit of pleasurable masochism in before the miserable masochism of enforced family time begins!' Sapphire would joke. But I knew she had a point.

It was now that awful maudlin point in the year when Christmas is aching for New Year, and New Year knows it's going to disappoint Christmas. Christmas was hard enough with half my family on the other side of the world, but this year was my first for several without Christos and I missed him terribly. I struggled through the compulsory jollity, resenting it all. Everything served to remind me that this time last year I was deeply in love with the only man I thought I could marry. But after a tearful Christmas Day, I steeled myself. Christos and I were over for good reason, and I had a life to be lived – and it was an exciting one, at that.

Fortunately, business had slowed but not stopped completely. The clients who came to us at this time tended to be melancholic and lonely, single men for whom the holiday stretched out in an empty waste of solo drinking sessions and hastily declined invitations to share home-made mince pies and carol-singing with their colleagues' children. I could empathise all too easily.

But it was impossible not to be cheered by the countless Christmas gifts we received from clients: perfume, chocolates, Kurt Geiger shoes, thoughtfully selected books we'd mentioned we wanted to read, leather boots and jackets. Admittedly, my vegetarianism struggled with the leather but then the animal was already dead, right? It would have been a waste of a good hide, I decided.

'A good hide for a good hiding!' Sapphire reassured me.

We were also cheered by the number of party invites we received. One night just before New Year's Eve, Sapphire and I found ourselves at the office with nothing to do after a client had cancelled on us at the last minute.

'We've got three options,' Sapphire informed me. 'So there's that cocktail party in Green Park that Roger invited us to, but I'm not sure how we pretend we know him, and besides, it will be full of old men.'

'Young people! I want young people, please!' I pulled a mock pout.

Sapphire nodded knowingly. 'Hell, yes. Hmm, well, there's drinks in Camden with my friend Rosie. She works in TV, you knew some of her friends, don't you remember? Or we could go and hang out with Violet and Co. somewhere up in East

London. She's having a party in that monstrous dilapidated townhouse she shares with about fifteen other people. Knowing Violet, it'll also be full of her male dom exes from across the global fetish scene, so be prepared for your sweet-looking little self to be accosted, Nichi! You know that, outside of work, she's obsessed with being dominated herself, right?'

I nodded. Whenever we had lunch with Violet she would talk as much about her 'Masters' as her clients, of how they would tie her to the bed, force her to suck them off and slap her face, bottom and breasts when she didn't comply. It might have sounded alarming if it wasn't for the very obvious pleasure that possessed her face as she told us about her latest conquering. Intriguingly, the more domming she did professionally, the more she herself wanted to be dominated. That interested me a lot, and I wondered if it was only a matter of time before I became similarly 'wired'.

'That's fine,' I laughed. 'I think I have a few ways of pulling a wayward man into line these days!'

'Oh, don't get me wrong, it's not a "kink" party, and it's not that Violet is only friends with sex workers. But that just makes the conversation all the more fun when you start revealing details about what you do, right?'

Violet's townhouse was a lot harder to find than either Sapphire or I had bargained for. It took us a full twenty minutes, shivering up and down the same murky streets, before we chanced upon it, taking a left when we presumed it could only have been a right. The fact that both of us were wearing our domming shoes with needle-thin stiletto heels made the quest that little bit harder. Usually I never wore shoes I couldn't run in – that was the feminist compromise I had made with myself over high heels. I just loved them too much to forsake them completely – but my KG stilettos were the only suitable shoes I had with me to wear with a black lace minidress.

Violet's house was indeed bizarre. She and her cohorts paid

a security company to let them occupy the house, and in return, got an affordable London rent. For some reason, though, there was no handle on the outside of the door. We had to ring Violet on her mobile to get her to let us in. 'Look up into the security camera so we can check it's you!' she trilled.

Sapphire was short-tempered after our odyssey in heels. 'Violet, who do you think you're talking to, you know it's me and Jade, who else would ever have access to THIS number? Now let us in, I need a drink!'

'You don't drink!'

Violet dared to wind up Sapphire in a way I never would have done.

'Exactly!' replied Sapphire and hung up.

Two minutes later and there was Violet, barefoot in a tight red dress and sheer sequinned leggings, ushering us across the threshold. She had the right wild hair and art-school style to pull off the outfit and made it look more quirky than cabaret.

'You understand now why I'm good in dungeon spaces, having to work this fortress entry system every day!' she joked. 'Lovely to see you, ladies, happy Missed-it-mass!'

We followed her along a high-ceilinged corridor, the walls of which were hung with exquisite collages and paintings of Indian goddesses. 'My friend Sebastian did them. Aren't they beautiful?'

I stopped in front of one particularly gory-looking image. It depicted an Indian deity I didn't recognise, her standing leg mounted on a copulating couple, head in her hand, and some kind of bodily fluid spurting out of her decapitated neck. I winced and thought back to the, by comparison, very tame statue of Kali we had on the office mantelpiece. 'There's a goddess more violent than Kali?' I exclaimed.

Violet came over to the painting. 'Oh, that's Chinnamasta. She's a figure of self-sacrificing sexuality. She resonates for me!' Violet laughed.

We passed into the main living area. It was a stunning open

space decorated with dressmaker's mannequins in vintage aprons and a clutter of mismatched sofas and armchairs. The walls were covered in snapshots of Violet and her housemates on their various travels around the world and about the capital. In the corner, the piece de resistance was a Christmas tree made of wire coat hangers and decorated with women's underwear. In the top left-hand corner of the room was the kitchen space, where at least half of Violet's flatmates were crammed, busily mixing homemade cocktails and carving up an enormous iced cake.

Violet ran over to them and threw her phone down on the worktop. 'Not the cake, not yet! We have to wait until everyone's here to serve it, especially Dan!' Sapphire turned to me and mimed a whip crack.

Suddenly Violet's phone started to ring again. Hands now covered in cake, she craned her head over the screen. 'It's Sebastian! I can't open the door sugared . . . will someone let him in?'

Nobody made a sign to move. Violet called out to me.

'Jade – would you be an angel? My friend Sebastian's at the front door now. Hang on, let me just check the screen.' She ran over to a small television screen which was linked to the outside security camera. 'Yep, that's him, lovely man, *beautiful* man . . . just make sure you come straight back here, yeah? Don't get caught out there in the corridor with him for too long!'

I tottered back down the corridor, taking care not to catch my heels in the strip of red nylon carpet in the now darkened passage. I had no idea where the light switch was. When I got to the door, I realised I also had no idea how to open it; there didn't seem to be a handle on the inside, either. I groped about the frame and then about the wall for something that would release it. Finally, I found a button and a resounding clicking sound suggested that I had made the right choice of fixture. I clawed at the letterbox and pulled the door awkwardly towards me.

If I'd known how to give a low, long whistle, I would have done.

Illuminated by the dull haze of a Victorian street lamp, a tall and beautifully built man, clad in an elegant full-length wool coat, stood on the doorstep. I drank him in. Black hair, shaved at the sides and left slightly longer on top, and a shadow of cultivated stubble that accentuated the planes of his incredible cheekbones and caressed his square jaw and defiant, dimpled chin. Then his eyes: electric blue and fringed with the kind of lashes that sweep you in. *Matia palatia*, palace eyes. That Greek phrase, which I had completely forgotten I knew, bolted back into my mind, and slunk down to my tongue. And finally, there was his mouth. Set in a sumptuous natural pout, his was the most provocative mouth I had ever seen on a man. So this was Sebastian.

He was so mesmerising that I forgot my manners and let him stand there, shivering in his own breath's fog, as I danced my eyes up along his exquisite face, and then caressed them down the hint of throat and clavicle that his coat's upturned collar revealed to me. Running my eyes down the full length of his body, the only other hint of clothing I could see were his grey trousers, artfully tucked into scuffed leather boots. He held, I noticed, a light leather briefcase that cut into the silhouette of his coat.

He looked right back at me, holding my gaze with an unbridled intensity. I could feel the colour creeping into my cheeks, as if he were shading them in with his stare. Then he smiled.

'Come in. Sebastian.' My lips tumbled about his name, transmuted to four syllables by my Yorkshire pronunciation.

His smile tightened apologetically, then he tilted his head to the left. 'I'm terribly sorry, I don't know your name.' A deep, soft voice with the occasional, abrupt clipping of a consonant. Like a tape recording of a wave washing on to shore, interrupted. I couldn't place his accent. Flawless manners, though.

'No, no . . . I . . . Violet just asked me if I would let you in.'

I took a deep breath, revived myself to full domme power, and held out my hand. 'I'm Jade.'

'Hello, Jade.' He closed his hand around mine reverently, as if taking care not to shock me with his touch, then strode gracefully across the threshold, and followed me down the corridor.

His footfalls seemed to chase upon me as we made our way, and I self-consciously clutched at the hem of my lace dress that was whispering about my thighs. As we passed the picture of Chinnamasta, I turned round to look at him. His downcast eyes shot up to meet mine. Was it my imagination or had I caught him watching my ass as I walked? No, he couldn't have been. He was far too polite and I was flattering myself.

As we entered the main room, Violet, who was now liberated of cake, flung herself at him. He kissed her warmly on the lips and gave her a long, enveloping hug.

Sapphire eyed them suspiciously and came towards me with a cocktail.

'Another one of Violet's former captors, I presume.'

I shrugged. 'No idea.'

'Come on.' Sapphire gestured with her head. 'You must meet Violet's friend Katia. She's from San Francisco. She's been making online fetish videos out there, and you *have* to hear some of her stories! I've had such a good idea for a new cuckolding scenario off the back of one . . .'

Half an hour later and Sapphire, Katia and I were still talking 'shop'. Or rather, they were talking and I was barely listening. I was tired and bored, and had a bad case of festive-season fatigue. I was ready for bed. I looked across the room to where Sebastian was engaged in fervent conversation with Violet and a handful of the other guests. I observed him for a minute or so. He spoke little, but listened intently. But when he had something to say, his soft, low voice was entrancing. I had to be a part of that conversation.

'Sapphire, I'm just going to go and talk to Violet for a bit,

I feel as though I've been rude not chatting to her properly all evening.'

'OK!' she shrugged. 'You don't need my permission to go and talk to her!'

As I moved over the tiled floor, my heels tap-tapped in time with my heartbeat. Oh my God. I'm nervous. Get a grip, Mistress.

Sebastian looked up as I approached. That cobalt blue stare again. Were those eyes even natural? Perhaps he wore coloured contact lenses.

Violet, who was thoroughly alcohol-sodden, came over and flung her arms about my neck. She was at least five inches taller than me, and was failing to keep her cleavage out of my face. 'Jade, lovely little Jade. How can you be a mistress when you're so CUTE!' She pinched my cheek theatrically and kissed me.

Then she turned to the group, 'Isn't she the cutest dominatrix you ever saw? She's Sapphire's trainee. Honestly, the way that woman corrupts innocents!'

Playing along, I placed my hand on my hip and fixed her with a domme-glare. 'I'm not as cute as I look, Violet!'

'What do you think, Sebastian? Is Mistress Jade mean?'

'I bet she's terrifying when she's angry,' he replied. Was that meant to be sarcastic? It certainly wasn't ingratiating. His face gave nothing away. Then he gave me a sideways smile. 'How long have you been working as a dominatrix?'

'Not long, a couple of months. Although it feels much longer.'

He nodded knowingly. 'My ex was a domme. Harder work than it is fun, right?'

His ex was a domme? Did that mean he was a submissive? I still found it hard to second-guess people's D/S preferences. It wasn't as though there was a physical type of man that preferred it one way or the other. And good looks had nothing to do with it, as the variety of our client base had shown. Still, for some unfathomable reason, I wanted to know.

'Depends on the client,' I replied. 'There tends to be a correlation between how good-looking they are and how much hard work it is.'

He laughed softly. 'But it's always good to know someone is holding to account the wayward cocks of the world. Vengeful women have their work cut out, it would seem.'

So that meant he must be a submissive. An iridescent bubble, similar to when you realise the sexiest man in the bar isn't looking at you after all, burst softly over me. What was I disappointed about? It's not as though I wanted to find a kinky play partner outside of work. Was it?

He was without his coat now, and wore a smooth, tight black jersey which clung around his copious biceps, and highlighted every muscle that ran up along his strong shoulders and down across his chiselled chest. He leaned towards me in his chair. It startled me and I stepped back involuntarily.

Violet slunk over, and flopped on to the sofa next to Sebastian. 'Don't listen to a word he says, Jade. Sebastian is the most dishonest-honest man I know.' Sebastian laughed at her and shook his head in protest.

'What does that mean?'

'It means,' said Violet, placing her fingers around his throat, and looking up into his eyes, 'don't let him distract you with his veneration of the vagina. He's a Dom dressed up in submissive sentiments.'

'I'm sorry,' he said, 'so I like roughing up women. It's just how I am.' He looked right at me as he said this. His beautiful mouth seemed almost to snarl as it passed through a smile and back into its default semi-pout. 'Doesn't mean I can't appreciate the feisty ones. Besides,' he added, turning back to Violet, 'if there's no fight, what's the fun?'

I was confused. I thought male doms liked good girls they could lead by their hair, tie up and spank without much whimpering. Did this mean there was room for more disturbance in the power-play?

'OK, OK, so you're a little "switchy",' Violet drawled. 'But you know ultimately you're going to get your way.'

'Yeah, Violet,' he murmured at her menacingly. Then sat back, clutched on to the sofa arm causing him to tense his biceps, and affecting a mock Southern US accent said, 'No little lady's getting away from these guns.'

'Oh my God, Sebastian,' Violet groaned and shrieked, playfully pushing him away by the head as he smirked at her. Without missing a beat, he grabbed her by the arm she'd raised against him and pulled her across his knee. She shrieked again, this time in genuine shock, and he laughed at her, a deeper, nastier laugh. This man! This man was impossibly sexy.

Sapphire shouted at Violet from across the room. 'Violet, start behaving! Isn't Dan going to be here any second?' Sebastian put a finger to his sumptuous lips and 'ssshhd' commandingly in Violet's face, before carefully guiding her back up to the seat next to him, keeping one hand on the hem of the dress as he manoeuvred her, in a curiously polite bid to help preserve her modesty. He straightened out her hair, patted her on the head. 'Good girl,' he intoned. Violet clumsily punched him in the chest, and he laughed at her affectionately.

Sapphire came over to me. 'Jade, are you ready to go? We've got a ten a.m. tomorrow, and we don't want to miss the tube.'

'I know, I know.'

'Say your goodbyes!'

I frowned. Why was Sapphire treating me like her little maid all of a sudden? I waved at the group of other people I'd barely introduced myself to, then turned back to Violet and Sebastian.

'Thanks for having us, Violet. You cheered up that truly awful time of year.'

Sebastian smiled and nodded fervently. 'Tell me about it. I'm keen to get back to work.' He looked up at me quite seriously. 'A pleasure to meet you, Jade. I hope we meet again.'

I couldn't bear it. I had to tell him. I took a deep breath. 'My name's not Jade.'

'Oh?' He looked puzzled, then taken aback. 'Have I been calling you the wrong thing all evening?' So well mannered!

'No, not at all. Jade is just my domme name. My real name is . . .' I paused. Something in me decided not to tell him. I needed some leverage here. I needed to create a reason for him to think of me again. He looked up at me expectantly. 'It begins with N. Take care, Sebastian.'

Back home I shook off my shoes and lay down on the bed, fingering the hem of my lace dress. Sebastian. Sebastian, Sebastian. Was he the most beautiful man I'd ever met? Sure, he was stunning-looking but there had to be something else that explained why I'd been so transfixed by him. After all, I didn't know anything about him, and I hadn't even asked. Not where he lived, not what he did for a living. And yet somehow none of these questions had seemed relevant. All I'd wanted to know was what he liked in bed. I shook my head at myself. Come on, Nichi, you think about everything in terms of people's fetishes since you started domming.

I couldn't be bothered to get undressed, and shuffled myself into bed, lace and stockings prickling against the cotton duvet. In my mind's eye, two scenes played over again and again. The first was Sebastian hauling Violet across his knee. His stealth. His grace. That awful, sexy laugh as he held her there over him. And then the way he'd looked at me when I'd opened the door to him. And then it dawned on me.

I wanted Sebastian. I wanted him to dominate me.

Chapter 12

January was a quiet month. All the clients, even the very richest, were watching the pennies after the financial excesses of Christmas, and the pennies did not extend to submissive 'treats'. After all, our services were not something you could offer up in the January sales. The lull in bookings gave me a much-needed time to reflect on where I was headed with the domination.

Sapphire had only been showing me the bondage ropes for two months but my apprenticeship had been so intense that I felt as though I'd been embroiled in the world of pro-domming for much longer. My language, which had once been peppered with Greek, was becoming saturated instead with domme-speak. My chats with Gina were full of references to 'foot worshippers' and 'panty sissies', and phrases such as 'topping from the bottom', which referred to the way a submissive might try to surreptitiously run the show. In some sense, all the clients ran the show, of course. After all, as Sapphire had pointed out when we first met, they were paying us to enact their fantasies. But the most genuine submissives handed over their free will along with their white envelopes. I never felt as though we were catering entirely to their whims because we had so much creative control over the content of the sessions.

Even if my daily life was radically different to how it had been just a few months before, my sexual morals and my sense of how people deserved to be treated had not degenerated one jot. If anything, I was even more compassionate towards other people's sexuality, and the battles they faced in reconciling what society told them it was OK to want with what they actually wanted. I had often reflected on the limitations of women's sexual roles, but domination suggested to me that men were just as restricted. My understanding of what was meant by mutual respect and consent had also been strengthened. In most cases, the clients were far more respectful than the men I met when I went out dancing with Gina, for example, because the boundaries were explicit and the terms of the sexual-economic contract we were entering into were clear. I thought back in particular to that one obscene night in Soho. No, I felt no shame about anything I was doing.

And yet I knew that society thought less of me for it. I knew now that there were men who would never date me because I had sold sexual services. At the pop-up blood donation centre I was turned away because I couldn't answer the question, 'have you ever had sex for money?' with a straight 'no'.

'Even if I've never had penetrative sex with someone for money?'

'You can't donate if you've exchanged sex for money. They're the rules, it's not defined any more specifically than that I'm afraid,' the receptionist explained.

This baffled me. I understood that the restrictions were based on statistical rather than moral reasoning. This was why men who engaged in 'male-to-male sex', as the NHS pamphlet put it, couldn't give blood either – because it was easier to catch the HIV virus that way. That said, I hypothesised that people who had lots of unprotected sex were surely the most high-risk group of all, regardless of whether it was with men or women.

'But why would it matter if I had had sex for money? Surely the more important issue is whether I used a condom or not?' I asked the receptionist.

'We don't condemn anyone's lifestyle choice,' she replied, robotically trotting out the equal opportunities phraseology that somehow managed to sound weighted with condemnation, 'but you belong to a high-risk group.' To this day, I have never been able to give blood.

I would reflect on my newly acquired 'whore' status sometimes as I took a white envelope stuffed with £20 notes to pay
in to the bank once a fortnight. There would be a plethora of
other freelancers not on PAYE paying in their weekly earnings:
child-minding women with other people's babies in fashionable
pushchairs; tradesmen in paint-splattered, sand-blasted overalls,
and, often, some other girl my age, dressed innocuously in jeans
and flats, concentrating hard on transferring from her own
white envelope to the bank's paying-in kind a similar bundle
of banknotes. I would look at her and want to offer a comradely
smile, but, even if she suspected I too was turning tricks, we
never acknowledged one other, such was the secrecy and the
social stigma of earning a living from sex work. I had managed
to secure another, more prestigious internship starting at the
end of February. But it was still unpaid. So this was what I
had to do for at least another three months as I pursued my
final career goal.

Although Sapphire and I made amazing money by many
people's standards, our hourly rate actually wasn't as sumptuous
as it first appeared. Five to ten clients a week didn't mean five
to ten hours' work. There was prep to do; session planning and
tidying up afterwards, research into new sex toys and the latest
BDSM kinks.

What's more, Sapphire invested much of the money she
made back in to the business, buying new equipment and
costumes for the two of us, where required, and spending
money on her website, advertising and professional photos.

Our beautification routines – shaving, moisturising, nail-
painting – were, like our daily wardrobe, not much more than
the basics most women performed just to go to work at the
office each morning. We perfected our own manicures and
pedicures and I got a trainee hairdresser friend to give my
dark-blonde hair some free highlights. I became even more
convinced that most beauty rituals really were carried out for
the benefit of other women, not for men. Interestingly, despite

the fact Sapphire kept her knickers firmly on for domination sessions, she purposefully maintained a well-groomed but full thicket of pubic hair. 'These guys love to see the suggestion of a hairy bush,' she told me. Even if they didn't, she really didn't care. And they never complained about this or any other aspect of our appearances, lending credence to my belief that domming was about much more than surface sex appeal.

The funds were never guaranteed, of course, and there was no way of guarding against session cancellation. We couldn't take a deposit from the clients as this would have involved them giving us their actual names and bank account details, and most of them were as secretive about their real identities as we were about ours.

Sapphire was incredibly good at weeding out the 'time-wasters' – men who had no intention of booking a session, but just wanted a free thrill from a bit of email communication with us. But from time to time we would still find ourselves waiting anxiously at the office. As I quietly fretted about how I would manage to pay my rent that week if this was the start of a trend, an irritated Sapphire would pluck her eyebrows into arched perfection as she gave the imbecile just five more minutes, then finally scowl and swear into the mirror when it became apparent that we'd been duped. 'I could have booked that slot five times over today; I tell you, if I ever catch the cowardly little cunt . . .'

In the meantime, I still hadn't forgotten about that night at Violet's party, and the delicious Sebastian. Truth be told, he'd become my new favourite masturbation fantasy. It had been five months since I split up with Christos and I was finally ready to stop looking back at the 'what might have beens' and focus my energies on the 'what may bes'. Now I was cursing the fact I hadn't somehow procured his number. Anxious not to give away my crush to Sapphire, I had a roundabout conversation with her about it on our first day back in the office after the New Year.

'Sapphire, I'm beginning to get curious about the whole submission thing. I'm wondering if I might like to try it myself.'

Sapphire raised her eyebrows. 'Well, try it if you like, Nichi, but seriously, I think you're like me. You can play kinky but really you're just a passionate vanilla. All this faffing around with crops and paddles and ties. Honetly, all I want when I go home to Matt is a good old plain shag! And a decent cup of tea afterwards.'

Matt was Sapphire's long-suffering boyfriend. She rarely talked about him, even with me, despite our growing closeness, and I found it quite touching that there were clearly still some elements of Sapphire and her life that were non-negotiably private.

'Anyway, you see what happens with Violet. She becomes utterly consumed with these bastards and they're never really nice to her. And then she ends up heartbroken and doesn't eat, and she loses her tits, and her clients cancel because she looks so morbid. You don't want to get in to that. *I* don't want you to get in to that!'

Later that week we had lunch with Violet and Angela again. It was the first time we'd seen Violet since the night of the party. She was utterly morose.

'Jesus, girl, not another one!' Sapphire sighed.

Violet's eyes started to fill with tears. 'Sapphire, don't say anything! Don't say I told you so! I know I'm a fool.'

Angela put her arm around Violet and tucked her hair behind her ears maternally. 'No, you're not a fool. You just, you just give too much of yourself, Violet.'

'What happened?' I asked tentatively.

'Oh, I don't know. One minute Dan and I are having this amazing hot D/S sex, spending every weekend together and making summer travelling plans, and the next he's disappeared.'

'What do you mean, disappeared?' Sapphire asked.

'He's gone off to South Africa. No reason. He just rang me up from the airport, and was like, "take care, doll, see you in March. I'm off to join Sebastian in South Africa".'

'Sebastian?' exclaimed Sapphire.

'Yeah, you know. Sebastian's working on an art project out there. He's got a commission to paint the daughters of some rich white Afrikaaner family or something. Dan said he was going to work as his assistant.'

'And Sebastian didn't tell you this? I thought he was meant to be your friend, Violet!'

Violet shrugged again, biting back fresh tears.

'I've tried Dan's phone and his email but he hasn't responded. I guess we'll just have to wait until they get back. Originally, Sebastian was due back for this big spring fetish ball, you know the one. But who knows now. No doubt they're plotting to seduce the daughters and tie them up.'

Sapphire pursued her lips in disgust. 'Are we done with dominant men now, please?'

One wet evening in mid-February, one of those evenings when you feel spring has decided to take a sabbatical in the Caribbean and will never return, I arrived at the office to find Sapphire in a truly foul mood. Business had started to pick up but this meant our delayed 6 p.m. was going to back into our 7.30. Sapphire had painful, spasming RSI, initially contracted from too much typing as she replied to the dozens of slave-mails she received each day. It was being exacerbated by all the corporal punishment she was having to deliver, for alongside working with me, Sapphire still saw the same number of clients alone. The money she was making was obscene, but I did worry about the toll too much domination was taking on her health. It wasn't as if there was a HR department to check up on her.

At least our 6 p.m., when he did arrive, would hopefully relax her. Jack was a strapping Canadian businessman with the body of a paratrooper and a boyish face, tanned and dimpled. He also had an unapologetic foot fetish. He would pay us to spend a full hour examining, stroking and massaging our feet. We had even trained him up to give us pedicures. At first his hands had shaken too much to do a good job, he had been so in thrall to us and absorbed in the privilege bestowed upon him. But with practice he had improved – mainly because he knew that he would feel the force of our wrath if he didn't. His adoration was so intense, and so pure, that it was almost impossible not to feel genuinely warm towards him because of it.

I would make sure that Sapphire got the first foot massage. We now had access to a second room, which we used as a bedroom, complete with wrought-iron four-poster double bed. Sapphire reclined on it stiffly.

When Jack arrived, he came with his head hung in apologetic deference. 'Mistress, I'm so, so sorry I'm late.' He ran his hand through his hair and tugged at his tie. He'd clearly had a harried day at the office, too. 'I've brought you a gift to say sorry.' It was a Coco de Mer perfume she loved. Did he know that she had nearly run out of her current bottle?

'Yes, I mentioned it in passing last time, didn't I? And he remembered, like the perfect slave he is.' She patted his tanned and dimpled cheek.

Jack was perceptive, and evidently he could see that Sapphire was tense. 'You look like you've had a hard day too, Mistress.'

'Damn right,' she snapped back. 'Honestly, the pain I put myself through for you deviants. My shoulder is killing me.'

Sapphire was struggling to lie flat. I took a spare black velveteen cushion off a nearby chair and gestured that she might like it underneath the offending shoulder. She waved me away before I could get to the bed.

'Don't bother, Jade. It'll only set me at an even more awkward angle. I should have gone to Pilates this morning but instead I waited in for some spineless sissy that I was interviewing to be my cleaning maid. He never turned up. He can forget trying to rearrange that. Now, Jack, be a good little pet and come and do what you're good for!'

Jack approached the bed. He had already stripped down to just his boxer shorts. He clearly had been rushing to get to us. The sweat glistened in tiny beads across his soldier's body, and down the centre of his chest. He never needed to be asked to strip. The routine was always the same when Jack came to serve. I would let him in and he would give an adoring and adorable smile, blue eyes beaming out from beneath his black hair. Once inside, he would place his white envelope on the mantelpiece, or the dressing table, depending on which room we were in, soundlessly take off most of his clothes, hang them on one of the provided hooks and ask who required service first.

Despite his size, Jack was very gentle. But he had simply enormous hands. Both Sapphire and I, by contrast, had rather small feet and he could massage the whole length of one with a single hand, they were so big. Jack cradled our feet the way a love-struck seventeen-year-old cradled his girlfriend's cheek, and stroked our toes with similar adoration.

Jack took Sapphire's left foot to begin with. After a few undulating strokes I could see she was beginning to relax. I relaxed at the sight of that. She slipped back soporifically into the pillows, which were made out of violet sari fabric and coordinated with the curtains. As Sapphire smiled, so did Jack, both of their bodies softening in tandem. Jack got as much out of giving the massage as Sapphire did receiving it. I unscrewed the top off a pot of rose-scented moisturiser to use on Sapphire's feet and passed it to him. Maintaining the massage with his right hand, Jack took some of the lotion in the fingers of his left, then held it in the palm of his hand for a few moments so as to take the chill out of it before he applied it to Sapphire's foot. He really was one of life's pleasers.

'Jack, are you single?' Sapphire queried.

'Yes, Mistress,' he replied in his low Canadian lilt.

'Why?' I exclaimed. Then felt slightly embarrassed. That had been a little overeager.

Jack had the grace to blush, and let out a short laugh.

'Oh, same story with all the guys my age in my line of

employment. We work too much! A pathetic excuse, I know, but there we are.'

'Well, I would say not having a girlfriend was a waste of a good foot fetishist, but I know that's not true,' purred Sapphire. 'I never want you to stop coming here.' The foot massage was having a restorative effect on Sapphire, returning her to her more usual flirty self. 'And that's an order!' she added. We all started laughing.

Jack now moved on to Sapphire's right foot, again warming the lotion in his hand before applying it with conscientious strokes.

'OK, Jade, your turn. I'm very reluctant to hand him over tonight. Don't say I never do anything for you!' That was something I would never have dreamed of saying to Sapphire. She'd given me the means to support myself in London, and to pursue my journalistic goals. I was nothing but grateful to her.

Sapphire shifted over on the bed and patted the mattress. 'Up you get!' she ordered me.

I hopped up obligingly, pulling down my skirt as I did so, so as not to reveal my stocking tops. For some reason, in front of certain clients, I became strangely coy. Sapphire saw me and laughed. 'Oh, Jade, there's still a bit of vanilla in you yet! I'm sure someone could be troubled to beat it out of you!'

'I'd rather not, thanks!' We laughed and as I lay back next to Sapphire she patted my hand affectionately.

Jack smiled at the pair of us stretched out like a couple of Persian princesses and approached the foot of the bed again. I was wearing stockings. He hesitated for a moment, unsure of what he was required, or perhaps, allowed to do.

Sapphire became aware of his stiffness and lifted her head awkwardly up off the pillow. 'Jack, just ask Mistress Jade if you want her to remove her stockings. Or better still,' she added slyly, 'ask her permission to remove them.'

'Mistress Jade, what would you prefer?' he asked me.

'Oh, I don't care,' I said breezily, then thought better of it. That wasn't very assertive. 'Remove my stockings, Jack. But be careful not to ladder them. They're new on.' Sapphire and I got through stockings like most women got through tissues and chewing gum.

Jack gingerly extended his hands up to the lace tops. Then, with his fingers whispering about my thighs, he removed first one stocking and then the other. I started at his touch. Despite the well-heated bedroom, I could feel myself goose-pimpling.

Suddenly, I felt Sapphire stiffen beside me. She flicked her head over to face me. 'What's wrong, Jade, you're not cold are you?' I turned my head in her direction, but couldn't bring myself to meet her gaze. 'A bit,' I lied. Any other time I would have given Sapphire a knowing look or mouthed 'HOT!' to her. But something told me I couldn't possibly let her know that Jack removing my stockings had turned me on.

Jack took my right foot in both hands and ran his thumbs up the centre of my sole, all the while watching my face for a pleasurable reaction. I had never had a professional foot massage, but I couldn't imagine any masseuse surpassing his sensual strokes, his hypnotic technique. I watched as the muscles all the way along his fingers, wrists, forearms, biceps, and finally his naked chest tightened in a bid to ease my tension.

Sapphire turned her head to face the ceiling again and lay there in tranquil repose. She was trying to take a catnap. When Jack left, we literally had a five-minute turnaround before the next client turned up.

'You have truly beautiful feet, Mistress,' Jack murmured.

'Not as beautiful as mine, of course!' Sapphire tinkled, still with her eyes closed. It may have sounded like a joke to Jack, but there was an uncharacteristically snide hint of competitiveness in her remark. Sapphire was never like this with me. Had I done something to offend her without realising?

'Well, of course, you both have exquisitely beautiful feet!' Jack explained. 'It's why I love to serve the pair of you so much!'

But that wasn't good enough for Sapphire. She sat straight up.

'Let's have a competition. Here, Jade, put your foot next to mine so that we can compare properly.'

She slithered down the bed and thrust her right foot forward next to mine, forcing Jack to cease his massaging. 'Take a good look, Jack, and tell us – whose foot is sexier?'

'Sapphire . . .' I gave an uneasy half-laugh. I was sure that Jack was similarly uncomfortable. But if he was, he didn't show it.

'Mistress,' he replied calmly. 'You know how much I adore worshipping your feet, how beautiful I find them. You have such perfect, white soles. But Mistress Jade's feet are just so tiny. And that instep . . .'

I may not have had Sapphire's long, slim legs but a combination of dwarfly genes, years of childhood dance lessons and a (quite literally) overarching love of vertiginous heels had made me a foot fetishist's wet dream. Any other time I would have welcomed compliments for an asset I didn't even know I possessed. But right now, this asset was a threat to my friendship with Sapphire.

She rose up off the bed imperiously. Uh oh. This was just what we didn't need. How could I pull this back? She floated towards the bedroom door, then paused, and looked contemptuously at Jack from over her shoulder.

Then Sapphire said something I had never heard her say before. 'Well, Jack, I'm afraid that's it for today. Your time is up.'

As soon as Jack had left, Sapphire immediately began to complain again about how much pain she was in, and how enervated she felt by the stress of having to deal with so much admin.

'Well, is there anything I could do to help?' I offered. In several senses of the word, I really couldn't afford for Sapphire to be irritated with me.

'Maybe you could start answering some of the emails for me.' She'd clearly already been thinking about this. 'I could pay you a little to do admin. I mean, it's not like you have any other work on the go, is it?'

Oh bloody hell, I still hadn't told her about the new internship. It was going to be a set three days a week so I would no longer be available every day for domination. After everything that had happened this evening, I was even more reluctant to tell her about it. But if I didn't tell her now I risked seeming as though I'd been hiding things from her. Something told me concealment would irritate Sapphire even more.

'Well, actually, it looks as though I've just got a part-time internship. Starts at the end of next week. So I'm only going to be able to work Mondays and Tuesdays from now on, plus evenings and weekends, of course.'

Sapphire was busy at the dressing table. She had taken off her jacket while she touched up her make-up, and the black lace camisole she wore underneath exposed her trailing tattoo. I saw it so infrequently that it reminded me of the first elusive glimpse I had of it – and of Sapphire – the night we met. As I watched her apply a gloss to reawaken her crimson lipstick, I realised I was genuinely afraid of how she might respond. Sapphire may have been my boss and my co-conspirator but she had also effectively become one of my closest friends. Yet, even now, she was somehow just out of emotional reach. As I waited for her verdict, my heart felt as though it were over-beating.

The seconds hung between us like a rope bridge until finally Sapphire merely shrugged and said, 'Nichi, it's fine. It was always a matter of time before you got another job.'

'But it's not a full-time job, Sapphire, just three days a week. I'll still be available much of the time.'

She turned round and smiled at me. It was a genuine smile, if a little stiff. 'Well, maybe it's time for you to start working by yourself, anyway. You can domme without me.'

Was Sapphire sacking me? Or promoting me to autonomous domme status? I couldn't quite tell.

'But there are loads of things I still don't know how to do. *Shibari*, for example! I'm hopeless, I never remember the knots.'

Shibari was the art of Japanese rope bondage, and was one of the most specialised domination skills, whereby the submissive was tied up by the dominant in elaborate, aesthetic rope holds. Sapphire had taken a couple of classes a while ago but since we rarely got asked to perform even the most basic of knots, she always hesitated about offering it.

'Nichi, when do we ever do *shibari*? There are specialist mistresses you can go to for that. It's actually called *kinbaku* by the way, *shibari* is what the moronic San Franciscan kink hipsters decided to call it, for some reason. Anyway, no one's going to ask you for exquisite Japanese rope work. You're always going to be a more sensual, vanilla domme, just by dint of your looks.'

'What do you mean?'

'Oh, you know, small, round face, curvy . . . you don't exactly look like a hard bitch.'

Was Sapphire really reducing me to the role of play-domme because I looked as though I couldn't command authority? I bristled. If anorexia had taught me one thing it was never again to become hostage to my own perceived bodily limitations or inadequacies – and certainly not hostage to anyone else's pronouncements on them.

Sapphire continued. 'Well, you know how it is with the clients; sure, you're great at teasing, CBT and particularly at scathing verbal humiliation, but I've lost count of the number of times one of them has asked me if you switch.' Switching meant when you let them dominate you within the course of the same session. Nowhere in any of our advertising or correspondence with the clients did we offer switching. Few serious dommes did. It wasn't exactly wise to let a man you didn't know go to town on you.

'But what does it matter? It's up to us to exert control! It's up to me to make them believe that I have no interest in being

flung across their knee just because I fit some physical carica-
ture of a female submissive.'

The doorbell rang. Our next client already. These bloody
submissives and their timing. I didn't understand this conversation. However well Sapphire had taken my news, there was
some other odd dynamic at work here. From time to time I
had suspected there were some subliminal tensions between us.
I had often wondered if I provoked her to tartness, as well as
being caught in its crossfire. Evidently there'd been more to
my suspicions than mere paranoia. Although even if this were
true, I didn't understand why.

'Well, look, don't worry about it now,' she said. 'Anyway, this
next session is going to be very interesting. In all the rush
tonight I forgot to tell you about it – although I know we've
discussed it before hypothetically, and I know you want to do
it.'

What was Sapphire talking about? A session with a couple,
perhaps? Or was it the handsome James again, returning for
me to tie him to the X-cross this time? I just wanted to get on
with it. Anything to move us on from the alarming altercation
we'd just found ourselves in.

'Mistress Jade,' she announced with mock gravity, 'prepare
to lose your reverse virginity.'

From the top of the weaponry rack she reached up for the
harness with the attached dildo, the one I remembered marvelling at the first time I had ever sessioned here. I saw now that
the belt was folded back on itself and extended out so that it
could easily fasten around my waist. 'Here.' Sapphire handed
me the strap-on. 'It's time for you to "take" your first man.'

Like Jack before him, Christopher was broad-shouldered
and built like a Titan, standing at least six feet three inches
tall. But where Jack was boyishly buff, Christopher was rugged,
with sun-bleached hair and fine furrows about his mouth and
eyes that suggested a few too many debauched nights along
life's way.

As soon as Sapphire saw him, the strained mood that had prevailed in the office just seconds before evaporated, and she settled herself in the throne for once, leaving me to sit on one of the tattier armless chairs we used for spanking.

'So, Christopher. Your email was very candid. And very brave. I haven't had time to share it with Mistress Jade though.' I noted I was back to being referred to as Mistress. 'Do you think you could possible explain a little for both our sakes?' That pearl-knife smile of hers.

Christopher exhaled world-wearily and settled himself into an available chair, legs astride in fatigue. He ran a hand through the frosted tips of his hair.

'Well, Mistresses. Do I call you Mistresses?'

He paused.

Hadn't this man been to a dominatrix before?

Christopher was a barrister. A rather brilliant one, or so he assured us. Somehow his arrogance was not self-mythologising but endearingly matter-of-fact. He talked about himself as though he were relating a well-worn tale about a childhood friend who exasperated him.

'You see, all my life I've been kinky, but I've somehow kept meeting beautiful, brilliant women that just weren't into the same things I was, and then marrying and having children with them anyway.'

'How many times have you been married?' Sapphire asked.

'I'm on my third marriage. And I have four children. Don't get me wrong, I love my children, love them to death. And I've loved my wives. But I've never been able to tell them what I want sexually. Only because I knew they'd never find it erotic. And they'd never be able to find me appealing after I'd confessed it to them.'

Sapphire stole a sideways glance at me, then looked back at him and bit her bottom lip, absent-mindedly touched her chignon. I knew what she was thinking. She was thinking, 'Honey, why don't you make me number four. *I'll* understand.'

'And what exactly is it that you require, Christopher?' Sapphire asked him, her long slim legs tucked up underneath her at a purposeful, thigh-flashing angle. But Christopher didn't look at her legs. He hadn't come to us merely to be teased.

He continued. 'I mean, what is it that women want? They want a sperm donor, a bag carrier, a walking, talking, limitless credit card. They want to be cherished and adored and loved. And they want you to be ready to ravish them at a moment's notice.'

I was aghast at Christopher's cynical sorrow. 'Not all women are like that, Christopher,' I challenged him. 'Sapphire and I earn our own money and always would. We've got no interest at all in being "kept".'

Sapphire nodded vigorously, and added, 'We understand that some people have different sexual needs to the ones society sanctions. Especially,' she licked her lips, 'men like you.'

Christopher smiled with a slight reverence.

Sapphire had heard enough of the pseudo-therapy session. I could tell she wanted to get down to the business of sodomising. And I knew she was amusing herself with thoughts of five foot nothing me pressed up against six foot something him.

'So, Christopher. You've come to us to get a little of what no other woman deigns to give you.'

With no effort at all Christopher fell to his knees. The rapidity of his submission was actually alarming.

'Please, Mistresses,' he begged, hands clasped as he pleaded with us, 'please, mistresses, I need to feel myself possessed by you. I need simultaneously to be your slave and your desperate servile pet, and your adoring little slut, owned by you both.'

He looked to the floor as if to compose himself, then uttered, 'I long for you to take me.'

It wasn't what he said but the way he said it that was startling. Christopher sounded as though he'd stepped out of the pages of a nineteenth-century novel by way of a hardcore kink porn film. And I'd never known a man sound so desperate for anything.

Sapphire stood up and placed one hand on her hip. Then she lunged towards him and pulled him up by his hair's frosted tips. As she thrust his head back towards the light, the contrast of her dainty, white hand against his rough stubble and sun-drunk skin aroused me. Sapphire reminded me of a sorceress beguiling an awestruck knight. But there was no more beguiling to be done here. He was already thoroughly beguiled. All Christopher now needed was ravishing. I went over to them both.

He looked up at me. His eyes were wide as pools, and as wet. He whispered, 'I am your fuck-toy. Do whatever you will with me. I implore you both.'

Sapphire turned to me and pursed her lips playfully. 'What do you think, Mistress Jade? Do you think he deserves to be our little fuck-toy?' She bent down and whispered in his ear, loud enough so that I could hear, 'I know Mistress Jade has a toy she'd certainly like to fuck you with.'

Christopher shuddered. We hadn't even touched him and his forehead was already saturated with sweat, his stubble glistening with it, too. It was now strange to see a man on his knees in clothes. Sapphire must have thought the same thing.

'Well, Christopher, while Mistress Jade is thinking about whether she's going to "treat" you or not, why don't you relieve yourself of some of your vestments.' She was gently mocking his archaic-sounding words, but he was too dazed to notice.

When the doorbell rang earlier, I had placed the strap-on carefully on one of the armless chairs. Now it arrowed at me accusingly like a spun bottle. How difficult could a bit of repeated thrusting be, I thought to myself? I turned back to Christopher who had just finished fervently unbuttoning his shirt.

Christopher's body was something to behold. In complete contrast to his stubbled face, he had the smoothest, most gleaming chest I had seen, with gorgeous, warm coppery coloured skin, and impossibly sculpted pectorals.

Sapphire didn't even try to stop herself and went right over to him, digging her nails into his golden chest as though she were pricking dough. 'Oh, you're just ripe for objectification, aren't you?' she smiled.

His eyes lit up. Objectification. There it was. The experience he'd clearly been waiting to have all his sexual life. 'Oh God, Mistress, you have no idea how many times I've fantasised about being paraded about on a lead by someone like you, before being handed over to someone like . . . Mistress Jade.'

I bristled. Please don't let Sapphire get annoyed at that, please don't let her get all competitive again. But Sapphire was in her element. 'Pimping men out', as she called it, was one of her favourite fantasy games with the clients.

'Stand up,' she ordered him. She went over and tugged at his fly until it was half undone, revealing a small V of white fabric. I could just about make out the shadow of an erection.

Then she hovered her fingers over the tip.

'I wonder just exactly how hard you are at the thought of this. Lose your trousers.'

Obediently he yanked them down to expose his colossal, rugby player's thighs. And then I noticed it. He was wearing women's knickers. White satiny, lace-trimmed knickers with a tiny sparkly bow, behind which the head of his cock rose.

Sapphire bit her bottom lip and shook her head at him. Hardly designed to accommodate male anatomy, the knickers emphasised his straining erection. His balls were also bulging out of either side of the gusset. Sapphire took one scarlet-nailed finger and traced along the bulge, then feigned tucking it back in behind the fabric. It was no good. There was far too much of him to fit into a pair of female panties.

'Do you like them, Mistresses? I thought it might please you to see me as a real whore.'

I'd never found the idea of men in women's underwear erotic before. But there was something about Christopher's gleaming, coppery body, his skin as smooth as the satin he was encased in, and the fact the knickers couldn't contain him, that looked so deviant, it was delicious. It cried out for him to be touched.

Without waiting for an invitation from Sapphire I slunk over to him and slid my hand up the inside of his thigh. God, he felt better than he looked. He wanted this so badly, his skin practically hummed at my touch. I let my fingers explore the novelty of the feminine fabric framing such a hard, muscular male body.

We locked eyes. I needed to establish my authority over him, and I wanted him to relinquish his control to me from this moment on. He attempted, for a few seconds, to return my unremitting gaze. Then he looked at the floor pitifully, then back up at me again timidly from under his lashes. So he'd conceded. Then he moaned as if to vocalise it.

'Mistress Sapphire,' I said. 'I think this little . . .' I paused. Saying the next word felt so wrong '. . . slut . . .' but God, it was exhilarating, 'needs putting to the test.'

Sapphire looked at me admiringly for a moment. See, Sapphire, I thought to myself. I can be a seductive bitch, too. 'I'm glad you said that, Mistress Jade. I was just about to invite you to assume the position.'

I'd never seen Sapphire this excited before. We'd often talked about what it was like to fuck a man and she described in graphic detail how you judged what size dildo the slave could take, how you lubricated them up, and the best position to use depending on their level of experience. I'd even watched explicit femdom videos on my and Sapphire's favourite kink porn site. But I'd never actually seen Sapphire do it. Usually, the clients who came to her for strap-on play wanted no one witness to that level of submission.

Sapphire glided towards the door, her tattoo glowing like neon strip-lighting as she passed underneath the bright white bulb in its red shade. She turned and looked at Christopher from over her shoulder, beckoning him. 'It's time, little slut.'

Then he looked up at me and I realised he was seeking my

approval to follow. What Jack had started, Christopher could finish, I thought.

'Get up, then,' I commanded softly. He rose feverishly, and in his haste, brushed his face against my top as he did so. He smelled like leather, and expensive cologne. His trousers were still loitering about his ankles. 'Permission to unhook myself, Mistress?' he asked me.

'Obviously,' I replied. 'I'm going to need to you to be able to spread your legs.'

Sapphire came back in. Her desire to see the main event was making her impatient. 'Hurry up, we don't have all evening, you know,' she snapped at him. He shook off his shoes then yanked at his socks and trousers and padded after her into the bedroom.

I took the strap-on from where it lay on the chair and analysed how I would slink into to it. Perhaps it was better to put it on under my skirt now, I thought, lest I fall over or get tangled in it or do something that would break the spell and compromise my authority. I slid first one bare leg and then the other into it, catching my right heel in the gusset strap for a moment as I did so. Then I guided it up around my bottom. I went over to the mirror and took a look at myself from behind. It was made of exquisitely soft leather, with carefully crafted adjustable side straps, so that it hugged my curves as well as any silk thong. Then I turned around. Full frontal. I was a not insubstantial eight inches long. I wrapped my fingers around my cock for a moment and felt a surge of power. I was indomitable.

In the bedroom, Sapphire had already ordered Christopher into position for me. Up on the bed he lay, on all fours, with his head resting in the purple pillows, presenting his perfect ass to me. He was still wearing the women's knickers. Only now it was clear that they weren't actually proper knickers but the skimpiest of thongs.

Sapphire went over to him and spanked his bottom a few times for good measure. 'That's why you've worn these provocative panties, isn't it, Christopher? Because you want to feel the sting of my hand on your exposed ass.'

Christopher mumbled something indistinguishable into the pillows, making his answer known instead by undulating back on to Sapphire's hand as she stroked him between slaps.

Sapphire turned back to look at me. I had had to roll up my skirt about my thighs in order to accommodate the strap-on's punishing angle. Sapphire noticed it poking out from underneath my skirt.

'Now, Christopher, Mistress Jade is here and ready to begin your deflowering. And what a sight she is, too.' She sighed as if she were a proud mother admiring her daughter dressed for her first date. She gestured for me to go and flaunt myself to him. I edged round to where his head lay on the pillows.

Christopher looked up at me with adoration. 'Please, Mistress, may I touch it?' This amused me. He reached out his hand in reverence.

But just before his fingers reached my tip, Sapphire pounced forward and slapped his hand away.

'Christopher, didn't anyone tell you it's very rude to fondle someone else's cock?'

I was confused. Didn't Sapphire usually let them do that? In fact, didn't she usually make them give her head, as she put it?

I looked up at her, and she tapped her finger to her wrist, gesturing to an imaginary watch. Damn it, she was right. There was no time for foreplay. We needed to cut to the main event.

'Now, Christopher, Mistress Jade has never done this before. She's actually losing her strap-on virginity tonight, so do bear that in mind, won't you, if her thrusts are a little . . . unnatural.' Wasn't this whole thing pretty bloody unnatural, I thought to myself. I supposed Sapphire was only trying to cover our backs in case the experience left a lot to be desired, but it irritated me. I was determined to do a good job.

Sapphire took a bottle of lube from the table and, after

removing his thong until it lay around his knees, binding them, began fingering his ass. 'Oh my,' she exclaimed. 'He's very open already. You've been using butt plugs, Christopher, haven't you?' He nodded vigorously into the pillow. She slapped him hard. 'You really are a little slut then. Let's see how hard Mistress Jade can fuck you.'

I went round the back of the bed and clambered up on to it, positioning myself in between Christopher's splayed legs. He was shaking. I placed my right hand gingerly on to his bottom. He jerked, and startled me. His movements were so bold, and so unrestrained. At any moment, I thought, he could rise up, turn over and haul me down on to the bed, pinning me under him. Thinking about this possibility made knowing that it was I about to fuck him even more exciting.

Sapphire approached the bed. She was holding a condom. She unwrapped it and rolled it on to my cock. How surreal, I thought to myself. A woman has just sheathed my prosthetic penis. She looked up at me reassuringly. 'Now, remember everything I've ever told you, Mistress Jade. Go steady to start with, and find your rhythm.'

I took a deep breath and eased the tip of the strap-on into Christopher's anus. Sapphire was right. There was hardly any resistance. It slid right in, almost up to the hilt, immediately. Christopher moaned. He moaned the way I moaned when a hot man slid himself into me that first time when you begin to have sex. His moan aroused me. It made me want to make him moan again. I inched back and slid myself gently into him again. And then again. And then, slowly, I started to rock my hips back and forth, attempting to build up a rhythm.

At first the motion didn't come naturally. My hips were too used to gyrating circularly, like the way I moved when I danced. I tightened my core and tucked my pelvis under. Then hesitated. I thought of the time I had learned to walk on stilts at circus camp in Italy. 'Until the stilt becomes an extension of your leg, you will not move naturally with it,' the instructor had told us.

I wondered if this applied here, if I had to claim the cock as my own temporarily, to make the motion work.

I tried again, imagining the strap-on was a real extension of my body. That was it. I had it. And then just as quickly I lost the rhythm again. Jesus! Was fucking really meant to be this hard work? Were men actually putting a hell of a lot of effort in to do something that we women though was instinctual to them? Thank God I did yoga. There's no way a weak core could work a strap-on.

Sapphire looked at me with encouragement. 'You're doing a great job, Mistress Jade. Trickier than it looks, isn't it? How is it for you Christopher?' she enquired teasingly. I had become so absorbed in perfecting my technique that I had almost forgotten there was a man on the receiving end of my thrusts.

'It's heaven, Mistress. Pure heaven.' Sapphire and I both laughed at the surrealism of it.

'So I can work you harder, Christopher?' I demanded.

He arched back on to my cock. 'Oh God, Mistress, yes, please, please give it to me even harder. I'm your adoring slut and I deserve to be pounded.'

I found my rhythm again and resumed fucking him, gripping on to his hips the way I liked men to grip me. God, was this how inert we females were? How merely receptive? No wonder fucking made men feel dominant.

Then, another realisation. The harder I pounded up against Christopher, the more the strap-on was inadvertently stimulating me. Even with my own knickers forming a barrier between me, the strap-on and Christopher's body, I could totally have an orgasm like this if I wanted to. I was turned on and alarmed by it. I couldn't let Sapphire realise this. And I certainly couldn't let myself climax in front of her, even though the harder I went at it, the more I wanted to let myself. I was going to have to hold myself back. This really was like being a guy!

As I became more excited so, too, it seemed, did Christopher. He had reached back and was clenching on to his own cheeks now, as if presenting himself to me. In my determination to control myself I grabbed on to his hair and pulled him hard up towards me.

'So you like that, you little whore? Is that what you've been waiting for all your life? For a woman to come and take you the way you've been forced to take woman after woman? Is that what you've thought about every time you've been up inside them? About getting pounded yourself?'

I reached between his legs and grabbed his cock. It was rock hard. It was such an ego trip to be able to fulfil someone's long-held fantasy like this.

'Oh, Mistress,' he pleaded, 'if you touch me there, if you touch me like that I'm going to cum.'

'No, you're not.' I took my hand off his cock and gave him a single, exacting spank. 'You don't cum until I say so,' and instead began increasing the vigour of my strokes, digging my nails in to his backside to anchor myself as I worked him even harder.

As if in direct contravention of what I'd just said, Christopher started to tremble violently. Oh God, please don't say it was too late already, that in ordering him not to climax I had somehow pushed him towards it?

'I'm cumming, Mistress, I'm cumming, I'm cumming.'

How could that momentary tease of his cock have produced this? They could be such indulgent little pricks sometimes, these submissives.

Suddenly, alarmingly, Christopher burst into violent climax and cried out in pleasure, hauling himself up by the bedstead, pulling away from me and my strap-on, bucking, and shuddering and squirming as he did so. I'd never seen a man climax like this before. This was more like a full-body orgasm, more than a mere physical release.

When his orgasm was over, Christopher released his grip on the bedposts, sank down to his knees, and then rolled on to his back, utterly enervated. There were tears in his eyes. Of relief? Of despondency? I sensed no trauma. Still, he had an erection. *How?*

'But Christopher, your cock is still hard!' I exclaimed. I didn't understand this.

He looked at me as if I'd just asked him why he wasn't speaking Greek when he'd already told me he only spoke Russian.

'Oh, but I didn't cum like that, Mistress Jade. That was an anal orgasm.'

I turned swiftly to look at Sapphire. She had never warned me about *that*.

With impeccably poor timing, or perhaps it was impeccably good timing, Sapphire's BlackBerry cried out from the other room. It was unlike her to forget to put it on silent. It distracted the clients and made them feel as though we weren't paying them enough attention. Ever the pro, she averted the faux pas by saying nothing and merely sweeping out of the room.

I turned to Christopher and began the usual post-coital pleasantries.

'Would you like a shower, Christopher? There are fresh towels laid out in the bathroom. Or is there anything else you require?'

He looked at me intensely, gravely, even. He looked as though he had something serious to say. Uh oh. Had I done a bad job? Worse still – had I hurt him?

'Was that OK?' I hazarded.

'Yes, Mistress. It was exquisite.' He was nodding rapidly, his breath still shallow. '*You're* exquisite. I have to see you again. Would you come visit me at my flat?'

'Well, of course. Sapphire and I are always happy to do outcalls . . .'

'Not Sapphire. Just you.'

Chapter 13

Domming with Sapphire was never the same after that night with Jack and Christopher. The comments she had made about my lack of authority really stung, and I couldn't help thinking she might be right that it was time I struck out on my own. I owed Sapphire a huge debt of gratitude, and always would. There was no way I would have been able to stay in London after I broke up with Christos without her, much less continue to pursue my dream of becoming a journalist. But it was time to fly solo with the sex work. Once the decision had been made and we discussed it, there was no tension in those final sessions. The intimacy of our curious friendship was changed, but it was time for us to part company.

I did feel a little guilty for stealing her client. Not that I exactly engineered it. A few days after that session, Sapphire forwarded me a thank-you email from the eloquent Titan himself. It came complete with an attached picture, a gratuitous thong-clad, bent-over-bed shot. But I only had eyes for his email address.

Christopher became my first regular. His working hours meant that finding time to dominate him could be tricky. Luckily, I have always been an early riser and he liked nothing better than a bit of morning strap-on sex. So every couple of weeks I would find myself boarding the tube at 5.30 a.m. with only a black belted mac covering my highly immodest underwear. With each visit my strap-on technique improved, and I also got better at remembering to transfer one of the £20 notes from the requisite white envelope into my purse before I tried to buy breakfast at the Pret round the corner afterwards.

By 8 a.m. I had earned half a week's wage and was free to work on the increasing number of freelance articles I was now getting commissioned to write, following my most recent, and very successful internship. I'd saved the day helping to pull together a new feature article just hours from going to press when it turned out our lead piece had already run in another magazine. Even so, most of the work I was doing was unpaid. Would I ever be able to give up domming entirely and make a living out of journalism?

Though actually, I wasn't ready to give up on the domming just yet. As well as my bank balance, sex work had transformed my libido. I thought back to the days of my anorexia when I was as asexual as a tablecloth. Every so often I would have sex just to test whether the desire had returned and find, disappointingly, that the most pleasurable bit was the post-coital cuddling. Later, Christos had rekindled the flame of my desire and I had always adored sex with him. But it was domming that had truly stoked my sexual imagination. I had never felt better about my body, my mind, and how the two coalesced. I had come into my sexual power.

Sometimes I would get on the tube and find myself packed against some old lech preparing to creepily press himself up against me. I would angle my elbow just so, and if the driver pulled on the brakes too sharply at Stockwell, well, I always had the excuse of accidental impact. Drunken men on the night bus got a withering stare and a stiletto-stamped foot if they tried it on with me. From time to time, when I was feeling particularly imperious, I would catch some pinstriped, professional gent lingering his gaze on me just that little bit too long – and I would know immediately he was but a slave-in-waiting. Some days I was so confident in my domme powers that, given the right set of circumstances and prop-concealing lighting, I believed that 90 per cent of men could be persuaded to submit to me.

The only real problem I had with sex work now that I was my own boss was that it troubled my socialist conscience. My vast hourly sum was completely unjust when compared with the minimum hourly wage. I thought about my hard-grafting Labour family, imagined my ancestors turning in their graves at the fact I had become such a fearless free-marketeer. Of course, I justified it with the fact I was still not being paid for my actual career. But still, it troubled me. And so I came up with the concept of charitable domination, whereby every couple of months or so, I would get my clients to donate to various charities and emergency appeals in the wake of flood, famine and civil war. On occasion I also chose anti-trafficking charities, which I supported myself. I was painfully aware that my sex-worker status was one of luxury and choice, a rare thing in a global industry full of individuals who were far less lucky than me. I remembered the character of Belle, the prostitute in *Gone With the Wind*, who is far more giving than the heroine, Scarlett O'Hara, and smiled at the tart-with-a-heart stereotype. I hoped my own Maid Marian act was, however paltry, at least one way of helping out those a lot less fortunate than myself.

Although I was a lucky sex worker, I wasn't a lucky journalist, and I still didn't have a job. I had set myself a deadline of 30 April. If I hadn't found a full-time paying position by then, I decided, I had to seriously reconsider my career choice. And domming was not to be a permanent alternative option.

One thing that had become apparent now that I was domming alone was that boundaries were getting more fluid. When I first started working with Sapphire I had come up with the slogan 'we sell boundaries not services'. What I meant was that it was safer for a client to get his kicks with us than with an extramarital affair or a play partner. We knew where the emotional lines were when it came to BDSM, and we never crossed them. In some instances though, it was clear both you and the client wanted to cross a boundary – the boundary dividing a professional relationship and a real friendship, for example. Eventually, some of my regulars became dear friends, people that, to this day, I could call upon for anything from help putting a bookcase together to their opinion on a new personal relationship. But only once they weren't clients any more. I learned this the hard way when Christopher and I found ourselves in a grievous misunderstanding.

One Sunday at the beginning of April, Christopher texted me to ask if I was in London. 'Sure. Do you want to meet up?' I replied. I was surprised that he hadn't travelled back to Hastings, where his wife and children lived, for the weekend. 'Would you mind coming round? It's just, I don't know what to do. My wife has found out that I'm into domination and she's devastated. Wants a divorce and sole custody of the children.'

Oh God. Poor guy. I grimaced. Desperation seeped out of each electronic character. How could I say anything but yes? That evening, dressed in jeans, knee-high boots and a fitted checked shirt, I turned up at Christopher's flat. His eyes were practically swollen shut with a day and a night's worth of sobbing, yet he was still genial, and immediately offered me a drink. All he had was champagne. 'That's a barrister-who-lives-alone's fridge for you,' he joked sardonically.

As Christopher hunted for champagne flutes, I went to sit down in the living room, and tried hard not to drink in the idyllic photos of him and his Monica Bellucci-alike wife on their engagement; him and his wife at a ski lodge in the Alps for New Year; him and his wife holidaying on a yacht in Capri with his three catalogue-cute children, all wind-whipped hair and blithe smiles.

'How are you?' I asked him when he finally came and sat down with our drinks.

'Oh, you know I didn't really want to go there. But I just . . . well, who else can I talk to about it?'

Over the course of the next half hour he described a torturous evening where his wife had found his collection of anal toys and confronted him about them. At first she had been convinced he'd been having an affair, 'which would actually have been more palatable to her', and that he'd been using the toys on another woman. 'But when I explained to her that it was just my kink, she told me I made her feel sick, that she didn't want me near the children any more.'

'Well, it's probably more the shock of her finding out that she didn't know you as well as she thought she did that upset her, rather than what she actually found out.'

I didn't really believe what I was saying, but I had to try and offer him some comfort, some hope. I didn't want to compound his sense of shame. If only he'd been able to tell his wife in the first place.

'Would you dominate me, Jade? It would make me feel better.'

I hesitated. I wasn't keen on using domination as a kind of emotional therapy for someone so clearly distressed. In fact, it had always been one of the rules. Don't dominate someone if you think they run the risk of harming themselves with it.

'Are you sure that's a good idea, Christopher?' I asked him. 'Do you think you're in the right headspace for this?'

'Oh, I think so. A bit of self-abasement couldn't possibly make me feel emptier than I already do.'

'You'd better lose some clothes, then,' I ordered him, snapping into character. We would start, I decided, but I would scrutinise his every slight response as we played, and if I had even the smallest suspicion he was not OK, I was going to stop.

Once Christopher had stripped to his briefs, male briefs for once, I ordered him to bend over the bed and began hand spanking him. He was very quiet. After a minute or two I asked him if he was OK. 'Yes,' he replied simply. Then he stood up. 'But you're right. I'm not really in the headspace for it.'

Phew. Thank God he'd had the self-awareness to recognise that. I gave him a hug. 'Let's go back next door, and just have a drink, yes?' He nodded and smiled. I could see that he too was relieved.

Settled on the couch, Christopher began talking about his marital problems again. For nearly two hours I sat and listened and nodded my head sympathetically as he traced back through every detail of detachment and discord he'd experienced with his wife. And then the wife before. And then the wife before that. Eventually he was analysing his relationship with his mother. 'You know, she was just so hard to please. She never told us she loved us or that she was proud of us and I only remember her kissing me once. When I broke my leg. I was six.'

Listening to Christopher made me feel terribly sorry for him but I also felt uncomfortable. I was effectively playing the role of counsellor here, and I wasn't qualified to do so.

'How do you think I can win her back, Jade?'

Oh God. How the hell could I answer that?

'I think you have to wait for her to come to you now. And take some time for yourself.' It was awful, generic advice but surely he couldn't come to any harm if he followed it. This was exhausting. I had to get him on to something else. Finally, he changed the topic.

'So what are you going to do about the domming when a handsome man threatens to ride off into the sunset with you?'

I laughed. 'Like that's going to happen! I don't think I'm the type to be kidnapped!'

'You're not dating anyone then? No one in mind?'

'No, no,' I replied. 'Although . . .' I wasn't going to tell Christopher about Sebastian. I knew he wasn't due back from Cape Town for another month. And yet, three months since I'd met him, I still couldn't shake him from my daily fantasies.

'Anyway, how's the Bar? Tell me about any scandalous trials you have coming up . . .'

'Well, you know I can't divulge proper details. But since it's you . . .'

After twenty more minutes of relaxed chatter, I decided that I'd successfully distracted Christopher from his impending divorce. Time to go.

'Thank you for coming, Jade. I really, really do appreciate it. Could we do it again sometime? You're such a good listener. I went to a counsellor once, cost me heaps of money, but they didn't get me the way you do.'

I hesitated for a second. This really wasn't the way to let a relationship with a client go. He was paying me heaps of money too, wasn't he? I supposed there was no harm in just chatting, so long as he didn't actually expect me to give him detailed advice.

'Sure.' I smiled, a little reluctantly.

As he walked me to the door, I waited for him to offer the money he usually kept rolled up on top of the bedside cabinet for me. Only, thinking back now to when we'd been in the bedroom, I couldn't remember seeing any money. Shit.

'Well, take care.' He hugged me to him once again. 'Do you need something for a taxi ride home?' I nodded dumbly. So that's what he meant about the counsellor. Clearly he had no intention of offering me anything here. I knew what Sapphire would have done. She'd have politely but firmly explained that her time always came at a price. But I couldn't. Was it even up to him to realise that, or up to me to have clarified it before I arrived? The boundaries had been blurred before I'd even arrived.

I waited until the taxi had pulled out of view of Christopher's flat and then asked the taxi driver to drop me off there instead. I might as well save the £60 fare and get the tube. At least I wouldn't have 'worked' entirely for free.

On the way home I thought over the evening's events. I was angry with myself for spoiling a perfectly good professional relationship by trying to be Christopher's friend. But then, what else could I have done but offer Christopher comfort? I could *not* have gone. But that didn't feel humane. He was a reasonable man, I was sure the money issue could have been rectified with a quick phone call. But for some reason, I was disinclined to do that. Instead, I took the evening's mishaps as a sign that it really was time for me to move on.

Thankfully, I met my self-imposed deadline. On 30 April I found out that I secured my first proper full-time paying journalism job on an independent politics publication. When I rang my dad to tell him, I laughed with grateful relief. So did he. 'Just your brother to worry about now!'

Once I began the job I was more tired, more stressed, and had a lot less fun than I'd enjoyed while I'd been domming, but finally I could relax about the direction my life was taking. And yet still I felt a yearning. I no longer missed Christos, exactly, but I missed the joy and intimacy of that relationship. Perhaps I was destined merely to have a string of perfectly pleasant but innocuous relationships. Perhaps I'd had my fill of love.

I talked about it with Gina as we browsed the Victoria and Albert the weekend before Easter. 'It's not as though I believe in the One, you know I don't,' I told her. 'But when you've had such a perfect relationship, is everything after doomed to dissatisfaction?'

'But it wasn't perfect with Christos, Nichi,' Gina wisely pointed out. 'You know very well it wasn't.'

'Well, as perfect AS then!' I replied. 'Anyway, I'm not looking for perfection. I'm looking for real, raw passion and a soul connection. I know you're going to think this is stupid, Gina, but that guy I met at the end of last year, I, I . . .'

I didn't dare say the next bit out loud.

'Sebastian, wasn't he called? You think he had it?'

I couldn't look at Gina. 'But Sapphire and Violet quite rightly tried to put me off him. I mean, I've heard so many horror stories about BDSM relationships, "lifestylers" you call them. I'd be stupid to go there. You think I'm stupid.'

'No of course I don't! Look, forget about the BDSM bit. Sometimes you just get a feeling about someone. I'm sure even kinksters get that!'

'Yes!' I said with relief. Being able to admit this to Gina stopped it from feeling so delusional. My thoughts about any potential connection with Sebastian were becoming an obsession, despite Sapphire's warning.

'But the thing is, the feeling I got about Sebastian was

different from how I felt with Christos. It wasn't that kind of romance. It was . . . it reminded me of this John Donne poem, "The Ecstasy" I think it's called. "Our eye beams twisted and did thread our eyes upon one double string".'

Gina raised an eyebrow at me. The Metaphysical poets weren't really her forte. I pressed on.

'There's something about the idea of twisted eye beams that's so, well . . . it's about something darker than love.'

'Well, then,' Gina teased, 'I suggest we get out of this place. Something tells me you're not going to find Sebastian here.'

A couple of days later, Sapphire called. She'd seen from my Facebook status update that I had a proper job and phoned me to ask how I was getting on. I was glad she'd rung. Hearing her voice made that recent, if surreal, part of my life feel less cut off from my current reality. 'So how's life as a real slave, Nichi? Not tempted back to the dark side?'

'No, thank you,' I replied. 'Although I do miss the dressing up!'

'Well, you should come to this spring fetish ball I'm going to on the weekend! Remember that fetish club where we sometimes used to tout for clients? Well, they're having what I'm assured will be a splendid kink party on Saturday night. There's a lot of great stage acts too, male burlesque and amazing go-go dancers.'

I was a little wary of seeing Sapphire again. We hadn't actually met up since the night I lost my strap-on virginity.

'Besides, I miss you!' she said, as if sensing and seeking to quell my anxieties with one simple phrase.

'I miss you, too.' It was true. We had become so close over the course of my apprenticeship in domming. And hang on a minute, wasn't this the party Violet had mentioned over lunch when she'd cried over Dan? The party that Sebastian was due back in town for?

'Is Violet going?' I asked. If Violet was going then there was the chance, just the minutest, grain-of-sand, inkling of a chance, that Sebastian might be there too.

'Yeah, of course! She's currently got some new Master – not Dan – play-pimping her out. They go to these parties and he offers her up to the highest bidder!'

'The highest bidder?' I was horrified.

'Oh, not like that! I mean, some guy propositions her with a domination offer. She has to relay it to her Master and then he decides whether he thinks she's "earned" it or not in service to him.'

'Doesn't Violet wear herself out with these complex D/S games?'

Sapphire laughed. 'You know how it goes. Once you get suckered into these kinds of relationships, you're always looking for the next high!'

'What are we dressing as?' I asked Sapphire.

'Ha! Good girl! I don't know. Why don't we just full-on fetish it up? You can wear my rubber prom dress if you like.'

'You're on.'

But the fetish night never materialised. On Saturday morning Sapphire texted me to tell that she had a truly appalling migraine and that she was going to have to cancel.

It was a good thing she didn't call. There was no way I'd have been able to hide my grievous disappointment. I was so eager to see Sebastian again, and the idea that he might go and meet some other curious little thing with submissive tendencies roused me to a sense of very slight, but very real, jealousy.

This was silly. Why was I wasting my time fantasising about someone I might never meet again?

I had to see him.

I was going to chance it. Violet would give me his number, wouldn't she? Come on, Mistress Jade, take the man if you want him!

I toyed with the idea of asking Violet for his number for the best part of a day. What could I use as a pretext? I know! The painting he'd done for her!

'Hey Violet, it's Jade, hope you're well. Could I possibly have your friend Sebastian's number btw? I know of a commission he might be interested in . . .'

Perfect, perfect. Innocuous. Valid. There was no way she would suspect a thing.

Violet replied within a few minutes with the digits. Then she followed it up with this: 'Commission? To spank your ass I presume? ;)'

Damn it! Had it really been that transparent at the party that I was knee-shakingly, lip-poutingly, eyelash-flutteringly head over heels in lust with him? Apparently so.

But who cared. I had what I wanted.

Now, to text him. I agonised even longer over this. I didn't want to pretend I had a commission for him. I was just going to be bold and ask him if he wanted to have a drink. But what if Violet told him what I'd done? That would make me look stupid. Although I'd look stupider if I misled him with the offer of work. No, I just had to play this straight.

I wrote the message out six times. Then I got a grip. 'Hey Sebastian, it's Jade. Hope you're well and that Africa was' . . . was what? A great place to serve your sex drive as you tied up a multitude of women? Let's not mention Africa. 'Hope you're well. Would you like to meet for a drink some time? x.'

Simple is best. Send. Send it, Nichi! Finally I sent it.

Now I had to switch off my phone and forget I had one. Or . . . or I could just read his immediate reply!

'Hey Jade, lovely to hear from you! A drink would be great. Next Friday? Sx.'

Chapter 14

Our first date was scheduled for the following Friday evening. It was the end of a torturous week at the office for me; press week at the magazine, which meant 7 a.m. starts and 10 p.m. finishes. On deadline Friday at around 1 p.m., the office erupted into a volcano of stress when it turned out that one of our contributors, whose 5,000-word feature had yet to materialise, had actually barely started writing it. But I managed to agree a new deadline and broker peace between him and my editor. Chanelling my erotic energy into professional problem-solving kept me from falling into a nervous haze of fret and over-analysis about my date with Sebastian. It also stopped me from sneaking off to the toilet to examine my face and figure in the mirror for the eleven-hundredth time.

Hour conceded to hour and eventually it was 5.03 p.m. and there were just fifty-seven minutes separating me from the sight of the lustrous Sebastian. Was I suitably dressed, I wondered? I didn't want it to be totally obvious that I'd been waiting for this ever since the party at Violet's, so I'd decided not to change my work clothes, consisting of a black sheer silk shirt, black lambswool sweater, tight black pencil skirt – which admittedly did hug my bottom just so.

My only concession to datedom was to wear stockings rather than tights. It was a mere mental boost. I was adamant there would be no other need for them.

On top of that went my scarlet Cossack coat and a tawny Russian hat. It should have been spring but along with a resur-rected Lord, Easter had brought snow, and there were still icy clots of it on the ground. Before I left the office I swapped my riding boots for monochrome snakeskin heels – albeit heels with straps, which should ensure I could navigate through the snow without falling over.

My boss smiled at me on the way out. 'Well, you look nice, Nichi. Off out for drinks?' It was a perfectly innocuous enquiry but I blushed, in spite of myself.

'Yes, just going to meet a friend.'

He smiled at me, nodded approvingly. 'Lovely hat. You look like . . .' He twisted his lips as he searched for the correct comparison.

'An oligarch's mistress?' I substituted for him teasingly.

'No, no, I was going to say a Russian princess. Or at least a heroine from a Russian novel.'

OK, Nichi time to go. I often found myself engaged in these inappropriately suggestive roles with older men. Damn the domming, I thought. I was still adjusting to regular working life.

Sebastian and I had arranged to meet at Oxford Circus tube. It was a short walk from my office. As I marched along, I tried not to let my nerves seduce my composure.

Was this even a date? Maybe he just thought we'd arranged a friendly drink. I mean, nothing had actually been made explicit. I tried for the umpteenth time to read the signals of that last conversation, as we were saying goodbye at Violet's. My treacherously swollen pupils, the licking of my lips and lowering of my gaze at regular intervals could have given my intentions away. And what about him? Why would he have hung around talking to me for so long if he wasn't interested in spending more time with me?

The tube station came into view. I fiddled in my coat pocket for my mirror and lipstick. Still perfect. Or as perfect as it would ever be. Get a grip.

I crossed the penultimate road on to a pedestrian crossing. I couldn't see him. We'd said six, right? I pressed the button on the traffic lights with the tip of one leather-gloved finger, and waited there, poised to cross. As soon as the green man flashed up, Sebastian came into view. Concealed by a fog of evening shoppers, he'd clearly been stood there a while, as straight-backed as a statue, clad in that heavy coat again, hands thrust deep in his pockets in protest against the early evening chill.

Even from across the way I saw him see me. He fixed me with that long, intense stare of his. As I approached him, his handsome face broke into a broad smile. I'd not seen him smile like that before. My heart raced.

'Hello.' He kissed me. Or did I kiss him? No, I merely held out my cheeks in polite offering. He kissed me, slowly, deliberately on either cheek, his stubble teasing my hair to his face in a static caress.

'Hey, Sebastian. How are you?'

'Well, thank you. Yourself?'

'Oh, I've been on press and . . .' I stopped myself. Right now, I wasn't interested in my work. I was just filling the air between us with some kind of white noise in a bid to avoid betraying the deep lust I was feeling. 'End of a long week. I'm fine.'

I smiled. My breath came out in a quavering fog. How could I care about any detail of the daily grind in the presence of this mesmerising man?

'So . . . where do you want to go?' Sebastian asked me. 'I'll admit I don't have an insider's knowledge of Soho.'

That surprised me, given what Violet had led me to believe about what Sebastian got up to in his spare time. But then he wasn't originally from London, was he? In fact, where was he from? I didn't even know.

'Well, I know a reasonably OK pub a few minutes from here. It's a bit of a media haunt so as long as you don't mind that. The John Snow it's called. It'll be busy but then isn't everywhere at this time on a Friday evening.'

'The British love to booze!' he laughed.

We began walking. He kept his hands pressed firmly in his pockets.

'Where are you from then?' I asked him. 'If not Britain?'

'Oh,' he replied vaguely. 'Everywhere and nowhere. I was born in South Africa. But I grew up in Montreal.'

That explained the distinct lack of South African in his accent, and the hint of melodious transatlantic.

'Since then I've been a resident of a dozen or so other nations, none of which has loved me enough to give me a second passport.'

That was an odd way of putting it. 'Well, was there somewhere else in particular you wished would?'

'Oh, I'm not fussy,' he replied. 'But I like Britain the best. I relate to the grey, the genial cynicism of the people. It matches my character. And my wardrobe!' He laughed.

Sebastian had such a warm, open way of expressing himself, it made every statement of mild pessimism seem like a declaration of joy.

'What about you? Any second passports?'

'No,' I shook my head. 'My mother lives in Australia and I suppose I could apply for citizenship there if I wanted to, eventually. And I nearly ended up a Greek national. But that's another story.'

I gave a tight-lipped smile, then scolded myself. What the hell was I bringing up Christos for? I paid little attention to generally sexist dating rules but even I knew that you should never talk about exes on a first date.

When we reached the pub it was indeed fit to bursting, but so was every other drinking hole along the same stretch of Friday night Soho. Sebastian let me enter first, then was practically slammed into the back of me as another group of Friday revellers followed up behind us. Sebastian looked at me and raised his eyebrows. 'I apologise on behalf of my inebriated countrymen,' I said. We both laughed.

There were no seats so we shuffled ourselves into a nook

of the bar and Sebastian went to buy us drinks. I unbuttoned my coat but left it on. The number of people crushed up around us made it too difficult to remove. And my hat? What would my hair look like underneath? Maybe I could leave it on after all.

'Beautiful hat,' Sebastian offered. I blushed. Could he read my thoughts or something? He'd noticed the hat, that was good. I wondered if he thought I looked like a Russian Mistress.

'May I stroke it?' He held his hand up in front of me and ran his cool gaze over my face, awaiting my consent.

I laughed. 'Of course! Here!' I took it off and put it on the bar, forgetting about my hair in my bid to please him.

'Mmm, it's like a calico cat,' he sighed. 'Secret rulers of the universe, cats. I do miss having one to snuzzle.'

'Snuzzle?' I ventured, laughing. Was that even a word?

'Oh you know – it's a compound of nuzzling and snuggling. Do you like cats?'

'Yes, I do. I like neologisms, too!'

He laughed. Under the bar lighting, I could see that the light stubble concealed deep dimples. I'd not noticed them before. But perhaps he'd not smiled in a way to reveal them.

'Sometimes I wonder why I became a painter when I love words so much. Probably easier to make a living out of writing.'

'Oh, I wouldn't be so sure!' I laughed, through gritted teeth.

'That's your real job, right? Writing?'

'My only job now. I've given up domming.'

He gave a single nod and held my gaze for longer this time. I didn't resist it.

For the next hour or so we talked about my creative ambitions, and his, computer-generated poetry, the astounding variety of Greek swear words (it turned out he'd had a Greek ex, too), my obsession with sausage dogs and whether the kink practice known as 'forced bi', by which an otherwise straight man is 'forced' to give another man head, should be renamed 'encouraged bi' for the sake of political correctness. There wasn't

anything Sebastian offered up that didn't inspire me to instinctive agreement, contemplation or conspiratorial laughter. Who
knew we'd have so much in common?

After about an hour or so, I heard a male voice mutter, 'No
wonder it's called a bar with idiots like this blocking the way.
Can't even get the bloody drinks in!'

I turned around to see a bald older man, oversized and lairy,
scowling in my direction. Without warning, the domme in me
snapped to attention.

'I'm sorry, sir, but it's very busy in here tonight and there's
nowhere else to stand. In fact, as I don't know that there is a
law against standing in a bar, I really don't know what your
problem is!'

His female friend hit back at me. 'He hasn't got a problem,
love, or at least he didn't have until you were stood there.'

Oh God, I wasn't in the mood for a public showdown. I
glanced at Sebastian. He was staring hard into his whisky glass.
What? You mean you aren't going to defend me?

I turned around, swallowed my scorn and smiled pacifically.
'I'm sorry. I didn't know we were obstructing you.'

The couple were swallowed up by the swell of the crowd,
and I was left feeling the tiniest bit disappointed. Perhaps
Sebastian hadn't wanted to intervene because he thought I was
the kind of girl that did not take kindly to being rescued. He
wouldn't have been wrong – usually. But, well, anyway, I needed
to change the subject.

I glanced at him. He was staring at me admiringly, and grinning. When I met his gaze again he merely shrugged. 'You were
doing perfectly well by yourself there. Far be it from me to
interfere with a domme when she's in full flow. But I can fight
and protect when I want.' He winked at me, gave me a sexy,
sideways smile.

I caught my breath and had to look away for a second. I'd
never met a man who could wink without it looking sleazy. Was
that . . . was he trying to seduce me? No. That was just his

way. Besides, there was something about his manner that was both too considerate and too nonchalant. Suddenly I felt defiant. Well, fine. If he thought I was that easy.

'So you're a fighter, eh? What kind of fighter?'

'Fencing, mainly. And then I do a bit of boxing.'

So that explained the divine body, that compelling combination of indomitable strength and unequivocal grace.

'Do you enjoy it?'

'Yes. But really I exercise because I'm vain.' He shrugged his shoulders good-naturedly.

I laughed in surprise. It was so refreshing to hear a man confess that. Women conceded it to one another all the time.

'What about you?'

'Oh, the gym – I've just started working out with a personal trainer. And yoga. I know yoga is better for my soul.'

'Well, of course. I can't get through the day without meditating. And if I don't meditate . . .' He trailed off.

Suddenly my mind blazed with an image of Sebastian seated in cross-legged position, wearing some kind of loose-fitting trousers and no shirt . . .

'Have you been to India?' he asked me, interrupting my reverie.

'Not yet. I'm trying. I want to go work in a Goan brothel.'

Sebastian frowned. 'Really? Wouldn't you earn more over here?'

'Oh, ha ha! No, I didn't sell penetrative sex! I mean, I want to do aid work out there. You know there are these girls born into prostitution? There's this ancient tradition of *devadasi*, basically a religious sanctification of prostitution, and it can be used to justify what is effectively growing up in sexual slavery. You can go and volunteer and teach the girls English or other skills that will help them break out of the brothel if they choose. I mean, I was a sex worker with choices. Not every sex worker is in the same position.'

'That sounds wonderful.' Sebastian smiled at me. 'I hear

they're crying out for domme-angels. Northern British accents preferable.'

I flushed. He meant me, right?

'God, I must sound so bloody earnest!' I started laughing at myself.

'Well, if you'd said you were going to re-educate them about the sins of the flesh then maybe I'd agree. But you sound quite sin-friendly.'

I laughed again 'Ha! You could put it like that!'

'And I love a good sinner. "We're all sinners!"' Sebastian affected a preacherly quaver and held up his hands to the light playfully.

I remembered that the night we met he'd told me his ex was a domme. This man got it, then. He didn't judge me for anything I'd done.

'Would you like another drink?' he asked me. 'Same again?'

'Yes, please.'

Another glass of wine. My second and final drink, I told myself. He set it down in front of me. Already, I felt unusually light-headed.

I looked at Sebastian. This was so easy. It was so easy to be in his company.

'So why did you leave Montreal?'

'I wasn't happy there. A lot of things happened that took me a long time to come to terms with, even after I'd left, if you know what I mean.'

I did, and yet I didn't. He could have been talking about anything. My mind raced. Drugs, crime, seducing the wives of French-Canadian diplomats and leaving them broken-hearted?

'My daughter lived there. But then her mother took her away to Italy. Once she'd left I couldn't stay.' Sebastian's face seemed to solidify, agony seething beneath the surface.

'How old is your daughter?' I asked him.

'Seventeen.'

Seventeen. Seventeen?

'And I'm thirty-six,' he offered up candidly, trying to empty out the shock.

'Oh!' I said, as simply as possible. What else could you say?

He smiled at me. I thought I could sense a hint of relief at my response.

'Were you with her mother for a long time?'

'A couple of years.'

'What's your daughter's name?'

'Juliet. I named her.'

'Lovely name. Who after? Not the doomed Shakespearean heroine?'

'No, no! There are many reasons. It resonated.'

'Were you there when she was born?' For God's sake, Nichi. I shouldn't have asked that. This was such a personal conversation to be having with someone you barely knew.

'Of course,' Sebastian said, and smiled as though I'd just asked him if his heart ever beat.

He seemed willing to talk but the mood was threatening to darken. I didn't need to know this stuff now. What I did need to know was some more about the kind of kink stuff he was into.

Sebastian shrugged off his coat and laid it across the bar, then pulled the black lambswool scarf from around his neck. He was dressed in similar jeans tucked into boots again, and a thick charcoal sweater with a stylish row of buttons that came undone along one strapping shoulder. Concealed, his body was even more delicious. I needed an excuse to touch him. Or perhaps not. Well, he'd touched my hat, hadn't he?

'Mmm, that's cosy!' I squeezed the soft woollen fabric that shrouded his bicep. He tensed at my touch and fixed his eyes on mine as a rush of heat raced up from the pit of my stomach, flooded over my chest, wove round my throat and inflamed my cheeks. He saw it. I knew that he saw it. And I knew, too, that I was no longer imagining our connection.

But what now? On any other date the moment when it was

clear we were burning for one another would have been the point when I asked them if they wanted to come back to mine. But this time I didn't want that. Or rather, I didn't want only that. I couldn't remember the last time I'd felt this compelled, this captivated, this excited by someone.

'So what made you give up the domming?' he asked me. He leaned on the bar. Turned to face me. 'Realised you weren't naturally dominant after all?'

Oh God. He was going right in for it.

'I was never naturally dominant,' I explained calmly, although my heart raced like a looped electronic drum. Thank God I could still invoke my domme's composure when necessary. Although, Sebastian staring at me like that, with a hint of a cruel smile about his alluring lips, was testing every atom severely.

'I'm a switch,' I pronounced. I'd never actually said it before. And what's more, was it even true? Did I have a single dominant thought towards Sebastian?

'Switching is best,' Sebastian nodded. 'Like I said that night at Violet's' – that night at Violet's? So he remembered it too? – 'where's the fun if there's no fight?'

'Although . . .' Uh oh. Here comes the caveat. 'Sometimes I meet someone and I can't do anything else but pull their hair and fuck them senseless.' He smiled at me and finished his whisky. Another shrug. 'But generally I like a bit more rough play first.'

My hair. Oh God, to have this man pull at my hair, force my head up to him in a wanton kiss.

'Would you like another one?' he asked.

'Um, well, what time is it?'

Sebastian gestured to the bar clock. '10.45.'

'10.45?' How the hell had so much time elapsed without me feeling hungry, cold, or tired on a freezing Friday night? Without feeling much of anything apart from utter captivation with this man. And deep, dark lust for him.

I paused for a moment then shook my head. 'I'd better not.' Good girl. 'I should get home. Yoga in the morning.' That was the crappest excuse ever but I did have to get home. If I didn't I was going to drag this man into the bathroom with me, first date or no.

'Let me walk you to the tube, then.'

I picked up my bag and rearranged my hat, much to Sebastian's pleasure. Outside the street lights dimmed as if they were blushing. Sebastian pulled up the collar on his coat and then very deliberately offered me his arm, with gentlemanly charm. I took it. We walked along the icy cobbles back up towards Oxford Circus. Since there was no way I was going to make a fool of myself at this stage in the game, I took particular care, inching myself down the steps into the underground. Sebastian stood protectively behind me.

Before the ticket barriers, we braced ourselves for the goodbye. Or at least, I did.

'Thank you for a lovely evening,' I said, and beamed up at him.

His cheekbones had taken on a tinge of pink from the cold, highlighting their angular perfection even more in his beautiful face. His lips were pursed. Then, unexpectedly, it came.

'Would you like to come back to mine?'

I thought my heart might spring out of my chest and into his arms. 'Oh!' My eyes fell to the floor in prostration. I wanted it. I wanted him. So badly. But I had to stick to my diktat. I didn't want to become one of his one-night stands. He had to know I wanted more.

'I'd love to,' I replied, placing as much stress on the love as I could muster without it sounding like mad desperation. 'But I, well. I've said I won't do that any more.' I looked up at him.

His gaze was as level, as genial as before. He got it. I think. Did he?

'Well, we'll have to do this again sometime.' His voice purred like a car pulling into a drive.

'Yes. Let's. Definitely.'

And then we kissed. Just his mouth full on mine. A lavish yet simple lips-meeting-lips kiss, a few seconds that spilled over and magnified in my mind as I replayed it on the way home.

Next time.

Chapter 15

The next morning I called Gina.

'How did it go?'

'You remembered?'

'Er, this is the man that has stalked your dreams since December. How could I *not* remember? So, how did it go?'

'Yes. Stupendously. He . . . it's . . . oh God, Gina, there is so much chemistry there! On my part anyway, I swear he's the most beautiful man I've ever met.'

'Yeah, we know that bit already, Nichi. What did you talk about? Hang on a minute . . . are you even alone?'

'Gina! Yes, I'm alone! He asked me, but I said no.'

I didn't always indulge myself to my loins' content. Although generally speaking it was true, if I wanted sex I had no problem with having it on a first date. These old-fashioned, moralising rules about what women should or shouldn't do if they wanted to avoid been labelled did not matter to me. From that perspective, I don't know why I'd decided not to this time. Well, no, I did. I went over it again in my head. It's because I want more than sex.

'Oh my God, is this the first time you've ever NOT gone home with someone you wanted to shag into oblivion?'

'Yes, I think it probably is!'

Gina squealed. 'OK, OK, so what did you talk about?'

'His art. My writing. He has a daughter, Gina, a seventeen-year-old.'

'Jesus, Nichi! Please tell me know he's not secretly fifty-two or something!'

'He's thirty-six. I know it sounds crazy but honestly, you should have heard the way he spoke about her. Juliet, she's called. Her mother won't let him see her. Anyway, we only talked about his daughter for a bit, I felt awkward about it. Then we talked about sex.'

'What kind of sex?'

'Oh, you know. The bad kind.'

'Still up for it then?'

'Gina, I tell you, I've never been more up for it.'

'Did you kiss?'

'Yes. It was divine. I'm never going to be able to look at that spot in Oxford Circus tube the same way now. I have to pass it every morning on the way to the office! Oh God, his *lips*, Gina. But what do I do now? I just have to wait, right?'

'Yes, you just have to wait.'

'But what if he doesn't text?'

'Can you even hear yourself right now?'

'Yes, I know I sound utterly pathetic. But what if all he wanted was sex and now I've missed my chance of being . . .' I paused for a moment and imagined for the forty-seventh time since last night Sebastian pulling me in to kiss him, my hair wrapped round his hand '. . . of being ravished. And now he's going to move on to the next submissive and give her a punishing instead.'

'So you lost out on a hot night. You want more. Remember that. And this sounds like it could be more, anyway. Nichi, you did the right thing.'

I knew she was right. I knew I was right refusing to go home with him, even if I had simply got into my own bed and masturbated deliriously about him.

'Besides,' stated Gina, 'he's going to text.'

Three days later, Sebastian did indeed text. 'Hello. Hope you're well. Let me know if you're free this weekend. Drinks? Sx.'

I was at work when I read it and tried and failed to contain an 'Eek!' of joy. My colleague looked over the top of his computer screen at me. 'Good news, Nichi?'

'Good news.'

So it had worked. He didn't just want sex. He wanted me.

I managed to wait a whole eleven minutes before I replied. 'Hi, yes, that would be lovely. Where were you thinking?'

On Friday night, something suddenly occurred to me. Sebastian didn't know my name. Or rather he knew that Jade had been my domme pseudonym and that I was in reality called something else beginning with N.

I texted him to that effect.

S: 'Ha, yes, it did occur to me. But I planned on using my powers of clairvoyance to figure it out. N . . . hmm, let's see. Natalie?'

N: 'Nope.'

S: 'Not Nefertiti?'

N: 'Alas, no, something way more prosaic.'

S: 'Nancy? Nadia?'

N: 'No and no (oh, and it's not 'no' btw ;))

S: 'As you can see, I don't have a baby name book! Hmm . . .'

N: 'Well, do you even need to know? I'm sort of amused by the fact you don't. Let's stretch it out a bit longer.'

I mean, I would need to tell him my name eventually. Or how else could he call it out?

Saturday arrived. What to wear? Since last weekend, spring had danced in seemingly from nowhere. I pulled out of my wardrobe a dress I'd bought the last time I'd gone to visit my family in Australia. It was backless, with a black bodice and a netted, dusky rose-print skirt. With its stitched-in cups, the construction gave incredible cleavage, and the back, a generous and provocative display of flesh. Shoes. Hmm, snakeskin heels? The colour of the rose stamen matched the shade of snakeskin. Anyway, I didn't want to be too matchy-matchy and black was boring. And then there was an angora cardigan, with a plunging neckline, which fastened at the waist with a single satin button. Layered over the dress, the effect to my shape was of soft corsetry. It tied at the back with a luscious inky ribbon and begged to be stroked.

But really, I had no idea what Sebastian liked, or what he would like me in. It was still cold enough for stockings. Of course they went on, too. And black lace knickers, which could never be wrong.

It took me two hours to get ready properly for a date. But before I could prep myself I had to clean the house and my room. And change the sheets. It didn't mean anything, of course. I was resolved not to sleep with him until the third date. They just had to be changed.

We'd arranged to meet at London Bridge tube station at 6.30 p.m. Prom prep, as Gina called it, took longer than I had anticipated. Twice. Twice I moved our meeting back. 'Chronos has kidnapped me,' I texted him. Would he know who the Ancient Greek god of time was? Let's see. 'Yeah, that guy's always causing trouble. Not a problem. See you soon!' So he was as smart as he looked. But was he always so genial, so laidback?

At the station, Sebastian was nowhere to be seen. Then there was a text message. 'I'm right in front of the escalators, near the annex shop.'

Did I have to go and fetch him? Why couldn't he come to me? He had me skivvying about after him already. I scurried through the station and took the escalator up to where I knew he'd be waiting. Suddenly a half-remembered feeling seized me. What? It was . . . wow, no, really? I had butterflies. I hadn't felt like this since Christos.

I stepped off the escalator and scanned the station, spinning on my heels. I was on tenterhooks. Suddenly an arm cinched about my waist and reeled me round. It was him. Sebastian beamed at me, his blue eyes burning. He kissed me on the lips. More butterflies.

'Shall we?' He offered me his arm once again.

The pub was unusually quiet for a Saturday night. Sebastian held open the door. 'Watch your step in those shoes.' He smiled, first at me, then the shoes, then at me again. Did that mean he liked them? Did he have a shoe fetish?

'What would you like to drink? Wine again?'

He'd remembered. Shame it wasn't actually my usual. 'Gin and tonic, please.'

He ordered that and a whisky for himself. The man at the bar gave him a stingy double and so I decided to turn on the charm to get him a top-up of the extravagant Scotch he'd chosen. The double soon became a generous triple.

'That's enough to get me absolutely wasted. Thank you!'

Really? A tall, muscular man like him with his boxing- and fencing-honed body was wasted on three whiskies?

'I don't really drink any more,' he explained. 'I can't paint when I do.' He raised his glass.

I liked that. Dedication to the things that mattered to him. He was wearing the jersey he'd worn the night of Violet's party and my eyes devoured once more the way it accentuated the hard and handsome outline of his chest and biceps.

As before, our conversation darted about as regularly as our eyes. We discussed the artists he loved and the ones I did, our favourite Greek myths, how little we understood about Middle Eastern politics and how much we loved living in London.

Sebastian had a real gift for exuberant impressions. Of rock stars, politicians, African dictators. 'Sebastian, you're better than me! And I was going to be an actor!'

'Oh, me too, at one point!'

'I blame it on my obsession with the eighties film *Labyrinth* with David Bowie in it. Do you remember?'

'That film was amazing. If only for Bowie's crotch. If I'd been a girl I would totally have crushed on Bowie.'

After two and a half hours together it became clear that we couldn't have another date like this. Every question, every anecdote, every accidentally-on-purpose brush of my breasts against his biceps was biding the time before we finally had sex.

I turned to Sebastian and smiled. He smiled back at me, his eyes heavy with anticipation. I had really intended to wait. But I couldn't. Why deny myself this? Why deny him? We wanted each other so much. And if he only wants to fuck me anyway, aren't I just delaying the inevitable disappointment for myself if I stretch this to a third date? I focused on the rapidly melting ice in my glass. Finally, without looking at him, I said, 'Do you want to come back to mine?'

'Yes,' came the reply, before the last word was fully out of my mouth.

I looked up at him. Those dimples again.

On the tube back, a bunch of boorish boys were disturbing the carriage. Sebastian teasingly dared me to chastise them. 'I'll step in if they turn on you this time, I promise!' They got off before I could think seriously about rising to him. Instead, I turned my ire to how infuriated I became with people who didn't reply to my text messages. 'Noted,' he winked. We stood at the end of the carriage, not touching, just looking into one another's faces, full of expectant lust. There were only eight stops to go until we reached my flat, a seventeen-minute journey with a nine-minute walk once we got off.

It may have been the longest journey home of my life.

When we finally made it to my bedroom, I kicked off my shoes. Sebastian stared at them again. 'Those shoes are very hot.'

I laughed. I'd guessed correctly then.

Without being invited, Sebastian went over to the bed and lay down, his head propped up on the pillows. Ordinarily I might have been offended at someone's presumption in my space but this time I couldn't wait to join him, and settled myself alongside. He slid his arm around me, pulling me gently in to him so that I had to lay my head on his chest. He smelled so fresh, I thought for a moment it was the laundered sheets. How could anyone smell so pure? As he heaved a sigh of contentment I could feel the muscles contracting and releasing across his chest, and out along his shoulders. Even just lying on his strong supple body was turning me on. He stroked my hair with expert ease. Finally, he spoke. 'So, how do you want to be topped?'

Oh God. There, there it was. So he did want to dominate me after all. Every fibre of my body wanted to kowtow to him but already I sensed that our dynamic was built on something more complex than that.

'Who says I'm going to be topped?' I teased back.

He raised his eyebrows and stared at me for a moment, bemused. Then he got up and went round to the foot of the bed. He stood there, lavishing his eyes over my body for a few moments. Then he lunged at me and ripped down the bodice of my dress, exposing my breasts, caressing and kissing them roughly, greedily sucking at my nipples.

I ran my hands over his face, down the back of his neck, along the groove of his spine and then round and forward along his achingly athletic arms and torso, appreciating every sinew of hard flesh as it passed under my fingers. I clawed at his jersey and we freed him of it together. Around the top of his right arm were a series of electric-blue tattoos. I had never seen such artful tattoos before.

'I had no idea you were inked! Intelligent men with glasses and tattoos do it for me every time!' I told him.

'Well, then I'll make sure I wear my glasses next time!'

Next time? I couldn't even think about next time. I was consumed with this time. I lay there drinking in his warrior body; his pale chest glowed in the lamplight, his massive inked arms threatened to heave me up and over his knee like that night I'd watched him haul up Violet, and so I was caught off-guard when he suddenly decided to fling up the skirts of my dress, running his fingers up under the fabric of my lace knickers. He looked up into my face as if seeking permission, paused for a few seconds, then, deciding he didn't need it, yanked them down deliberately. Then, finally, he plunged his tongue into my wetness, moaning as he took that first taste of me. 'You're fucking delicious.'

I could only endure his licking for a few more seconds before I had to push his head away. 'You have to stop, I'm going to cum,' I gasped. 'Oh, and that would be too terrible!' he laughed, bearing over me and kissing my lips once more. His laugh was the wicked, sexy snigger that I'd first heard at Violet's. It mesmerised me. When it came to this man, I had no resolve. But I wanted to make this last. Playfully, I pushed his face away with my inner thigh, then scrambled up to strip out of my dress. As I leaned forward to fling it off the bed, he wrestled with the rest of his clothes, whipping off his belt to release his fly. Trousers, briefs, socks and shoes all came off in a rabid tumble.

I let my eyes linger over the bounteous sight of Sebastian fully naked. Then he reached out for me and very lightly slapped his hand on my bottom, spun me round, then grabbed on to me by the hips and slid me back towards him, before easing first one, then two, then three, then four fingers into me, I was so wet and so open for him. I arched back and started to work myself back and forth along his hand, then turned to glance at him over my shoulder. He was gasping now too, and had his cock in his other hand, masturbating himself as he fingered me. We locked eyes and I felt myself flood with desire.

We writhed like this for a few more minutes until my need to taste him overcame me. Abruptly I pulled away, then rose up on to my knees and turned around to face him. Then I placed my fingers on his throat and guided him on to his back so that I could control his entry into my mouth. Slowly, deliberately, I licked my way up along the centre line of his balls, then along his shaft, teasing the head of his cock with the slightest strokes of my hot tongue without taking him full into my mouth. He was already wet with pre-cum, and, as if there were a golden thread connecting my arousal with his, tasting him made me even wetter. I guided my face up to his. He looked me straight in the eyes. 'I need to fuck you.'

He kissed me with increasing urgency now and slid his hands up along my body as if I were a new canvas he were preparing to paint. As he kneeled up and then around me, I reached for his cock and stroked my hand all the way up along it, marvelling at its perfect girth and perfect length. Then fixing his electric eyes on mine, he eased his way into me, and I clawed at his shoulders and then his ass as I felt him fill me for the first time. Sebastian held me there for a moment then began to thrust in and out of me. He felt like hot, pulsing marble between my legs.

We fucked for nearly a full hour, continuously urging each other to the brink of orgasm, Sebastian withdrawing every so often to lick my clitoris until my whole pussy throbbed for him to be inside me again. He went so rapidly at the start I was worried it would be over before I'd even got to fully enjoy him. 'That's not going to happen,' he said, and smiled at me. 'I take a while to cum.' 'Lucky for me then,' I smiled back, then gasped as he angled up my hips and entered me again, even more deeply. After all that licking, this had me fighting off my own orgasm. But I couldn't delay it indefinitely and soon began clawing at Sebastian's shoulders and back, involuntarily thrusting up to meet his hugely swollen cock.

Realising how close I now was, he eased out of me, and sprang up off the bed. He stood at the foot of it, scrutinising me for a moment. I lingered my eyes over his tattoo again. Then with one swift movement he reached forward and seized me with his muscular arms, clamping one hand on my hip, the other on my thigh, and dragged me down the sheets to the edge of the bed. Keeping one foot on the floor for anchorage he began to drive in to me with the most deliberate, consummate strokes, rocking my body so that I had to cling to his neck to anchor myself.

Soon Sebastian's controlled thrusts gave way to his frantic lust. He kissed me urgently. 'I'm cumming, I'm cumming,' he choked into my neck, clutching me to him as his whole body started to quaver. I was so overwhelmed by the sense of him coming inside of me, that for a moment I didn't realise that I too was climaxing, and couldn't even get the same words out before we had both surged into an explosive orgasm together.

Afterwards we lay entwined, two springs uncoiling. I couldn't remember the last time I had climaxed like that. He slid his hand under my neck and fondled it, holding me to him as he lay on top of me.

After a few minutes he got up to go the bathroom.

'Would you like me to turn off the lamp?' he asked as he came back into the room, ever courteous.

'No, don't worry, the switch is just here.'

Plunged into darkness, I lay there, spent and smiling to myself. Then it occurred to me. Sebastian hadn't actually dominated me after all. It was impossible to feel let down after sex like that, but I wondered why he'd decided against it. Perhaps he was anxious about going to town on me when he knew I was new to submission. Well, if that was the case, I was going to need to give him a little encouragement. I didn't want him thinking I was nervous about it.

'Sebastian?'

'Mmm? What's up?'

His chest, on which I lay, rose up and down more slowly now, but he wasn't about to fall asleep just yet.

'So I guess I never answered your question. About how I like to be topped.'

'No, I guess you didn't.'

'Well, I'm hypothesising a little; I mean, I know I've never experienced it before, but I'm certain I like having my hair pulled.'

'Mmm, go on.'

'And being pinned down.'

'Of course.'

'And having my thighs forced apart . . . In fact, just generally being forced.'

Sebastian patted my thigh. 'All the good things.'

The next morning I woke in a delicious wooze, the way you do when you've fucked into the small hours with someone luscious and still have them in bed with you. I chanced my fingers down Sebastian's tattooed arm, in part to admire him again, and also to test if he were awake yet. He turned over and smiled at me. 'Good morning'. He reached out to cup my breast, then looked apologetic for having groped me without asking first. I giggled sleepily and rolled over so that he could hold me properly, sliding my hand up along the chiselled curvature of his chest.

We dozed for another twenty minutes or so, then suddenly, Sebastian spoke. 'Nicola.'

I pushed myself up, hovered over him. 'What?'

'Your name. It's Nicola. Or maybe Nicole.'

'You cheated! You must have seen it written somewhere.'

'I didn't cheat.'

He had guessed it. It was auspicious. It had to be.

'It's Nichi, actually.'

I lowered my head to kiss him, and slid my small body up along his much larger one. His morning erection prickled against me, and I wrapped my fingers around it, feeling him swell in my hand. He skated his hand down along my hip and then up in between my thighs. Before long, we were masturbating one another, kissing and clawing at each other with a rampant need all over again.

As Sebastian played with me, he moved his mouth alternately from my lips to my breasts. My super-sensitive nipples hardened at once under his tongue. He dared to bite them. It made me swoon. The more he bit, the more I moaned, and soon he was nipping and sucking and biting me until I winced in pleasurable discomfort. Abruptly he pulled away. 'More?' he asked me.

I hesitated for a moment. He slid his hand up under the back of my neck and stroked me gently.

'More?' He repeated the question. Only this time it seemed as though I had less choice in the matter. He asked me still with that low, soft lilt but something in his face had changed.

He didn't wait for my reply. He knew he had my permission to do what he had come here for, to do what I had been willing him to do since he crossed the threshold of Violet's house, what I willed him to do every time he touched me. Without waiting another moment he grabbed my hair with his right hand as if it were a rope, wrapping it round his hand twice in quick succession, then yanked on it, forcing my head to the side, my right cheek down into the pillow. Keeping a firm hold on my hair, he then seized me roughly by the wrists with his left hand, and pulled my arms in the opposite direction to my head, pinning me to the bed in twisted submission. I couldn't get out of this grip. My heart was racing. Was this a result of our conversation last night? Or had he been planning to do this all along?

'This is what happens, Nichi, when you tell me what you really want,' he said, then wedged his right knee in between my unsuspecting thighs, prising them apart. Instinctively I went to close them and he whipped his right hand down to give my right thigh the lightest of slaps, then yanked at my hair again. It shocked me. But before I could even catch my breath, he had thrust his cock into me and begun fucking me, rocking his hips against mine at a relentless pace, causing my cries of pleasure to catch in my throat.

Every so often I would test his grip, pulling away from the hand that held my hair, twisting my wrists under his fingers. But each time he tightened his hold.

'Oh, you're not going anywhere.' He laughed, that dark, mesmerising laugh.

So this is what it felt like to be forced by Sebastian. He was more abrupt than I could have imagined, in the best possible way.

After a few more minutes of this, he withdrew, then pulled me up by my hair and kissed me slowly, allowing me to catch my breath. But soon he used his legs to force me on to my side, and started fucking me that way with the same pace and intensity, his groin slapping against my ass as he did it. It was a stark, raw sound and made both of us moan with arousal.

'You've impressed me,' I ventured coquettishly. For a moment, he paused, bore right into me with those brilliant blue eyes and brought his face millimetres before mine, then dashed it to my ear and whispered, 'You had such a low opinion of me, did you?'

And with that he released me. First letting go of my hair, and then my wrists.

He grinned, with just the hint of menace, patting my cheek. 'You'll learn.'

Chapter 16

This time, I had no doubt that Sebastian would text again.

After we had sex that morning, I offered Sebastian a towel and asked him if he wanted to shower. 'Shower with me?' he replied. His request startled me, and I hesitated for a moment before I agreed. In the shower, stripped of make-up and my layered moisturiser and perfume seduction scent, I was plain and vulnerable. Christos and I had often showered together but it was such an intimate, sensual thing to do with someone you had just met. And yet I wanted nothing more than to be intimate like that with Sebastian.

Before we could even think about getting clean though, we were both yearning to touch each other once again. It only took a few minutes of frantic mutual masturbation until we both came again, Sebastian ejaculating up the length of my body, catching my breasts with his cum.

Afterwards, he asked me what 'feminine delights of cosmetics' I had in here, and I playfully scrubbed his face with my exfoliant. 'I think that's the first time I've exfoliated in about ten years!'

'Ha! Which means you did once upon a time!' I teased him.

'What can I say? I'm a narcissist! Anyway, shall we go get breakfast?'

In the café, we ate and joked over the turgid Sunday papers. I lounged on him and stroked the nape of his neck. For a moment I felt him stiffen under my touch. Perhaps he didn't like public displays of affection. But then he wrapped his arm around me and kissed my head. And when we kissed at the tube station, I had no doubt that he would be back. We hadn't arranged to meet again but it didn't trouble me.

Later that afternoon I texted him. 'So it's Nichi, btw, just in case you forget!'

'Oh I wasn't going to, don't you worry. But it's good to see it spelled because in my head I saw it as Nikki.'

'Like the Prince song ;)' I flashed back.

Three days later, Sebastian texted again. 'Nichi, hope you're well. Are you free next week post-Monday? Care to meet up?'

For the next two months Sebastian and I met up every week. Usually at the weekend, occasionally during the week, but always on an evening, and always for kinky sex. One time, when our schedules had forced us to go a fortnight without meeting, I invited him to have a coffee with me in the afternoon so that we could at least get to see each other before a full three weeks had passed. His artist's hours meant his work schedule, unlike mine, was entirely flexible and so it was easily enough done. But he declined and asked to wait until the weekend instead. For a moment I wondered anxiously if this meant he still only wanted sex with me, but the nights we spent together were as full with conspiratorial laughter and constant conversation as Sebastian pinning my hands above my head and commanding me to suck his cock. I knew this wasn't just about sex for either of us.

That said, the sex was only getting hotter. If I'd had any misgivings about my spiral into submission, Sebastian had seduced them out of me. I was utterly intoxicated with him, and it. Already, he had trained me to take a lot more pain than I could ever have imagined being able to endure, let alone found myself actively yearning for. 'Take it for me,' was an expression he'd often murmur to me, in between kisses and slaps. And I did. I loved to see the titillation he got from watching me wrangle with that line between pleasure and pain. The more aroused he became, the more it turned me on.

Everything Sebastian did, he did with safe, consummate control. Sebastian was an expert restrainer. He now pinned my wrists down with his knees when we had sex, the way I had seen done in kink porn films. He had no trouble wrapping his large dexterous fingers around my upper arms and would grip me so tightly that the next morning I would often wake to find myself marked with a bracelet of bruises. They usually faded quickly and were almost entirely painless.

One particularly forceful weekend, Sebastian had been very insistent that I didn't get my hands free, first bending me over the bed and spanking me, then turning me on to my back and teasing me remorselessly with my vibrator, holding me down as he did so to prevent me from grinding myself on it and climaxing. As a consequence, I was still a little coloured in come Monday morning. Because it didn't hurt, I forgot that there was anything to see until my boss asked me what I'd done to myself, pointing at my violet and damson arm, and I felt myself flush from the neck up and stammer out some hasty excuse. Later I stroked over the bruises. A little bit of Sebastian left on me until the next time I got to feel his unyielding grip again.

Despite the roughest sex of my life, Sebastian was one of the gentlest people I'd ever met. He was a 'rabid snuggler', as he put it one morning.

'Do you know what I would love to set up if I could free up some capital from my art business? A snuggle shack.'

'A what? Please expand.'

'Basically it's like a purely platonic cuddle brothel, where all you can get is a hug.'

'Mmm. That's nice. But do you think it's possible to attract the right patrons in the first place?'

'Are you kidding me? I know loads of men – and women – who'd be up for just a snuggle!'

'Hmm, I suppose I agree,' I conceded. 'You can get by without sex. But you can't get by without snuggles!'

'Well, I can't get by without sex,' he confessed, 'but I would never confuse the two. I would be an exemplary snuggle-shacker.'

He squeezed me to him and nuzzled me in sweet, platonic demonstration. I started laughing again. It wasn't just Sebastian's body that made me swoon.

What I really wanted, though, was to expand the repertoire of our activities. I talked about it with Gina. 'I know that it isn't just about sex, Gina, else why would we go for these long brunches? We're usually together for nearly twenty-four hours when we see each other. It's crazy the ground we cover in conversation. But I want to do cultural things with him. We spend so much time talking about culture it seems odd that he never suggests anything.'

'So find an exhibition or event you think he'd enjoy and ask him if he'd like to go.'

'Argh, I can't! What if he says no?'

'Why the hell is he going to say no? Unless it's an artist he doesn't like. Just ask him.'

'I suppose it's that a tiny part of me resents having to do the asking. Shouldn't he be asking me by now?'

'Nichi, he's not a mind reader. Maybe he's just not too good at formal dating.'

'I guess. I hardly am. OK. I'm going to email him.'

'Why don't you just phone him?'

'Because we don't phone each other. And I'm not about to start now! He has to make the first phone call.'

'How feminist of you . . .'

'It's not about that. I just want to know that he wants me.'

I knew Gina was right. I just had to ask him, but still I agonised over my choice of exhibition. I was desperate to minimise the chances of him declining. But why the hell did I have the feeling he might? I was just being paranoid. I knew it was early days but our connection was heady, intense and very, very real. I hadn't met anyone since Christos that I felt might be perfect partner material and I was determined to give this every possible chance.

Finally, I made my selection: a retrospective of the Japanese artist Yayoi Kusama's work. I was sure Sebastian would appreciate it, unless he'd already been. To make it even more difficult for him to say no, I told a white lie and said that I had press tickets.

'Yes, let's do it!" he replied, within a few minutes. 'Always good to see what the fellow obsessives are up to!'

Why had I worried so much?

The Saturday before the date I decided to go and have my hair blow-dried. It was an indulgent treat I'd only recently been able to afford, now that I finally had a decently paid job, and I'd never have felt the need to bother when I was with Christos. Yet despite his warmth and that dimple-flashing, beaming smile every time we met up, I realised that Sebastian had never actually paid me a proper compliment. I had no doubt that he found me attractive, but I still wanted to make the effort, and to entice him to remark.

Again, we met at London Bridge station, near to where the exhibition was being held at the Tate Modern. In the end I had opted for a tight black pencil skirt, stockings, black heels and a sheer, grey, leopard-print shirt. And fuchsia pink underwear, nails and lips after an amusing conversation we'd had in bed one morning about how the sight of bright, feminine colour worked Sebastian up into an even more dominant state.

This was the thing about being submissive; it made me want to desperately please Sebastian in a way I'd never felt like doing for any man before. It unnerved me, but already I trusted him implicitly and yearned to explore it.

Before I left the house I reconsidered the knickers. I decided to leave them off and smiled to myself slyly as I reached for my leather jacket and bag.

When I got to the station, Sebastian was already waiting for me, dressed in his usual monochrome, accessorised with the odd splash of grey. I tried not to race to him. He reached out to hug me and kissed me lavishly. And then he did something he'd never done before. He took my hand. Who cared if he thought it didn't matter to compliment me. This was the only kind of compliment I was really after.

The exhibition was quiet with just a handful of other visitors mooching about.

'Do you know much about her?' Sebastian asked me. I shook my head. 'So you can't be my expert guide?' he teased me.

'Well, I was very much hoping you could be mine, Mr Pro-Artist!' We looked at one another and laughed, then kissed spontaneously. Another first. Why had I left it so long to ask him if we could do something like this?

Kusama's formative work consisted of drawings she'd done as a teenager growing up in Japan. They were full of darkly sketched organic shapes. She had suffered from hallucinations most of her life and that psychic distress seemed to manifest itself in her work.

'It reminds me of the kind of thing I used to produce with my art therapist when I was anorexic,' I said, and grimaced. 'Just in terms of the obsessive, repetitive, bodily forms.'

I'd told Sebastian that I'd been anorexic during one of our late-night conversations, and he'd implicitly understood that it was little to do with vanity and far more to do with control. He nodded now.

'Yeah, I think I have a few of these locked away in my vault. All done during my Lana period, of course.'

'Lana?' I asked hesitantly.

'Oh, Juliet's mother.'

Ah. That conversation on our first date now made a little more sense.

'Was it a difficult relationship?'

Sebastian sighed and spluttered out an awkward laugh at the same time.

'That's one way of putting it. For years she used to drop in and out of my life on a whim. I used to constantly worry about the impact on Juliet. I was crazy head over heels in love with her. When she came back it was always the same. "We should be together, Sebastian, let's get married, Sebastian, I love you Sebastian." But then I'd wake up one morning sometimes weeks, sometimes just days later and she'd have vanished again. It went on for years. She even lived in Thailand for two of them and we resumed the relationship all over again when she returned.'

I listened solemnly. Even now Sebastian's story percolated pain.

'What was her reasoning?'

'Well, I think she had a few undiagnosed mental health issues, but that's not really for me to say. But she couldn't empathise, and she couldn't commit, not even to living in the same place for more than a couple of months at a time. And she could hurt me over and over with no sense of having done anything wrong.'

'That sounds awful. Did you have anyone reassuring you that it wasn't your fault? What did your friends say?'

'They would badger me repeatedly about her, urge me to end it. Until they met her of course . . .' Sebastian trailed off and smiled ruefully.

I couldn't be sure, but something told me that Sebastian was referring to the hypnotism of her beauty. For a moment I felt uneasy. But then I felt honoured that he found it so easy to talk to me like this. I ran my fingers down the outside of his arm in comfort. Suddenly a more sensual picture caught Sebastian's eye. 'Aha! A pomegranate. A particular favourite of mine. I like to think of it as my spirit fruit.'

'You know it was a pomegranate that had Eve expelled from the Garden of Eden, right, not a apple?'

'No, I didn't know that.' He smiled, seemingly impressed with this arcane snippet of knowledge, and then came up very close behind me as I examined the picture, and whispered flirtatiously into my ear, 'Trust you to know that, Nichi.' I felt his breath, that sharp smell of his, and I longed for him to touch me. But instead he moved away and gestured his head towards the next room.

The culmination of the exhibition was an installation called the Infinity Mirrored Room, a mirrored labyrinth decorated with hundreds of tiny coloured balls that hung like suspended firework spray from the ceiling, the rainbow lustre magnified in every direction. It was like floating through a sugar-hued hanging galaxy, a magical experience, and as I walked ahead of Sebastian, I couldn't help but examine our reflections caught among the lights. He was a moving study in muscular grace, and the rosy lights picked up the colour in that sensuous mouth of his. Meanwhile, there was me, little curvy Nichi, trying so hard to offer myself up to him as an object of desire.

I noticed the matching grey and black of our garments, as if we were dressed in a lovers' uniform. Yet we stood there together, apart. I waited to see if Sebastian would catch my eye in the mirror but he didn't. Absorbed in the lights, his face locked in on itself the way I imagined it did when he painted. It was as if he were studiously refusing to meet his own reflection, let alone mine, and it left me with a curious sense of disconnection from him. Only minutes earlier he'd been revealing details of his emotional life to me in the most intimate way.

Sebastian was an enigma. Perhaps that's why I was so willing to serve him sexually. Because by trusting him to dominate me, I hoped that he might entrust me with access to the most intimate, vulnerable parts of him.

'Well, that was beautiful,' Sebastian said as we left the gallery. 'I'm really glad we saw it. Now, are we going to yours, or would you like to come back to mine?' He was testing me again with this proposition.

I thought about it for a moment. He'd asked me back to his numerous times but I preferred to be in my own space where I had ready access to my magic complexion-saving cream if I slept in my make-up accidentally on purpose. Or maybe I just preferred to have Sebastian in my space so that I could sleep the next night with his pine-river scent lingering about the pillows, have a little more of him etched on my life. No, going to his could wait.

'Not tonight. Let's stay at mine.'

No sooner had we made it through the door than Sebastian came up roughly behind me and began to grope my bottom. When I reached my hands back to stroke along his arms he grabbed those too.

I ground myself back into his groin and strained my head back to kiss him.

'Would you like anything?'

'Yes,' he replied. 'I'd like you to bend over the bed for me.'

My skin prickled. The sex games between us always started sensually, with some gentle kissing and fondling that worked itself up into a fever. Sebastian had never commanded me like this before.

I shuffled obediently into the bedroom and kicked off my shoes.

'A-a-ah! Did I say you could do that? Put your shoes back on.' Sebastian came up behind me and placed a strong hand on the nape of my neck, then stroked it down over my collar-bone, then my cleavage, until his fingers slid under the fabric of my top. His breath was cool on the back of my neck. Yet I burned as he blew on me. 'You know how much I love high heels. And you really do have a penchant for slutty ones, Nichi.'

I thought about retaliating for a moment but Sebastian was caressing me to distraction already, inching his fingers down into my bra and stretching out the cups so that he could pull on my nipples.

'You could probably make me cum just like that,' I told him between snatched breaths.

'That's if I let you,' he replied immediately.

Suddenly he slapped me hard on the backside.

'Ow!' I cried out and swooned back into him.

'What did I say about your shoes, Nichi?'

'You didn't give me a chance!' I retorted.

Sebastian whipped his hand out from underneath my bra and clamped it back around my neck.

'So let me help you,' he said, rearranging my shoes in front of my stockinged feet. 'Step up!' I slipped them back on, nervously resting back on to him for balance as I did so. God knows what Sebastian had in store for me. The feel of his body behind me filled me with delicious apprehension.

Then, he brought his curling lips back to my neck, and whispered, 'Whoever knew you were this contrary?'

I was breathing hard now, the movement of my chest causing my bra to protrude out of my shirt where Sebastian had pulled it back. 'But I'm not,' I retorted weakly.

Sebastian thrust me face down into the mattress. I was bent over the bed now, ass in the air for his delectation.

He fondled his hand approvingly over the thin fabric of my skirt then lavished the tips of his fingers up along the insides of my thigh. I quivered under his touch, braced myself for the spanking I knew I was due any minute. Then Sebastian wrenched up my skirt, over my hips, arranging it in neat creases over the small of my back, until my bare white bottom was completely exposed.

'Oh, *Nichi.*'

Shit, of course! I'd completely forgotten that I wasn't wearing any knickers.

'You mean to say you went all the way round a civilised art exhibition with me without wearing any panties?' His soft, wave-breaking voice had lowered a tone. I'd gone commando because I thought it would titillate him when we finally made it home. But maybe, secretly, I had also hoped that he was going to use it against me.

The delicious anticipation of my first proper spanking had me quivering. And the quivering betrayed my lust, betrayed my need to have Sebastian honour it with his hand.

For a split second, I wondered if Sebastian would do to me now what I had once done to my clients, putting them into position then backing off to heighten the anticipation of punishment. But the sight of my smooth white skin, the spongy curves of my generous ass, must have implored him to strike it and without giving me a moment to brace myself, Sebastian's rampant hand came hard down on my behind, sending that sensual heat coursing through my cheeks and down along the backs and insides of my thighs.

He slapped me two, ten, twenty times, staggering the spanks, increasing the strength until I was flinching away from him, each slap, each scolding kiss of his fingers on my stinging flesh leaving me a little more supplicant to his whim.

'This is for daring to try and play cock-tease, Nichi. You think it's original to go out without your knickers on?'

Should I reply? I had no sense of what was the right answer any more. Whatever I said would be used against me. And I wanted it to be.

Sebastian grabbed hold of my hair and used it to twist me around, still on my knees, to face him. 'Are you going to suck me off really nicely now? To say thank you for that spanking?'

I nodded frantically and looked up at his eyes, seeking his approval, then started kissing my way up his cock, losing myself in the task of licking and sucking him to oblivion. Soon Sebastian was thrusting into my mouth, with increasing urgency. Momentarily I wrenched myself off him, 'I want you to cum in my mouth. Please. I want to taste you,' I begged. He shook his head defiantly.

'Oh, no, that's not how it's going to happen. Up you get.' Sebastian wrenched me to my feet by a fistful of my hair then pushed me back on to the bed.

I reached out to his cock again.

'But I want—'

With no warning, Sebastian clamped his hand over my mouth. The sheer eroticism of his overpowering me like that was almost too much to bear, and my body seemed to crumple into the bed in compliant lust. I had wondered when he might eventually gag me.

'Don't say another word, Nichi. Or you're not going to get an ounce of pleasure yourself.'

Then without releasing his hand, he slid down the sheets and began to lick me out. Of all the men I had ever known, Sebastian gave the most exquisite head. He buried his face into my pussy with a reckless fervour, tongue-fucking me and dancing his fingers over my clitoris until I was bucking up to meet his mouth, desperate to cum.

But before I let myself there was something else I wanted him to do. The way he had clamped me quiet had unleashed my need for it.

'Sebastian!' He brought his dripping mouth away from me, and looked up into my face earnestly.

'Will you slap me?' His electric blue eyes sparked up, initiated into a darker kind of sexual service. He rose to his knees, bore over me. 'So you know what you deserve after all,' he leered, then whispered huskily up into my face, 'you little bitch,' and struck me lightly across the bottom of first one cheek, then the other. Then he did it again, more rapidly, returning one hand in between my legs to tease my clitoris as he continued insulting me and striking my face with light slaps.

After that, it was as if Sebastian had created a direct line between the two. Every time his fingers slapped down hard on my cheek, I felt a yearning for him deep inside my increasingly wet pussy. This lasted for no more than five minutes before he'd brought me rapidly, rabidly, to the edge of my orgasm. Just as I was about to climax I cried out 'Harder!' and for the first time, Sebastian struck me fully across the face as I began to rock around his other hand, crying out in abandon and trembling with obscene pleasure. As my breath settled itself, Sebastian kissed my burning cheeks tenderly.

Afterwards, I went to the bathroom to examine my cheek. It felt far redder than it looked. I knew from slapping the clients how quickly surface colouring went down. Sebastian really was so good at this.

I went back into the bedroom and climbed into bed beside Sebastian. We lay there stroking one another's shoulders and chatting about the worst sexual experiences we'd ever had with people.

'Do clients count?' I asked him.

'Sure!'

I told him about the old gent I'd once dominated who shouted 'Fiddlesticks!' when he ejaculated. Sebastian convulsed with laughter and pulled me in tightly to him with affection.

'What about you?' I asked him.

'Oh, well, you know me, I'm always very appreciative of getting laid!' He patted my hair. I playfully hit away his hand.

'So rude!'

'But I'd say probably all the times when women have said things like, "Make love to me!" or "Tell me I'm beautiful!"' He burst out laughing.

I winced. What? Did Sebastian really find it funny that the women he'd slept with might want to be considered attractive by him? I mean, sure, people fishing for compliments could be a little bit of a turn-off but wasn't that just indicative of human vulnerability? I wanted to say something but I didn't know what.

Sebastian interrupted my thoughts. 'I'm going to brush my teeth. Do you mind if I borrow your robe?' He gestured to an embroidered satin kimono hung on the outside of the wardrobe door. He got up, put it on, and gave me a mock bow. Then before I'd had a chance to make a joke, he shook a finger at me. 'Don't think I'm into dress-up though! My ex tried that on with me and she got nothing but the back of my hand for it!'

The next morning Sebastian and I woke for our usual second sex session then promptly fell back asleep. When I woke again, Sebastian was still dozing. I carefully slid out of the bed, trying not to disturb him. I must have fallen asleep last night before he'd made it back into bed. My kimono was hung up on the wardrobe door, arranged perfectly, with the belt tied in an elaborate knot. I smiled at the care Sebastian had taken in rearranging it.

'Where do you think you're going?'

'To get some water. To have a shower. Is that against the rules?'

I stretched, then went over to my drawers and began fiddling about for a white lace negligee I had spent a ridiculous amount of money on a couple of weeks earlier, partly, I hated to admit to myself, in a bid to please Sebastian. As I slipped the nightie over my head, Sebastian paid no attention to it whatsoever and instead grabbed me by the wrist and pulled me back towards the bed, allowing him to catch hold of the other wrist too, and from there, roll me on to the duvet and then into him. He held me, arms twisted behind me, my head face down in the pillow for a few moments, then bent down to kiss my bottom. Then he smacked it sharply. 'You know, I don't exploit your ass enough.'

What did he just say? Ha! Finally!

'Wow. Careful there, Sebastian,' I said. 'That was almost your first compliment.'

'What are you talking about?'

'You know, you nearly paid me a compliment. Or did you perhaps mean that my ass is only worth exploiting?'

'What? Of course I've paid you compliments!' He looked uneasy and genuinely shocked. Did that mean he'd thought things he'd not expressed? I hoped so. But he needed calling out on this.

'No you haven't,' I retorted. The conversation last night, his mocking the women he'd slept with, had been the first thing I'd thought about when I woke up, and I still felt troubled by it.

He stared at me stubbornly. Then he shrugged his shoulders. 'Anyway, compliments are overrated. You never get the compliments you want in life.'

What an odd thing to say. Weren't all compliments gratefully received? They certainly were by me.

'Fine, I'll remember not to pay you any from now on!' I teased.

Chapter 17

For the first time after one of our dates, I decided not to text him that afternoon. I realised that while he replied to any text message or email I sent, always conscientiously and with verve and affection, he never initiated contact, unless it was to fix up the next time we were going to have sex again. We'd been dating for several months now. Wasn't it a little weird to hear absolutely nothing from someone you had such a connection with, from week to week? This time, I had to wait.

Monday came and went. On Tuesday, there was still no text from Sebastian. At work I switched my phone off until lunch in a bid to stop me from constantly checking it. In the afternoon, I was fact-checking a piece about artistic censorship in China, and was sure Sebastian would know the answer to an ambiguity I was puzzling over. I thought about texting him to ask his expert opinion, but stopped myself. That evening Gina called me to ask how the art gallery date had gone. I told her.

'Lady, you need to relax. That sounds emotionally sound and mighty hot. I can't believe you went out *sans* knickers! Actually, knowing you, I totally can. Very sad about Juliet's mother though. So what's the deal? Does he see Juliet now?'

'I don't think so. His ex is married to someone else, has other children with him, and they're seriously difficult about Sebastian seeing her. They Skype but what's that compared to spending quality time with your daughter? He's missed out on so much of her life, I can't imagine how guilty he must feel. But Gina, I have to tell you something . . .'

'Uh oh. You're not pregnant are you?'

'God, no!! But . . . but . . . I don't know how to say this, and I don't even know where it's come from, but for the first time in my life, I actually feel like contemplating that kind of long-term future with someone . . .'

'Nichi!'

'I know, I know . . .'

'You barely know the guy!'

'I KNOW. But I can't help it. It's chemical. There's something about his whole body that just makes me relinquish a part of me to him. And when I hear him speak about Juliet it just tugs at my heartstrings.'

'Well, all I can say is that I hope to God this guy pulls his finger out and starts texting you. I've just heard something I never thought would come out of your mouth! You've got it bad!'

On Wednesday morning there was no text. Work was quiet and so I raked through every one of my email folders on the off-chance that a missive from Sebastian might have made its way into one or other of them by mistake.

On Wednesday evening I walked home and found myself fighting hard to swallow the hint of a lump that rose in my throat as I passed the Tate, where we'd spent such a beautiful evening the previous Saturday.

On Thursday I had managed to channel some of my old domme power and felt withering towards Sebastian. If he texted now I was going to make him wait for it.

On Friday morning, at around 11.32 a.m., finally, there it was. No explanation. No apology. Just his usual 'Hey, hope you're well! Are you free to meet up next Wednesday? Sx.'

My heart heaved with relief. I made him wait a whole seven hours for a reply. 'Hello. Wednesday. Not sure yet. x.'

Immediately he responded. 'OK, well, when might you know? Perhaps it's time you crossed my threshold?'

Wow. So he was really pressing this issue of me going to his. That must be a good sign, right?

'We'll see. I'll let you know tomorrow.'

'Be sure to! Xxx,' came the reply. Good.

The following Wednesday, Sebastian met me after work at the tube station nearest his flat. I'd had the afternoon off and had taken even more care with my appearance than usual, exfoliating and moisturising every inch of myself, selecting a low-cut black netted top and a tight plum skirt that zipped down or up the front, according to your intentions. Purple suede skyscraper heels completed the outfit. My nails were a deep damson. It was getting too warm now for stockings but still I wore them.

I had perfected my lipstick by using the darkened train window as a mirror, but I was less nervous this time, for some reason. I had decided that Sebastian had something to prove to me, and this, combined with the rather more vampish outfit choice, was filling me with a rare forthrightness. In fact, I felt more as though I were off to meet an old client than Sebastian.

Sebastian was waiting at the other side of the barriers for me, and lunged lightly forward as I passed through, placing a hand on the small of my back as he came in to give me a long, deep kiss. I pulled away first and gave him a cool stare. For a moment, Sebastian looked almost nervous. But perhaps that was just the novelty of his pale eyes peering warily at me from behind his glasses.

As we walked out of the station, Sebastian looked unsure as to whether he should take my hand or not. I didn't offer it, and purposefully kept a few feet between us as we made our way along the main road.

Suddenly, a gaunt woman in her early thirties looking slightly the worse for wear came up to me. 'That's a lovely skirt you're wearing!'

'Oh!' I laughed a little and blushed. 'That's kind, thank you.' Compliments were compliments, even if they did come from passing inebriated strangers.

t

Then she gestured to Sebastian. 'Does he tell you you're beautiful?' Sebastian looked at first embarrassed and then rueful. Ha! The domme in me shook her head with laughter. I glared right at him, sucking in my cheeks. 'No, he doesn't!'

Sebastian, surely, had to take the point this time. We continued to walk down the road, at least two arm's lengths apart. Then Sebastian spoke. 'I was just about to say you looked gorgeous.'

We had dinner at one of Sebastian's favourite local Turkish haunts before heading back to his. The terrace of the restaurant was decorated with coloured glass hookahs. I hadn't had one since that night Christos and I had dined with Layla. For the first time, I spoke vividly about Christos, and Sebastian told me about his Greek ex.

'Do you know much of the language?' I asked him.

'Hmm,' he pursed his sumptuous lips, 'just *malaka*!' He made the appropriate offensive hand gesture and I started to giggle. 'What about you?'

'Well, I was pretty good, I guess. Not fluent by any stretch of the imagination, but it's a beautiful language. Underrated, in fact. I do miss being called Nichi *mou*!'

'Nichi *mou*?'

'You know, it's just an endearment. Means "my Nichi."'

'Oh, *mou* like that! Of course.'

I was beginning to thaw now. There was no way I could keep up the domme act with Sebastian. I craved his company when we weren't together. He started telling me a ridiculous story about a friend of his who made robots and had wondered if he could make his own living doll, one of those life-size Barbie-alikes that people use as sex toys. He mimicked his friend agonising over the ethics of using his technical skills to satisfy his lust. The animation in his handsome face was utterly comedic. I loved so much how Sebastian's mind worked. It was so similar to mine.

'What have you been working on?' I asked him.

'Oh, nothing much. I'm struggling to get funding for one particular project I really want to get off the ground. Any idea how I can raise a grand at short notice?'

It was a rhetorical question but still I gave it real consideration. I did know. Of course I knew. The quickest way to get money was still the quickest way. I placed the tip of my tongue behind my teeth for a moment to slow me down before I spoke. And then I offered up my suggestion. 'Well, I could tap up some of my old clients for you.'

'Ha! Nice try, Nichi! I've always suspected that you'd secretly love to see me worked into some little "forced bi" scenario of yours . . .'

'Sebastian, what are you talking about, you know I don't domme any more.'

'What do you mean then?'

'I mean that I could dominate some of them into giving to your project. Just like charitable domination, really. Only you're my pet charity.' I was toying with him. This was so naughty. I bit my lip in excitement.

Sebastian's eyes had taken on that dark glitter the way they had when he'd slapped me in the face for the first time.

'So Nichi . . .' He sat back in his chair and gazed at me. I could tell he didn't know whether to hug me for trying to help him out, or ravish me roughly for trying to control his fate for once. '. . . you're going to pimp yourself out for me?'

'No, Sebastian, I'm not going to pimp myself out for you!' I retorted. 'Think of me as your artistic tax collector. I don't have to do anything for the money. I mean, theoretically, I've already done it! Now, how are the donations being collected?'

'We have a donations page. Here, I'll send you the link now.'

Sebastian texted me the URL. All I had to do was compose a message to my various clients and pass it on with a command for them to donate. Done.

'Now, let's eat and we can check your donation page after dinner.'

When the waitress came to clear our plates, Sebastian ordered us tea and I went to the bathroom, taking my phone with me. It had vibrated repeatedly with text messages through dinner and I was curious to see what the clients were coming back with.

Several of them sent a simple 'Anything for you, Mistress.' But others were cheekier. 'What's your bra size again, Mistress, 34D? How about a pound for every inch then?' And then, there was a more sinister message from one of my least favourite old regulars. 'If I donate £500 how about I get to do anything I like to you for once?' I hesitated over it. I was actually tempted to agree. Sebastian needed the money and I wanted to raise it for him. Suddenly I remembered Violet's comment about self-sacrificing sexuality that night at her party, as we'd passed the gory image of the Indian goddess. Was that what I was doing for Sebastian right now? And, even more frighteningly, was I, in some perverse way, getting off on it?

I looked at myself in the low-lit bathroom mirror. What was I becoming? It was as if I was bound to Sebastian in some indelible way. We still barely knew each other and yet I was acting as though I were his devoted wife, supplicant from here to eternity. I didn't even dare ask him if we were exclusive, for God's sake, although I was pretty sure we were. Only a couple of weeks before, when he'd stayed over, I'd wanted to know the time. 'Go and check my phone. It's in my jeans pocket.' You wouldn't let a woman you were dating check your phone if there was any chance there might be a message from another one there, surely?

But I had to get a grip. I deleted the offer of £500 in exchange for a nothing-off-limits session with me. I still had some boundaries, and I needed to remind myself of that.

Back in the restaurant, I showed Sebastian the donation page. In half an hour my clients had already gifted his project with £600.

'Nichi, this is amazing! I can't thank you enough.' Was Sebastian actually slightly in awe of me for once?

'You're welcome. Now don't say I never do anything for you!'

He levelled his gaze at mine. 'I never would,' he replied sombrely. 'But honestly, you've saved me a really tough job. The only other option would have been to sell myself into sexual slavery.' Sebastian grinned at me, then expanded on it. 'I don't fancy your clients, but I can think of a couple of women I wouldn't mind kowtowing to. Queen Rania of Jordan, for example.'

I started to laugh and nodded in agreement. 'Don't get me started on beautiful Middle Eastern women! You know how much I appreciate them!'

'Well, we might need you as their trainer, Mistress Jade. Although I've found that most women know how to ball-squeeze instinctively.'

I presumed Sebastian was being mildly misogynist and tutted at him. 'Oh shush, you little anti-feminist!'

'No, I'm serious! You think I'm a giver not a taker then, eh?' He winked at me in the crepuscular light.

Had Sebastian really just confessed to being a masochist as well as a sadist?

Sebastian had warned me that he lived in a temporary and ramshackle studio. It was pretty squalid. Not that Sebastian himself was ever anything but immaculate but he clearly didn't care about the dilapidated conditions he lived in, so long as he could paint.

There was a poky window and the funereal curtains looked as though they'd never been opened. The bed was similarly dark and spartan, dressed only with two flimsy pillows and a duvet drowned in black covers. 'Would you like me to take your jacket?' he asked with the utmost charm. I nodded and he opened the wardrobe doors to reveal a sea of charcoal clothing. The only colour in the room came from Sebastian's chaotic paintings, crammed around the edges of the room. How different it was to the way Christos had always lived. The conversation about Greek exes had him lingering in my mind. But Sebastian's paintings were so exquisite that I couldn't think about anything but his brilliance and his beauty.

Sebastian gave me a minute to acclimatise before he began winding me in to him.

'So, Nichi, you thought you were pretty clever there, demanding that your old slaves cater to your Mistress-whim. Did you tell them that you were raising money for your Master?' Sebastian used the term master mockingly. We laughed at people who used the terms Master and Slave ordinarily. But the truth was that, right now, to all intents and purposes, I guessed he was just that.

'No. I just told them I was helping a friend.'

Sebastian leaned in towards me and pushed me up against the wall, sidling his fingertips up along the outer curves of my body, resting his hand possessively across the top of my exposed cleavage. He kissed me demandingly. 'A friend, eh? A friend that likes to rough you up every now and then.'

My body heaved under his touch.

'They don't need to know the details.'

Sebastian raised his hand. I flinched. Sebastian's eyes lit up and he cooed at my reaction. I knew it had turned him on. Then he let his hand come to rest above my head.

'Awww, poor little Nichi!' he pouted and tutted at me. That mouth of his. I wanted to kiss it off. But instead I played up to my designated submissive role, lowered my head and widened my green eyes in placation. 'I was only trying to help you, Sebastian.'

'I know I know.' He fondled his fingers over my cheek, then with a deftness and speed I couldn't possibly anticipate, brought his taut hand hard down on my cheek. 'And I do appreciate you whoring yourself out for me. But I think you need to be

careful with it. I mean, you wouldn't want to become my donation slut, would you . . .'

My heart started at the words 'whore' and 'slut'. These taboos,
words that had once sounded so silly when used with the clients,
now made me swoon with a dark delight.

He slapped me again. Then smoothed my hair into a rope
between his fingers, before pulling hard down on it and kissing
my upturned mouth.

'So just in case you were thinking of doing it again, Nichi,
I think I'd better fuck a little sense into you.'

Sebastian walked me over towards the bed, still with my hair
in his hand. 'Kneel,' he commanded. I fell to the floor facing
the bed. 'Not that way.' He grabbed me roughly and turned
me round to face him.

'Now, take that filthy little top off. I want to see these provocative tits of yours properly. Although clearly I could see most
of them already.'

I peeled off my top in haste. Usually I revelled in showing
off my body but for some reason now I blushed at the thought
of my outfit being overly immodest to Sebastian, even if he
was just trying to humiliate me.

'Much better. And the bra.' I unhooked my bra and let it
fall forward of my breasts into my lap.

He took first my left breast and then the right in his cool,
rough hands and toyed with them, bouncing them up ever so
slightly in his palms. Then again with unaccountable stealth he
whipped back his right hand, before sensuously slapping both
of my breasts in quick succession. He'd never done that before,
and the novelty and the way he caught my nipples as he brought
up his fingers thrilled me. I felt a throbbing between my legs.

Next, Sebastian moved on to my skirt. 'That's coming off
too, Nichi. How easy it would have been for me to expose you
in the restaurant.'

He twisted the metallic zip between his thumb and forefinger
then slowly inched it up. Csszzkcsszk. The incriminating noise

was amplified by the silence of Sebastian's room, the only other sound being my increasingly rapid breathing, and his. He eased the zip up past my crotch. Then he tugged at it one final time, letting my skirt fall to the floor. Now I was kneeling in nothing but violet knickers and black lace-topped stockings.

'Time to get up, Nichi.' He took hold of my hair again and waited for me to mount the bed.

Then as if the whole undressing had been an exercise in restraint for himself rather than me, Sebastian pounced, wrestling me into the mattress, kissing me voraciously as though he'd never had the taste of me on his tongue before. First throwing my hands above my head, he then pulled down my knickers, leaving them above my knees.

Sebastian was still dressed. How was he going to free himself, I wondered? But he was already on it. He rearranged himself until he was straddling me and ripped off his white jersey revealing that glorious torso of his. As he wrenched at his belt I watched his inked biceps tighten and pulse angrily. With his chiselled chest, tattooed arms and spectacles, he was the perfect warrior poet. Then he laid his bare chest down on mine as he freed himself of his trousers and briefs. I revelled in the sensation of his naked skin on mine. I was hotter and hungrier for him than I could remember ever being.

Sebastian took my face in his hands and held it there for a moment, quietening me with his cobalt-blue gaze. He traced his fingers along where he'd pinkened the skin earlier and I prickled under his touch. Then he placed one hand on my throat in an exacting grip and began teasingly slapping my breasts again, this time even more sensuously, alternating the slaps with flickers of his tongue across and around my nipples. I moaned feverishly, my senses overloaded with the intermingling of pleasure and pain. Every time he thought I was enjoying myself that little too much, the hand round my throat tightened. The unpredictability of sex with Sebastian, of sex right now with Sebastian, made it excruciatingly erotic.

Finally, he released his grip on me, and broke the silence. 'There. Do what you will while you can. You only have a few minutes.'

With no knowing when I would get to touch him again, I clawed at his biceps, hooked my legs around his hips, forcing us tighter up against one another until his cock lay along my slickening pussy. I thrust myself up along his length, knocking the top of his cock against my clitoris, as though he were my temporary vibrator.

Sebastian soon put a stop to it and grabbed hold of me by the upper arms, throwing me back over the bed so far that my head hung almost entirely upside down. He slid his left hand under my head for support, then took his entire right forearm, braced it outwards and held it across my throat. I was utterly restrained. 'There's nowhere for you to go now, Nichi. Which means you're just going to have to be my little fuck-toy while I have you hanging there.' And with that he took his throbbing cock and sunk it into me rapaciously.

Sebastian fucked me like he'd never fucked me before until the sweat was dripping down the geometric perfection of his face and glistening in his stubble. Every so often we would strain our heads towards one another, our mouths meeting in bruised, desperate kiss after kiss. The suspension and the pressure on my throat was exhilarating, but despite his secure grip on me, the harder Sebastian fucked me, the further back I was slipping.

Yet the firmer he was with me, the more I wanted to fight back. Even just texting my old clients earlier for Sebastian had roused the domme in me. I had a wicked thought.

'Ow, Sebastian, you're hurting me!' I squealed, 'I'm going to fall off the bed entirely in a moment!'

Immediately he broke off his thrusting, and I saw a twinge of concern flash across his face. Cradling my head even more firmly with his left hand, he took his right arm from across my throat and wrapped it under my shoulders, heaving me back up towards him. Sebastian's readjustments gave me the few seconds I needed to reach out an arm towards his crotch and seize him, abruptly, by the balls. Sebastian swooned, and then swore at me. 'You little bitch!'

'Really? Didn't you say you were as much a masochist as you were a sadist earlier? Don't you like it even just a little bit? Doesn't it give you a thrill?'

'I hate it. But I love it,' he murmured as he buried his face into my neck and wrapped his arms underneath me. For the next few minutes, I teased his balls like this, grazing my nails along the skin, squeezing them over-tightly, and delivering the odd, gentle slap, soothing his face with loving kisses each time he winced. I knew that it was giving Sebastian pleasure, but his responses to being topped were more conflicted than mine. After a few more minutes, Sebastian backed away from my hands.

'Sit on my face?' he asked me, and lay back on to the bed.

'But I want to kiss the CBT better!' I replied.

'We can do both. You just have to turn around.' Sebastian guided me into position until I was facing away from him, my thighs astride his, perfectly placed to take him fully into my mouth. As I lowered my lips down to him, I braced my hips back and he slid his head up underneath me, licking backwards along my wetness. In tandem, we moaned in mutual pleasure and began to find a sucking, thrusting rhythm with our mouths and bodies. I urged Sebastian to cum whenever he wanted and soon I could feel his legs trembling beneath me in that way that signalled orgasm, his cock pulsating, and as he began to climax, I plunged my mouth down on to him so that he could flood it with his hot, ambrosial cum. The taste of him urged on my own orgasm, and I soon ground out the most intense climax on his face.

Afterwards Sebastian guided my leg back over his head and waited for me to lie on my back, then got up and covered my fatigued body with his. With his head buried in between my breasts, Sebastian sighed, and murmured, 'You smell so good.'

I nuzzled and clutched him to me. I could have said the same. Sebastian smelled like evening pine by a saltless sea, I had once told him. It was still true now.

The next morning Sebastian woke me with his avid caresses. He was clearly still turned on by what had happened last night, and I knew, after even just that little bit of switching, I was in for another thorough fucking. I fumbled for his cock, already rigid, and Sebastian groaned as I stroked my fingers up and down along his shaft then teased his balls with gentle rhythmic squeezes.

Sebastian's arousal aroused me, and he wasted no time working first his fingers into my rapidly slickening pussy, and then his cock.

'You thought you'd gotten away with topping me moment-arily, didn't you? Well, you're fucking wrong. Do you want to know what it feels like, hmm? Want to know what it feels like to have that sensitive place between your legs slapped?'

I shook my head. 'No, Sebastian, I'm sorry, Sebastian. I won't ever try and switch with you again.' The look of menacing disappointment on his face made me ache with an absolute desire to please him. At the same time the thought of him slapping my pussy as sensually as he had my breasts filled me with delicious dread. Maybe I could provoke him to doing it anyway.

'But Sebastian,' I said, daringly, 'you were hurting me. I had to make you understand.'

Sebastian laughed that dark mesmeric laugh. Oh God. He was going to give me what I wanted.

'Turn over. I said, TURN OVER, Nichi,' and he grabbed me by the wrists, pulling me up towards him and thrusting me down into the pillow, his hand pinned to the back of my neck.

'Put your ass up for me. NOW.' He slapped my cheeks to

make me assume the position. He began delivering a slow, teasing hand spanking, lifting his hand off me in between strokes until I was undulating up towards him to invite the next. He struck the flesh at the bottom of my cheeks. With each slap, he created an electrifying tingle which spread not only out along my bottom but inwards and down, as if there were a channel delivering the sensation directly to my pussy, creating arousing aftershock after aftershock.

The closer inwards he moved his hand, the more electric the sensation, and the wetter I got. Each time I swooned back towards him and begged him to fuck me. Sebastian had never spanked me to this level of pleasure before.

'You've had it too easy with the spanking. You thought it was all about me quietening you down. But I know,' he bent down to my ear, 'that you're secretly slutty enough to want me to smack your cunt.' He slid three fingers in and out of me in rapid succession. 'Oh, you want it all right.'

Just that phrase left me breathless and caused me to pulse around Sebastian's fingers. I was desperate.

'Open your legs wider, Nichi. That's a good little slut.' He spanked me again with precision, three times, four, in quick succession until the entire area between my legs was burning, until even the tops of my thighs were damp. And then he struck my pussy, allowing his fingertips to strike my clitoris, before he plunged his fingers back inside me. He repeated this ritual four more times.

'Sebastian!' I could barely get his name out. I gasped and shivered with electrified pleasure. Sebastian stroked my hair roughly, giving it a quick vehement tug, then traced his fingers down along the curve of my back. My perfect sponge of ass was still presented for him, and he began covering my cheeks in kisses, kissing in an inward curve, just as he'd spanked me.

'Now you're properly quiet for once, I see.' It was true. The spanking had utterly pacified me. Was this what it felt like to be in sub-space?

Sebastian put his hands back on to my bottom. I waited for him to penetrate me, and rubbed myself back on to his leg. Wasn't that what he was going to do?

'Oh, no, I want to see you.'

He spun me over and kneeled once again on my wrists, as he slid his massively hard cock into the wetness he'd created. We both moaned and clutched at each other as he sank up into me.

It didn't take long before Sebastian's whole body began to tighten and tremble in that way I now knew so well. He must have been slyly masturbating himself before he'd begun touching me. And then, just as he began to climax, he repeated under his breath, 'Nichi *mou*, oh, Nichi *mou*.'

My heart seemed to hit two beats at a time. I was so startled at hearing that endearment after all this time that I clamped my legs too tightly about his cock, oversensitive after his orgasm, which caused him to suck in his breath sharply between his teeth.

There was no explanation or comment on what he'd just said. He merely stroked a hand through my hair indulgently.

When I could move, I got up to go to the bathroom and steadied myself on the sink, trying not to peer too critically at my flustered face and sex-tangled mane in the mirror. Then I smiled in spite of myself. It must mean something, mustn't it? Sebastian had listened intently last night as I'd explained how significant that little phrase was to me and now he was using it.

Nichi *mou*. Was I really his Nichi?

Chapter 18

Later that morning Sebastian walked me to the tube station. It was raining and he carried an umbrella, valiantly trying to shield my revealing outfit and suede shoes, both utterly unsuitable for daytime, from the inclement weather. My eyes were smudged, my lips swollen. My hair had the kind of height whipped into it that only a night's worth of hard sex could construct.

Passing men, builders, students and a weekday morning's general ne'er-do-wells leched at me openly, despite my being on Sebastian's arm.

I giggled and played up to my newly acquired whore-about-town status. 'This is because you called me one last night, Sebastian! The world has picked up on it! Honestly, what kind of feminist totters about like this on a Thursday morning!'

Sebastian laughed. 'You're just a feminine feminist that likes being looked at. A femininist! Embrace it!'

We crossed over cobbles and Sebastian slowed down and held on to my wrist, concerned for my safety in the vertiginous shoes. 'Lean on me,' he urged.

'I don't need to lean on you!' I shot back. 'I've been wearing heels since I was seven years old!'

'Aw, come on, Nichi, I'm being romantic!' He was teasing but in the tease was a kind of confession. Perhaps this was Sebastian's way of saying, 'You deserve more.' Or could it be his way of ensuring I carried on dominating my clients to procure more funds for him? I didn't think so.

'Honestly, Sebastian, I have *no* idea how I've managed without you all these years.' I smiled slyly.

He put his hand on my face and kissed me. Once, twice, three times. Each kiss a little longer, a little more ardent then the previous one. We locked eyes for a moment. I saw something awakening in Sebastian's face: the realisation that I mattered to him.

When I got home there was already an email from him, with links to another art show he suggested we might go to. Then later that afternoon there was a text to say he'd had a lovely time with me and not to worry about flashing my tits along Kingsland Road. 'Think of it as a kind of community service, cheering up frustrated men on a wet Thursday!'

The next weekend we went to his suggested exhibition. It was rather lacklustre compared to the Kusama. But I didn't care. Sebastian, I felt, was opening up to me, opening up to our very real relationship. When we got home, he went into the kitchen to fetch some water while I started to undress. He startled me when he re-entered the room.

'Oh, I'm sorry, I've disturbed the lady in her chamber. Shame you don't have your unicorn to protect you!

I started to laugh. 'Don't you have be a virgin or something, according to legend?'

'Ah. I see. No, you're right, not much chance of that with your record. Well, maybe we can create you something else. How about a hornikorn?'

I started to giggle. 'A hornikorn?'

'Yes, it appears when you do something particularly depraved. The less innocent you are, the more likelihood you have of seeing it.'

'Oh my God, this is perfect! Can it be priapically purple, please? And have a black glittering horn?'

'A horn that's like a massive dildo? Absolutely!'

Sebastian harrumphed like a horse and squeezed me to him, playfully caressing my breasts. 'Yes. Definitely a sacred child of the hornikorn.'

*   *   *

The next morning I was sore from the vigour with which Sebastian had fucked me the night before. He offered to 'lick it better' but I had an overwhelming urge to lick him instead.

The more violent the evening sex, the more tender the next morning, I had realised, and right now I wanted to show him just how tender I could be. He stroked my hair as I kissed my way down along his chest, over his stomach and along his stiffening cock. I took him in my hand and slid the head of his cock back and forth along the length of my lips.

'Oh, Nichi, oh Nichi Nichi, that's so good. That feels amazing, don't stop.'

As my lips lingered over the head of his cock, he took his fingers and brushed them over my lips, so that he was part stroking me, part stroking himself. The sensation was exquisite. Every so often I would take him full in my mouth, then pull him up and out before encircling the head of him with my tongue and sliding him along my lips again, letting my saliva silken the end of his cock, before plunging him hard back down into my mouth, as far as my throat could accommodate him.

It took just a few minutes before Sebastian was ready to climax. 'In my mouth, Sebastian, go on,' I urged him, and in a few more seconds he had coated my lips and my tongue with his hot, sweet cum. No man had ever tasted better than Sebastian.

Afterwards he pulled me up to him and we kissed woozily. 'Thank you for that.' He kissed my head, before fixing his sleepy eyes on my face. Even half closed, they shone. 'That was beautiful. Just another reason why you're as unique as a unicorn.'

I felt a surge of joy rise up from deep within me and spread across my skin, as if I were suddenly bathing in a dazzling, warm turquoise sea. And then I knew it. I was in love with him.

Later that week we met up for a drink. I was dressed in a graphic-print frock with a plunging neckline, accessorised with black peep-toes and tiny quirky scissor earrings I'd found in the Victoria and Albert's haberdashery shop. I'd decided to tone it down a little after our last meeting. At least I could go to work in this outfit.

He kissed me in greeting, and immediately, and unusually for him, said, 'Nice earrings!'

I twiddled one, puzzled. I thought they were cute. They weren't the kind of thing that usually invited male attention.

Sebastian was smiling but he looked strained. 'How's your week been so far?' I asked him.

'Oh, you know, the usual existential struggles!' He grinned but I could tell he was tense.

'What's up?'

'Work's not going too well. Juliet was talking about coming over here for a visit but Lana is being difficult. And my visa is probably about to expire.'

His visa? God, of course. Not since that first date had we ever really talked about his residency.

'What's the deal with the visa?'

'I have until the end of the year, then if I haven't found anyone to sponsor me, I have to go back to Montreal. Or even South Africa. I have Lithuanian ancestry and can try and apply for an EU passport that way but there's no guarantee I'll get it.'

That sounded bad. I swallowed.

'And what about Juliet?'

'It means I'm going to have to wait until Juliet's eighteen before I can spend some proper time with her again. She was thinking about coming to work in London for a while but Lana's never going to have it. It's just to spite me. Yet again.'

Sebastian drained his whisky. He never drank this quickly.

'How can I help?' I asked.

'You can't,' he replied flatly, then opened his mouth as if to speak for a moment as he stared at my earrings again. Did he really like them? Was there something wrong with them? 'I'm going to get another one. You good?' I nodded. I'd barely touched the glass of white wine I'd asked for.

While Sebastian was at the bar my mind raced. So he was right, I couldn't directly help with Juliet but I could help with the visa. I mean, all I had to do to keep him in the country was marry him, right? It sounded rash, I knew. And yet the intensity of our connection over the past six months assured me it wasn't as insane as it sounded. There was nothing I could imagine more beautiful right now than marrying Sebastian. It had taken me three years to get to a point where I had seriously considered marrying Christos, but this was different. If Sebastian couldn't renew his visa, I'd lose him before we'd even properly had a chance to find out whether it might work. Juliet could come and stay with us. We could set her up here. I had a good job now, my career was relatively stable. I could do this. I had to think it through before I even so much as hinted it to Sebastian, though. But I flooded with a kind of love I hadn't ever imagined feeling at the thought of it.

Sebastian arrived back with his drink.

'Let's change the subject.'

'OK,' I smiled. 'Let's talk about . . .'

'Let's talk about those suggestive little earrings of yours. Where did you get them from?'

'The V&A,' I replied hesitantly. 'What's suggestive about them?'

'They just intimate threat. And sometimes I like a bit of threat. The right kind of threat, that is.'

'Yeah?' He was smiling more genuinely now. If this cheered him up I was happy to run with it. 'A bit of threat, eh? You mean you like to think about women armed with scissors, do you?'

'I do.' He moved in closer to me, and whispered in my ear, 'I like to think about castration-play porn, too.'

'Sebastian!' I gasped, and pulled away from him, only half-laughing. 'Don't tell me you've been watching it.' I'd seen some stuff in my time as a domme, but this was too extreme. It was the kind of thing I never understood people getting off on.

'No, I haven't been watching it. I've just been watching women's self-defence videos and wanking to them instead.'

'What?'

'You know, I love watching women learn to fight. Vengeful women do it for me every time.'

'Interesting. I've been thinking about getting my personal trainer to teach me to box.'

'Yep, well, there's little better than feisty women that might think about taking you on before you beat them down into submission. Feisty women that wave a pair of scissors around in front of your cock . . .'

Sebastian wasn't actually being serious. Was he?

'So if you were to wake up one morning to the sight of me brandishing a pair of scissors about your boxers, that would do it for you?'

'Shut up, are you kidding me?! You'll give me a hard-on. But Nichi . . .' He came in closer to me, I presumed, for a kiss. 'If you do start boxing you'll have to wear those earrings. I bet every man who sees them thinks, castration! And then promptly goes home to have a wank over them.'

I dissolved into a flood of perturbed giggles. Sebastian and I had had a few strange conversations in our time but this was definitely one of the most bizarre.

'Sebastian, let me tell you, as an experienced former pro-domme, castration play is not something I was ever asked for. You and all your imaginary sympathetic friends are on your own with that one!'

The next day at work, still wearing the scissor earrings, I started to think about the conversation in the pub. Had Sebastian been serious or was it just his slightly edgy way of letting off steam? He'd been increasingly moody of late. Not necessarily with me, but I knew, from the way he described his struggles to come to terms with what had happened between Lana and him, that Sebastian's dark moods were bile-black. I fondled the earrings and thought again about the night I had 'switched' the sex round and grabbed him by the balls, how his face had taken on a kind of peaceful suffering as I taunted him.

This just sounded too extreme to be a mere stress reliever, though. Imagining and wanking over this kind of extreme play was one thing, but acting it out?

Then again, hadn't I enacted mildly violent fantasies for my clients and never flinched when they asked me for things that would have seemed twisted to other people? Wouldn't it be hypocritical of me to moralise about it, just because this was someone I loved? And of all the people to do this, wasn't I the safest?

This was another thing, along with the idea of marriage, that I needed to think about thoroughly before I offered it up. I felt some reluctance on both scores but I could think of little I wouldn't do for Sebastian.

I decided to wait until I heard from him. These weren't issues you could discuss over text.

Five days passed and there was nothing but silence from Sebastian.

On the fifth day I wondered whether I should ring him. I was becoming genuinely worried about him. Then, on my way home from the office to the tube station, I bumped into Violet.

'Oh God, I haven't seen you for months, how's it going?' She gave me an awkward hug.

'Yeah, good!' I tried to fake a smile. I didn't feel so great, but I had no real reason to be overly anxious. Going days without contact, I had come to realise, was just Sebastian's way.

'So, what's going on with you and Sebastian? The last thing I heard, you were regularly stepping out together, and then last night I saw him at this gig I went to with Dan. He was in a weird mood and didn't mention you once. Are you still seeing each other?'

Jesus Christ, Violet could be candid. I suppose her honesty was to be admired. But right now, it just made me want to cry.

My heart hit the ground and lay there flailing about on the
pavement, imploring Sebastian to pick it back up

'We're still seeing each other,' I replied, a little too sharply.
'He's just, well, I guess it's just casual.'

'You guess or you know?' Violet tilted her head and looked
askance. 'Look, Nichi, Sebastian is a sweetheart but he's also
got some weird attachment – or rather – *detachment* issues.
Make sure you know where you stand with him.'

All the way home I played out the conversation I'd had with
Violet in my mind. I wanted to believe that Sebastian had just
not felt like being sociable when Violet had seen him but that
didn't explain the half of this. It didn't explain his worsening
mood and it certainly didn't explain why he went AWOL in
between dates.

I thought back to the first night I'd met him and how genial
he'd been, with everyone. Was it possible that our connection was
nothing special after all? The thought made me feel as if I were
losing all sense of what was reasonable. Maybe this was just what
he did: formed over-intimate bonds with people he didn't really
care about because . . . because what? Logic kept losing me in
the impossible labyrinth of Sebastian's emotional life.

Meanwhile, my heart felt as though he'd come over and
shaken it up. Despite the incredibly hot sex and the intimacy,
nothing seemed to hold his attention for long. I felt as if I had
to constantly provoke him in order to remind him to pay me
attention. I started to think about the scissor earrings again.
They had certainly captivated him. It was a desperate measure
but maybe this was what it was going to take to get him to
respond to me this time.

I texted Sebastian. 'So, Sebastian. I've been thinking . . . I've
got a little game we can play. It will involve me wearing the
scissor earrings.'

Immediately Sebastian replied. 'Hey! Really? That sounds
amazing and no less menacing than it should. When were you
thinking?'

'Well, when are you free?'

'I could fit some menace in on Thursday, Friday or Sunday. Or tomorrow, if that isn't too short notice.'

I was desperate to see him. I didn't care if he knew it any more. Before I had time to reply to his text he messaged again. 'Oh, God, I'm loving this already! *Way* too hard to meditate!'

'Tomorrow then,' I replied.

'Tomorrow then! I have just the scissors for the job ;)'

That night I lay in bed agonising over my decision until well past three. Was this the right thing to do, to try to satisfy one of Sebastian's ultimate and extreme fantasies? It was a bloody irony that the domme who had so vehemently stayed away from all forms of medical play was now finding herself about to enact perhaps the most sinister one she'd ever heard.

Well, that was another thing, I'd not actually heard it in any real detail. I had no idea how Sebastian envisaged this thing panning out. Which wasn't any different from any of the other sex we'd been having. That was the thing with embarking on this kind of relationship. You gave someone your trust, but if you'd plotted out every sexual encounter, it would have become pretty staid pretty quickly. The not knowing exactly how someone would dominate you was at least half of the point.

But why hadn't Sebastian texted me? How could he have called me Nichi *mou*, called me his unicorn, and yet still be treating me like a girl in university halls he hooked up with when he had nothing better to do? Where did all that hand-holding in the night, or the begging me to send him clips of me discussing the papers on Sky News because it really 'did it' for him, come from if not from a place of desire and deep feelings, of burgeoning love?

And what about the sex? The mind-blowing, soul-shaking sex? Sebastian was a phenomenal lover, but you couldn't have the kind of passionate sex we had without a real and raw connection, could you?

I lay awake for another hour, trying desperately not to cry.

I didn't want crimson-puff eyes tomorrow. Instead, I wanted to look knockout hot. I wanted him to remember the first time. I wanted him to think, I want this woman and everything she can offer me.

Sebastian was waiting for me at the tube station again. He had a look of fractious exhilaration on his face, and his blue eyes seemed to spark when he saw me.

In the end I'd decided to wear the outfit I had worn the first night we had had sex. The backless dress. The snakeskin shoes. Stockings. Only now I had a smoky-eyed red-lipped face, crimson nails and a look of impervious resolve.

Sebastian came forward to kiss me and took my bag. Like a gentleman? Or like a slave? I was tense. Is this how it was to be all evening? I needed to switch off the interior monologue and concentrate on making this experience as safe, sane and sexy as possible for both of us.

We'd arranged to go for dinner first. This time we went to a Cantonese diner with large, discreet booths and lax service. At least it gave us time to talk.

When we had paid the bill, split it as I always insisted we did, we made the short walk back to Sebastian's flat, talking about Iranian politics. 'How could a country so crazy produce all those beautiful women!' I joked.

'TELL me about it!' Sebastian seemed to swoon. 'That whole region in fact! You know how I feel about Queen Rania of Jordan . . .'

I laughed but inside I was crumbling. Why was I feeling so insecure? It was only Sebastian messing about. I mentioned other people I found attractive often enough. Didn't I? I tried to think of an example but my mind was blank.

'Yes, but I don't think she's into domination somehow,' I teased.

'Oh God, I'd never dominate her! Instead I'd lay her down by candlelight. I have reveries about her. In my mind she's always wearing a white angora sweater held together by a single button.'

In the flat, Sebastian's chatter gave way to nerves. 'I noticed your earrings as soon as I picked you up from the station. You don't know how many times I've fantasised about someone doing this for me.' He gazed at down at me with a look approaching adoration.

I could never be agitated with Sebastian for long. After all, I loved him. But he'd really hurt me this time. Did he have so little respect for me that he thought it OK to praise other women while offering me nothing in the way of reassurance? Was I just a willing mouth and a wet hole to him? Or in this instance, a pair of scissor-wielding hands?

Sebastian was fiddling about in his drawer of wicked tricks, as I had named it. In it, he kept rope, ties, a ball gag, crops. When we'd first met he'd told me how he had all the props he needed 'just here!' and kissed his biceps in jest. But I did wonder now why we'd never opened the drawer before. Not that it had ever bothered me. Working as a domme, I'd had enough of props to last me a lifetime. Which was ironic, given that now we found ourselves dependent on a domestic object to enact Sebastian's ultimate fantasy.

Sebastian stood with his back to me for a moment then exhaled loudly. Was it my imagination or was he actually shaking? He turned around and handed me the scissors. Oh my God. They weren't what I had been expecting, neither dressmaker's nor the standard paper kind. They were for cutting through chicken bone, and had ferocious-looking curved and serrated blades held together with a spring and safety catch. This was crazy. I wasn't going to do this.

'Sebastian! They're monstrous! Are you insane?' Sebastian shook his head apologetically. 'They're really not as bad as they look. You can't nick someone with them. Here. Try cutting a ribbon and see what happens.'

He handed me a red ribbon and the blades. I tried to cut with them. They chewed the fabric gummily.

'Oh! So they're not even sharp!'

'No, they only cut through if you apply absolute pressure. And you don't have the strength.' He smiled at me fondly, caressing my shoulder. 'They're completely safe, Nichi. I promise you. They're a visual aid to the fantasy, that's all.'

'OK. Well then . . .' Mentally I took a deep breath. 'Shall we begin?'

Sebastian undressed but for his briefs, and sat on the edge of the bed. If I wasn't mistaken, he already had a hard-on. I arranged myself, fully clothed, on the one chair. It was so long since I'd done this. It felt at once so familiar and yet so absolutely alien, especially given what I was about to enact. Hadn't you once dreamed of RADA, Nichi? Time to test your amateur actress's mettle.

I placed the scissors beside me on the chair.

I was going to have to feel out this dialogue by paying extremely close attention to Sebastian's reactions.

'So, Sebastian . . .' He looked up at me tremulously. 'I've been thinking. About that cock of yours. Is it really necessary?'

Sebastian took a sharp intake of breath. That was a good start.

'I mean, I know you're pretty good at fucking me with it, but I've started to wonder if you having a penis isn't a lot more hassle than it's worth.'

'What do you mean?' Sebastian levelled the question at me.

I hadn't bargained for that. It threw me for a moment, but I thought back to the times when the clients had done similar things. They weren't trying to derail the role play, just test your authority. I needed him to believe that I was guiding this, even though Sebastian was absolutely topping from the bottom.

'I mean,' I continued, 'that I think you in particular are governed by it a lot more than is good for you. I mean that you might feel easier without. Less burdened.'

'But I wouldn't,' Sebastian retorted, softly, childishly. 'I'd still have my balls. They'd drive me to distraction, encouraging me to think about sex knowing that without a cock I couldn't ever satisfy myself.'

OK. I was beginning to get more of a sense of where Sebastian wanted this to go. This was about Sebastian's subliminal concern that one day some woman might stop him from ever having sex again. But where was the erotic thread to this?

I inched my chair up towards him. He flinched as I stood up, then trembled as I settled back down, my stockinged knee now brushing against his bare one. I could tell from the straining under the fabric of his briefs that his erection had grown to a punishing proportion.

'But Sebastian, don't you think you might deserve it sometimes?'

'How could I ever deserve it?' he replied immediately.

'Well, might it not be payback for being such a beautiful bastard, for being able to have any woman you want without any real regard for them?'

I had no idea if this were true or not, no real idea of how many women had gone before me, but I wondered if, like that client James, my first verbal domination, the one that Sapphire had told me wanted picking apart, Sebastian too got off on being confronted with and then chastised for his own narcissism.

'But I've given them pleasure,' Sebastian replied.

'Well, sometimes pleasure isn't enough. Sometimes people need more than pleasure,' I retorted.

Sebastian looked simultaneously defiant and terrified.

Then it hit me. Oh God. Of course I could perform this role play. Sometimes people need more than pleasure? This was about us, about all the ways in which Sebastian was failing to give me what I needed. Perhaps it was actually going to be cathartic for me to channel my frustrations into something that would get him off. For the first time that evening I began to feel slightly less panicked. I could do this. I settled into my assumed role.

'Life isn't just about pleasure, Sebastian. Though you never seem short on pleasure-seeking. One of the first things I found out about you is that you took Violet's boyfriend Dan off to South Africa on a spanking tour.'

Sebastian balked. Oh, that was a little too close for comfort, wasn't it Sebastian?

'We didn't do anything too awful on that trip.'

'But you agree you were a bad influence on Dan. Encouraging him to abandon Violet like that. Was it fun tying up those innocent little South African girls?'

'We didn't tie them up,' Sebastian replied. I had no idea whether he was telling the truth or not but it hardly mattered. The point was that he was on the back foot.

'Even if I had I wouldn't deserve to lose my cock for it,' Sebastian said sourly. He wasn't a good submissive. Far too much defiance in him.

'If you say so, Sebastian.' I picked up the scissors nestling beside me. They were still cold, despite the proximity of my warm body.

Immediately Sebastian bristled. I looked at his crotch. There, on his ice-blue briefs, was an incriminating damp patch. God, it was incredible that even just the sight of the scissors like this turned him on. This was a full-blown fetish.

I rested the scissors lengthways across my lap and ran the tips of my damson nails along them, making a whisper of a scratching noise. The sound made Sebastian jump out of his skin and he fixed his eyes on the gleaming metal.

'Nichi, what are you doing? Why do you have the scissors positioned like that?'

I looked up into his eyes. My face was set in a Medusa-like mask. 'Because you want this.'

'No, I don't, I don't, I don't.' Sebastian repeated, shaking his head vehemently from side to side.

I was confused by his reaction. For a moment I couldn't tell whether this was Sebastian trying to end the role play. Then I realised what was happening here. I was letting my actual feelings towards him interfere with the play. Of course, in Sebastian's fantasies I wanted this and he didn't. That was the whole point. I wanted to punish him for untold sins against me and womankind and he was merely the hapless victim of my ire. But how the hell could I make this convincing? Whatever distress he'd caused me with his sporadic emotional distance, no part of me wanted to actually punish Sebastian for anything that had passed between us. Instead, every cell of my being wanted to love him, wanted to thank Fortune, whatever god I believe in, but mostly Sebastian for entering my life.

Sebastian spoke. 'Please don't do this, Nichi, please don't. I need to keep my cock. Let me keep it.'

I ran my nails rapidly up and down the scissors again, then spun them round so that the tips of the blades were pointing directly at Sebastian's crotch.

'I'm sorry, Sebastian, but you don't get a say in how this goes any more.'

His eyes widened again in fright. He bowed his head and placed his hands pleadingly on my calves. I slapped his hands and shook him off.

'It's too late, Sebastian. You need to man up and face the inevitable.' I took hold of the scissors in my right hand and took my left to the safety catch. It clicked audibly as it dropped, and Sebastian whimpered.

And then I realised something else. Fuck, we hadn't actually set a special safe word for this. Were we out of our minds? Sebastian was trusting me and I was trusting myself to not let this veer into unsafe territory. Well, we'd tested the blade. I knew I couldn't cut him. I'd never hurt a client and there was no way on earth I could hurt Sebastian. All I had to do was tease him a little with them. Perhaps rub them up and down his shaft a bit, maybe open them ominously. I presumed they made a suitably terrifying swiping noise as the blades came apart.

Focus on the role play, Nichi, make him cum and wrap this up quickly.

With the blades parted, I ran my fingertip along the dulled serrated edges. Sebastian was absolutely entranced, his cobalt-blue eyes burning like the heart of a gas-fired flame, and flickering rapidly between the blades and my face. His straining cock was poking out of the top of his briefs now. The sight of him turned on helped to convince me again that what we were doing was OK. All I wanted to do right now was give Sebastian pleasure.

I leaned forward, exposing my white cleavage in the dim light. Sebastian gazed at it greedily. Then I took my left hand and peeled back his briefs until they were resting halfway down his cock. I pulled back the waistband with my fingers, then took the scissors in my right and slid them along the inside of the outstretched fabric. Sebastian made a guttural juddering sound. I wanted to keep the scissors as far away from his actual skin as possible, and hoped that this action would be enough to stimulate his fantasy.

Then I pulled the blades back up for a moment, opened them slightly and clamped them down on to the fabric. Their dull teeth gnawed clumsily on the fibres. Even if I'd wanted to, I couldn't have cut through Sebastian's briefs for effect. I used the scissors to pull down the fabric until his whole cock was revealed. The head of it glistened urgently, and a single drop of pre-cum trailed down his shaft. I removed the scissors and took the fingers of my left hand to him instead, wrapping them tenderly along his length. Sebastian jumped away from me in fright but I gripped on to him by his cock, got up out of my seat and planted a leg either side of his right knee, sitting back on to his thigh to anchor him.

'You're not getting away from this, Sebastian. It's your fate. You know that, really. You also know deep down that you deserve it.'

I began masturbating him and leaned in to kiss him for the

first time. When our lips met it was electrifying. The inverted power exchange made this feel so dubiously erotic. Sebastian kissed me as if his cock depended on it.

'Please, Nichi,' he began again, 'please don't do this.'

'It's for your own good,' I repeated again. Then hesitated. What to do now? The role play was getting easier but the scissors in my hand still unnerved me. I felt as though I were armed with a weapon. But for this to work for him, I was going to have to touch his cock with the metal.

Closing the scissors, I took them gingerly to the outside of his skin and rubbed the outside of the blade along his shaft. Worried that Sebastian would jump at the sensation and inadvertently injure himself, I clung on first to the end of the blades. But Sebastian was lost in his own reverie now, and instead of trying to flee, undulated up against them. I breathed a long hot breath of relief.

'You could never really cut my cock off though, Nichi, could you?' Sebastian looked up into my face imploringly. 'You'd never try it, would it? You'd never actually put the blades around me?'

That meant he wanted me to put the blades around him. It must do. I was so loath to do this. But I thought again about the emptiness of the days when I waited for his messages, thought about the richness of my nights when I made love to him. Perhaps this was what he needed in order to understand just how dedicated I was to him, and to get him to truly commit to me. That's why I had to do this. For me, but more so for him. And so, still stroking him with my right hand, I opened the scissors once more and, taking the utmost care, wrapped them around the base of his cock with my left.

Sebastian couldn't have been more terrified if I'd put a gun to his head. In fact, I knew that this was truly more terrifying to him.

'Nichi, Nichi, Nichi, Nichi, Nichi,' he repeated, his entire body convulsing with fright, 'please don't, I'm begging you,

I'm begging you not do this,' meanwhile rubbing himself deliberately up against the metal blades and my fingers.

'Sebastian,' I gasped. I couldn't get another threatening word out of my mouth. This was so intense, so stupefying, I couldn't wait for it to be over. And then he said something that made me feel as though he'd just spun the scissors round and stuck them into my heart.

'How can you want to do this to me, how can you want to hurt me like this?'

I wanted to scream 'But I don't, Sebastian, I'm doing it because I love you and because I want to satisfy your ultimate fantasy and because I'd do anything, even a mad, unsafe, terrible, terrifying thing like this, if I thought it would make you happy for even a few moments.' But I bit my tongue, choked back the tears and increased the pace of my hand until Sebastian convulsed into a demented orgasm and ejaculated all over my fingers and the scissor blades.

We sat there for a few minutes, panting and staring at one another. I waited for Sebastian to smile and tell me that had been phenomenal. But he didn't. He merely looked up at me with fright and regret.

I slept poorly that night, lay there stock-still for most of it, deep in disturbed thought. Sebastian, meanwhile, was rigid as a corpse on the other side of the bed, and did not wake. Once or twice I kissed him on the neck and the shoulders but there was no response.

The next morning I woke first and lay there for nearly an hour before Sebastian stirred too. When finally he turned to me, even his eyes looked washed out. I went to pat his thigh affectionately. He flinched. 'Sebastian!'

'Sorry. I guess I'm just still a little wired up over what we did last night.'

This was exactly what I did NOT want to happen. Even now I was overwrought with exasperation. Come on, Nichi, have patience here, I urged myself. You would never have lost it with one of the clients, whatever their reaction. 'Would you like some tea?' I asked him, trying to be kind.

'No, thank you. I think I'm going to go back to sleep,' he replied without looking at me.

'OK, well, I need to get up and get on. I'm going to have a shower and then be on my way.'

In the shower it took me at least twenty seconds to realise that the water was burning me before I stepped out of the scalding stream, the delicate skin on my chest ablaze.

I hated the mirror in Sebastian's bathroom. The light was an inflammatory orange and highlighted every flaw, every blemish on my increasingly sensitive city-smoked skin. I dressed quickly and scraped back my flattened hair, then went back into the room.

Sebastian had fallen asleep again. I packed my bag as quietly as I could then leaned over to kiss him goodbye. His eyes sprang open again. 'I'm going.'

'Oh!' He sat up. But it was an involuntary rising.

'Do you have a busy week?' I asked him, trying to leave with the same parting questions I always asked.

He frowned. 'Yes. Too busy really.'

'Well, you know we don't ever have to make a proper night of it if you're short on time. I have a crazy amount of work too, now that I'm broadcasting as well as editing. You can always just come and crawl into bed with me one night. If you just want to snuggle . . .'

Sebastian didn't reply. My bruised heart heaved with fresh hurt, then sighed, dusted itself off once more. I decided to take another tack. Sebastian never arranged another date when we parted. He always left it to those delayed text messages. Well, I was sick of it. I was going to rectify it right now.

'Are you around at the weekend?'

'I'm busy,' he replied flatly. Then as if realising the curtness of his response, he added, 'Maybe the week after.'

I nodded numbly. I had to get out of here. I picked up my bag and fled down the stairs.

Outside it was a brilliantly sunny early summer day, with a gorgeous lapis lazuli sky. I passed under a cherry tree, which dusted me with its petals. It might as well have been raining black confetti. I had rarely felt so crushed. Now I knew it. I knew it all. Sebastian didn't love me. He didn't even care about me. He'd been so wrapped up in the pursuit of his own fantasy that I was a mere prop to that, a flesh-and-blood adjunct to what went on his head. I had never felt so used.

I must have stepped up on to the train and settled myself rigidly into a seat, but I don't remember how. Even the faded rose print of my dress seemed to taunt me with its cheerful romance. I buttoned up my black mac and shrouded it from view. Then I covered my devastated face with my oversized sunglasses and let the tears run where they may.

Chapter 19

When I got home I went to bed and slept for the rest of the day. It was the only thing I could think to do to put distance between me and last night's soul-shaking events. Every hour I came to and checked my phone. Nothing from Sebastian.

When I finally woke it was dark. I phoned Gina.

'Could you come round? I can't tell you this over the phone.'

'Oh, Nichi, I'm sorry, I can't! I've gone away for the weekend. I'm in Cardiff, remember?' I'd forgotten, of course. I'd become so enmeshed in the dramatic tensions of my own life that I didn't remember anything that my friends were up to any more. 'I can talk now if you want though?'

'No, it's fine, don't worry about it. We'll catch up later in the week.'

I hung up. Still nothing from Sebastian. I flung the phone across the room in despair. The tears started to run in rivulets down my cheeks once again. Who could I talk to about this? I had to talk to someone.

I crawled out of bed and retrieved my phone and then I called Gina back. 'I'm sorry I'm such a basket case, Gina, but if you can talk, I'd really appreciate it . . .'

She knew me well enough to know that I was really struggling. 'Tell me, lady.'

So I began to tell her what had really been happening over the past few weeks. I told her about the visa. 'Come on, Nichi! You don't marry someone just because they need a visa!' I told her about Sebastian's unpredictable moods and his withdrawal from me, interspersed with out-of-the-blue gestures like calling me Nichi *mou*. Gina tutted. I told her about our date last night and the endless references to dark-haired, dark-skinned beauties. She tutted again. I could practically see her shaking her head down the phone. I stopped at a full description of scissor sex, but I told her that the play had gone too far. 'It wasn't fun-scary, Gina. It was just fucked up.'

She was quiet a moment, taking in all I had said. I could tell that even she was struggling with a response. 'Look, Nichi, there is a huge communication issue here. Not just in the way he texts, the fact he's never phoned you, but because you have no idea what he wants or how he feels about you. And you really, genuinely shouldn't have this much insecurity about someone so significant to you. Look, I know it might be painful, but the only way to do this is be straight with him. "Where do you see this going?" Just ask him that. You'll have your answer in all of about five seconds.'

I knew Gina was right. I just couldn't imagine how I was going to set about doing this.

At around two in the morning I finally managed to settle myself to sleep. I lay in bed in a flimsy yellow vest and blue knickers. The last time I had worn these, Sebastian was here. Returning from the kitchen with fruit juice one morning, I had leaned out of the open window, the cheap, diaphanous fabric of the top enhancing the swell of my chilled nipples. Then I handed the juice to a just roused Sebastian.

'Did you make this?' he asked, with a smile.

I giggled back at him and shook my head. 'No. I'm not that servile yet.'

He drank and put the glass on the bedside table. He smiled at me darkly, beckoning me to him with his finger. Just that gesture made my heart race. I clambered back into bed beside him and through the fabric of my top, he gently bit my nipples. 'That's a provocative little garment you're wearing there, Nichi.'

Now, thinking about the image of Sebastian beckoning me

over to him aroused me. I stroked my hand over my breasts, felt my nipples stiffen. Then I slipped my fingers between my legs and imagined Sebastian caressing me there, with his slow, deliberate tease. Soon, I could feel myself quickening. I imagined Sebastian kissing me at first tenderly and then passionately along my neck, touching my willing mouth with his fingers and then his lips, holding me up to him, laying me down again, wrapping my legs around his waist and lavishing me with kisses. And then burying his head into my breasts and then my neck, and then taking my face in his hands and telling me . . . telling me that he loved me. As I orgasmed, my body shook. But not with pleasure. I had burst into tears.

The next morning, before I did anything else, I reached for my phone and texted Sebastian.

'Hey. I really need to talk to you about something. Would you meet me somewhere? I'm free after 5.30 p.m. today, or much of tomorrow. Nichi x.'

I made it brief and to the point. I hoped it conveyed some sense of urgency.

Sebastian was an early riser. He had replied within an hour.

'Hey, I'm free tomorrow (Friday) morning until about three or so. Could we meet near my studio? Otherwise, Sunday . . .? S x.'

Damn it. I couldn't leave work to go and have this chat with him. I was going to have to wait a few more days. Well, what did it really matter? I'd waited this long.

'OK, well Sunday then. Not sure where yet. I'll text you on the morning. X.'

'Sure, Sunday early afternoon is good. Everything OK? S x.'

'It will be,' I replied.

Later I called Gina.

'Hello chicken. I'm so sorry I forgot you were in Cardiff last week. You were an absolute gem for listening to all that in between family duties. How are you doing? Did you have a good time? You were there for your cousin's wedding, right?'

'Oh my God, Nichi, what a protracted affair. We didn't get to eat for six hours! But she did look gorgeous and they had an amazing band at the reception.'

'So you got to dance?'

'So I got to dance. I'm happy. Now. How are you? Not so happy . . .'

'I need to go shopping for a break-up outfit on Saturday, Gina. Are you free? I'm going to need your advice.'

I had tried to sound resolute on the phone to Gina, but my mind was shot to pieces. I knew I must first speak to Sebastian, though, and tried to focus on that. I became fixated on the question of what to wear. I kept returning to the idea of wearing white. I thought back to the way Sebastian had looked up at me as I removed the scissors from around his cock, the way he had jumped when I'd tenderly gone to touch his thigh the next morning. The scissors had toxified us. It had sullied all that was honest and pleasurable about our deviant sexual relationship. And I wanted to wear something that would help to purify it again, help to soothe the emotional chaos.

I rummaged through the clothes on the rails. A sliver of white caught my eye. It was the dress I'd worn that night at the hotel with Christos, the night we hadn't had sex. I had not worn it since because it reminded me too much of the tragedy of that episode in our relationship. And yet, staring at it now, it was infused with the very real love of those days, of the love that had nourished and sustained us. I pulled it out of the wardrobe.

I arrived before Sebastian at our meeting point in the park near his house. I wanted to find an appropriate spot to settle myself and gather my thoughts. Another pristine summer's day, hot enough for sunburn. This whole afternoon was going to be excruciating in every way.

Or perhaps it wasn't. Perhaps I was worrying for no reason. Here was Sebastian now, bounding gracefully up the bank towards me, smiling so that his dimples flashed up beneath his stubble. For such a hot day he was wearing a lot of drab clothes. An olive-coloured jacket. Grey jeans. A grey Fair Isle sweater atop some kind of similarly coloured shirt. He came towards me as he always did, cobalt eyes iridescent in the light. He kissed me full on the mouth, tenderly.

'Hey.' He sat down next to me. He looked at my face in blank expectation. Perhaps he genuinely had no idea why I'd summoned him, though I didn't think so. But it was clear that I was going to have to lead this discussion. There wasn't another moment to waste.

I started with something tangible. 'So, what's going on Sebastian? I find it a bit odd that after all these months you only still text me when you want to hang out. We've never even spoken on the phone. It makes me feel as though you're closed to contact with me in some way.'

Sebastian listened intently. He was tight-lipped, and his brow was slightly furrowed, but it was only the face he pulled when he was concentrating. He clearly didn't think this was odd.

I carried on. 'I mean, it's not that I need to be in constant communication with someone. It's actually quite nice not to have to be. But when we have a lovely time together, when we have the kind of sex we have together and then you just go home and never even say, "It was nice to see you," it makes me feel, I don't know, a bit used, and gets me to wondering whether you even care about me at all.'

'I care about you,' Sebastian replied, almost before I'd finished the sentence. But it didn't sound like a pledge of affection. It sounded like a defence. 'Of course I care about you. I don't understand how you could feel used, that's unfair. But there's something you have to understand, Nichi. I'm not monogamous.'

Oh God. So there it was. The first body blow. I paused for

a moment processing what that meant. 'So are you sleeping with other people?' was my next question.

'No.' He shook his head.

I scanned his face. What did I know of this man, really? How to catch him in a lie?

I believed him. 'So what does that mean then? Does that mean you have one relationship and the occasional other encounters on the side? Or that you see several people at the same time?'

In theory, this was no longer necessarily a deal breaker. Since the domming I'd begun to genuinely appreciate how one might get different things from different people, and in a way that was safe emotionally for everybody involved, subject to explicitly clear boundaries, absolute love, absolute trust and absolute honesty.

The problem was, Sebastian certainly hadn't been honest with me. And 'caring' for me was nothing like loving me. It wasn't exactly the best place to start from. But I'd be willing to consider it. I'd always believed that open relationships were not for me, but maybe I could do it for Sebastian. Maybe sharing him with other women was better than not having him at all.

Sebastian, however, shook his head at both of the options I offered. 'I can't be in a fixed arrangement with any one person, let alone a bunch of them. Non-monogamy for me just means that when there's an ex blowing through town, I usually hook up with them.'

I contemplated this for a moment. Why an ex? Why not a random girl you met at a party and wanted to dominate? There was a saying I'd once read on a gift shop postcard. 'Old flames are spent matches.' Why repeatedly return to someone who had once loved you?

'I mean, I haven't had a girlfriend since I was twenty-seven. I haven't lived with someone since I was twenty-three. I've had more exes than I've had girlfriends, if that makes sense.'

It did, and yet it didn't. I wondered how many of them would have considered themselves Sebastian's girlfriends. He and I had been seeing each other for six months and I certainly didn't count.

Sebastian paused and looked ahead. He seemed to be gazing right through me. 'I guess the question is, then, Nichi, how comfortable would you be with this kind of relationship?'

Hang on a minute. Was Sebastian actually trying to reframe this so that he was the one checking in with me?

Sebastian blinked, bowed his head for a moment, then lifted his eyes right up to meet mine again. That line from the Donne poem about the 'eye beams twisted' came to me again. Nobody else could look at me this way, with nobody else could I share this kind of connection. A part of me just wanted to find out whatever it was that Sebastian needed, and to offer it up to him.

My face must have given away my turmoil. As if by way of explanation, Sebastian began, unprompted, to talk more about monogamy.

'The thing is, I used to really love my girlfriends and would never have dreamed of sleeping with someone else.' He looked over the park. 'But when things went wrong, when the relationship inevitably ended, it would tear at me so deeply that I just got to thinking, what's the point being monogamous? So I stopped.'

It was just so depressing that Sebastian retaliated against the pain by running away from love. There was something about the way he had said those last three words, 'so I stopped', that I found particularly disturbing. I hoped he meant the people he got involved with afterwards knew he wasn't monogamous? But hang on, I hadn't, had I? Sebastian continued.

'I was seeing a girl a while ago, for about a year. She smashed my camera when she found out. That hurt me. I couldn't believe she could do that.'

'When she found out . . .?'

'That I wasn't faithful. That I slept with other people the whole time. When Zoe realised, she lost it.'

Oh my God. So the poor girl had been embroiled even deeper than I was with Sebastian before she found out. How the hell could he make himself out to be the victim here?

We sat there for a few moments in silence. Then Sebastian grinned at me playfully. 'Nice shoes. May I stroke them?' I nodded without smiling.

I looked at him as he petted them. If only he wasn't such a beautiful bastard. I thought about the concept of Platonic beauty I'd learned about at university, Plato's stupid idea that beauty and goodness were directly correlated. He'd clearly never met Sebastian. What had Sebastian ever done to deserve his looks? He just abused the power they afforded him.

He looked up at me as if to make some kind of joke about the shoes but I could tell he'd thought better of it. I was idly making a daisy chain, but the stalks were too short and I kept accidentally stabbing myself with my scarlet nails. I turned to lie on my front. Sebastian came to lie next to me. 'Do you want anything at all by the way? A pretzel or something?' Was that Sebastian's way of trying to show care, I wondered. In spite of everything, a flicker of hope rose in me.

We lay there together watching two sausage dogs frolic in the flowerbeds. For the first time in a week, I laughed, and Sebastian gave a silly commentary on their misdeeds to entertain me. Then, quite suddenly he asked, 'So what do you want to do? Shall we go get dinner?'

I didn't know what to say. My instinctive reaction was to say no. I should go home now. I should walk away from Sebastian here. Gina would have told me to do that.

'I'm not sure,' I replied quietly.

'I'm hungry,' was Sebastian's response. So the offer of the pretzel had been about his stomach not my heart. And it certainly hadn't come from anywhere deep within his. Or maybe I was just being oversensitive. 'Come on, Nichi. Have you eaten?

I bet you haven't eaten. It's a beautiful evening. It would be a shame not to go on somewhere else.'

It was indeed far too beautiful an evening to be moping at home about the abortive end of a barely formed relationship. For the first time in about twenty minutes, I looked directly at Sebastian. His eyes were even larger than I remembered them, two blue pools of apology. Everything about his demeanour seemed sad. I didn't want him to be sad, I didn't want it to end this way. And so I agreed to dinner.

We walked through St James's Park to Soho holding hands. We must have cut an odd couple, me in my white prom dress, leather jacket, zebra shoes and oversized sunglasses, he all in grey. I had spent a full half hour painting my make-up on with a rare precision, filling in my lips with red liner and lipstick, so that I was sure the colour would not shift. I caught my reflection in the odd taxi window as we walked up past Horse Guards Parade. I was perfected as if for a monumental first date.

A young fashionable couple passed us but I was too busy staring into the near distance to notice them. 'Oh they were VERY interested in you, Nichi,' Sebastian stressed as if intimating they found me attractive. It irritated me. Why did a compliment have to pass through the prism of someone else's appreciation? Why bother saying anything at all?

When we reached Soho, we walked along Wardour Street aimlessly, until Sebastian made a snap decision about where to eat. It was a Vietnamese place, cavernous, and quiet; the right kind of place to try to share a conciliatory meal together.

The waitress smiled at us warmly. She must have thought we were a couple. I felt like saying, 'Oh, don't worry, it's not nearly as romantic as it looks; he's just reassured me that he intends on sleeping with other people.'

The waitress set out the menus before us, then came back promptly with our drinks and to take our order. Sebastian offered up his choice first. It was the same thing I had decided

upon. Without thinking, I said as much. 'Oh!' he exclaimed
apologetically. 'You have it then! I'll have something else!' So
he was being deferential now too, was he? Better late than
never, I supposed. Only it didn't seem to come from a place
of genuine contrition.

The waitress went away again. 'How suppliant of you,' I
smirked. Sebastian stared back at me, the electric blue of his
eyes nearly obscured by the full dilation of his pupils. Was I
imagining it or was he turned on by my dismissive contempt
right now?

Dinner came. My dish, the one Sebastian had intended to
order, looked more appetising than his. He hadn't taken more
than a few mouthfuls of his food when he began to choke, his
cool angular beauty contorting into a red puffy mess before
my eyes. 'Too much chilli,' he explained. I sat there watching
him suffer and waited a whole thirty seconds before offering
him my sake to wash it down.

We finished dinner, splitting the bill as we always did. As we
waited for the tray with our change to be returned, Sebastian spoke.
'So, do you want to come back to mine?' he asked tentatively.

I stared at him. I had never failed to say yes immediately to
spending the night with him.

Now I shrugged.

For the first time ever since I'd known him, he actually looked
aghast. So he felt hurt and rejected, did he? Finally. A sign of
real concern. Inwardly I breathed a sigh of relief. So he wasn't
a robot. I knew all along he wasn't a robot. We couldn't have
had the kind of passionate, connected sex we'd had, couldn't
have lain there in one another's arms afterwards, stroking each
other until we fell asleep, if he didn't care about me, too.

We both needed reminding of that now, not the awful feeling
of lovelessness that the scissor sex had left us with. We needed
to go home and remind ourselves of how feverish and frantic
and beautiful sex between us usually was.

★   ★   ★

Back at Sebastian's, I kicked off my pinching shoes, settled myself on the bed and began to read the newspaper I'd asked him to buy for me at a shop on the way home.

I looked at the window. The funereal drapes. 'Sebastian, open the curtains.'

'I never open the curtains,' he replied.

'Well, please do it for me now. I'm asking you.'

Reluctantly, Sebastian opened the curtains then turned to look at me. 'You think there's something wrong with the way I live?'

'I just want to see the stars for once,' I replied gently.

He offered me an apple. 'Sorry it's not a pomegranate,' he said, grinning.

'I don't want a whole apple to myself,' I replied. 'Just a bite of yours.'

'OK, we can share it, of course, no problem,' came the reply. I tossed the newspaper on to the floor. He moved my shoes to the other side of the room, rearranging them reverently. Then he lay on the bed next to me and took a bite of the apple's waxy jade skin. Once broken in, he held the apple out to me so that I could continue eating it with ease. I took a small bite, dribbling juice down his fingers. 'I need more control of it,' I complained and clamped my hand around his.

'You can control it, that's OK,' he acquiesced. We locked eyes as I bit on it. It was the closest I'd felt to Sebastian all day.

When the apple was done we lay down side by side, and began to talk again.

'So are we OK?' Sebastian asked me.

I didn't know how to answer that. 'You mean, am I OK with the non-monogamy thing?'

'Well, among other things.'

The scissors. We still needed to talk about the scissors.

'Let's talk about the other things. The scissors, Sebastian. That was very intense.'

He nodded gravely.

'I mean, I think it was a little too intense, even.'

He nodded again, more hesitantly this time.

'I've played with a lot of people's fantasies, Sebastian, but that didn't feel like it came from a good place to me. And afterwards I got that real BDSM low, that thing I'd heard people talk about but never knew existed.'

'Me too,' he confessed.

'So why did you want to do it then? Why would you want to do something that made us both feel so terrible?'

'I didn't know it would make you feel terrible,' he replied. I started to feel bitter again. No, he didn't think about how it would make me feel. And he couldn't be bothered to ask either. 'But as miserable as I felt to begin with, you have to know, Nichi, it was so fucking hot to me. I've wanked about it every day since.'

'But we can't do it again, Sebastian.'

'Well, there's no point putting the scissors away now. It would like trying to stuff the genie back in the bottle. It's my ultimate fantasy and it always will be.'

I said nothing. What was there to say to that? I'd just told him that something we'd done together had really hurt me and yet here was he focusing on how many times it had got him off since, and how he wanted to do it again.

I looked deep into Sebastian's eyes. For the first time, I was starting to see a hollowness there I'd previously been blind to. And his beauty was rapidly deteriorating in front of me. I realised that I still had one question about the monogamy issue. I needed to ask him it.

'So, Sebastian, about the matter of monogamy. How does it change when you fall in love? Are you faithful then?'

'I don't.'

'Don't what?'

'Don't love.'

What? What was he talking about? How could he not love?

'I don't understand.'

'I don't feel romantic love. I haven't loved anyone since Lana when I was nineteen. My friends tell me it's because I haven't met the right person but I know that's not it.'

'Then what is it?' I asked in desperate exasperation.

'I just don't love.'

He stared at me defiantly as though he'd just informed me he really didn't like beach holidays. Or voting for the Tories. Or listening to hip hop. Not as though he had just announced he was inhuman.

My feelings for Sebastian, my respect, awe and admiration for him were fast unravelling. What was the point to life without love? There was none. What, then was the point for Sebastian?

Everything and nothing seemed to fall into place. Sebastian saw the disgusted shock on my face. He reached out to rub my shoulder tenderly.

We started to kiss. I am kissing a tin man, I told myself. See how it feels. Admire its novelty. But it felt no different to any other time we had kissed this way. Maybe I was being dramatic. Maybe this could still be OK. Sebastian rolled tighter towards me. Then he lifted up my dress and grabbed at my hips urgently, pulled at the fabric of my knickers clumsily so that I had to help him remove them. He undressed himself and I followed suit. In a minute or so, having barely taken any time whatsoever to touch his skin against mine, he had entered me and we ground against each other, urgently, hard and hot.

But it was like making love to a mannequin. No, forget the making love part. That was never going to come into it, was it? Suddenly I had never felt so detached from Sebastian. I seemed to be hovering a finger's breadth above my body, looking down on him touching me. He might as well have ordered me in.

As he began to slow-thrust me, I felt something in me release, as though Sebastian had quietly removed my newly acquired armour. His body coaxed mine into relinquishing to him, every single time. Even now, even after every awful desecrating thing that he'd said this afternoon and this evening, even as my head still resisted him, my body responded with love to his touch. His crotch ground tightly against mine, and caught my clitoris rhythmically. His strokes felt even deeper, more urgent this evening, every inch of my insides enlivened to the sensation of him urging up inside me.

And then, as if hit by a wave while I'd had my back turned against the tide, I was sucked into an aching orgasm, a rabid, intense G-spot orgasm, the first I had ever had with him. I lay there, panting. I was confused. Was that my heart's last-ditch attempt at trying to connect with him, even when my head resolutely refused?

Afterwards, I stared at the chink of moonlight that snuck through the gap in the curtains. Loving Sebastian was like letting him massage my heart with sandpaper. Only now he'd ground it right down to a single, tremulous vein.

I turned to face him. He was already asleep. How could he already be asleep? Why didn't he feel as though all future happiness had quietly, and quickly, just had its throat slit before him? Didn't he feel our abysmal loss?

I turned back to look at the curtains. What was I even doing here any longer? I couldn't carry on as if we'd had a minor tiff and agreed to work through it. I had to go. I had to get up right now and go and never come back. I lay there and counted to three. One. How I wish I'd never met him. Two. How I wish I'd never submitted to him. Three.

'I'm going to go.'

I sprang up out of the bed.

Sebastian's eyes opened.

'What?' he exclaimed. He was utterly confused, I could tell.

'I'm kidding myself if I think I can do this.'

'You're going to go now? I can sleep on the floor, don't go. I thought things were OK?'

I fumbled around for my clothes then flung them on clumsily, nipping my skin in the zip of my dress as I did so. Where were my knickers? Oh, who cared. I just needed to get out of here. What had Sebastian done with my shoes?

'Come on, Nichi, don't go like this. Look, let's just sleep and we'll talk about it again in the morning.' He looked up at me. 'Or not. You can just go then, if that's what you want.'

If that's what I want? So Sebastian wasn't going to even try to persuade me to change my mind? Did he care that little? Could he really be so fatalistic about this? Sebastian hadn't the faintest idea what I wanted or he would never have come out with such a blasé, feckless statement.

Well then. Might as well put it all on the line. 'Sebastian.' My voice was threatening to break at any moment. I wasn't sure if I could even get the next sentence out but it had to be said. 'I'm heartbroken.' I paused and forced a steady breath through the fast-forming tears. 'I never thought I could feel like this about anyone ever again after Christos . . .'

Sebastian lay stock-still on the bed, looking as though someone had just indicted him of a terrible crime he had not committed. And then he hit back with impossible coolness.

'I do care about you, Nichi, just not in the way you might want me to.'

At that moment, something inside me gave up. I grabbed my bag and edged out of the room. 'Honestly, I rue the day you ever darkened my door.' So it had been Violet's door but the point remained.

I thought back to that night. He'd positively glowed in the lamplight. He'd made me believe again, in just those first few seconds, that love at first sight was not just a naïve fantasy but a raw, real wonder that, when it came, could sweep your soul off its feet.

'Come on, Nichi!' He was defiant, irritable, almost angry. That kind of incantation, that desire to wish him away, had shocked him. Well, good. Maybe now he might start to understand what he meant to me, and what a terrible thing he'd done by leading me on all this time.

I felt one final sentiment in me rise, and let it burst out. 'You can't love me, Sebastian!' I waited for his rebuke. But it didn't come. Then I said it again in quiet agony. 'You can't love me!'

His silence confirmed the truth of my cry.

There was nothing more to say. And so I left.

Chapter 20

When I left Sebastian's that night, I knew the best thing from here on was for me to never see him again. The thought of not having him in my life was unbearable. But what good could come of any kind of relationship with an emotional leper? Still, the memories were seared into my body. Sebastian would be with me for God knows how long.

On Tuesday morning I arrived at work to find a large box waiting for me on my desk. My heart knotted around itself. There it was. My make-up bag, as requested. So Sebastian could at least do this for me. I approached the box and slid my fingers over the ends, holding the box there for a moment before I opened it, holding it where Sebastian must have held it before he sent it on its way to me. I felt as though my body might cry soft tears from every pore, and soak the cardboard.

He'd texted me again in the early hours. 'I've sent your things. Look out for the toothbrush; it's wrapped separately. Sx.' And then there'd been a second message. 'Let me know at some point if you want to meet up and talk, although I understand if not. I just hope last night was not the last time I'll ever see you.'

I opened the box. There, wrapped inside tightly scrunched newspaper, was my old dusky pink make-up bag, painted flowers flaking from its tired-looking leather skin, as if they'd withered away under the blast of the argument with Sebastian. The newspaper was the one I had flung away before we had gone through the motions of something other people called making love. My things were charged with Sebastian's loveless-ness. To touch them drove me to tears.

There was no note. I traced my fingers over my name written on the packaging in Sebastian's careful scrawl. I'd never seen his handwriting before. I lingered there for a few more seconds, then stored the cardboard box carefully under my desk. I would keep it there for weeks to come.

Once I had thanked Sebastian for the safe return of my bag, there was no reason to be in contact about anything else. And so we weren't. In the weeks that followed, I felt as though someone had gently draped a shroud over me and was waiting patiently for me to give up on life.

During working hours I somehow managed to muddle through. I worked ferociously until my eyes stung from staring at the computer screen, and broke only to make camomile tea and smoke. Bar the odd shared fag at a party, I'd never ever smoked before. But I may as well. What did it matter if I ruined my face with wrinkles?

I couldn't eat. Food felt as though it were feeding my agony.

My lack of appetite felt like more than the archetypal response to heartache. For the first time in years I was driven to actively starving myself again. I wanted to starve away the pain of Sebastian not loving me. But I also wanted to whittle away at myself until I resembled the radiantly lithe Queen Rania or any one of the slender, raven-haired, olive-skinned beauties who populated Sebastian's fantasies. As the time passed, my agony latched on to the memories of those awful humiliating discussions we'd had. I felt jealousy and heartbreak and self-loathing tearing at me. Late at night I lay awake and imagined Sebastian making love to other women. They were always exotic-looking. Back in the days when I had been domming, the clients had sometimes told me about their cuckolding fantasies, which involved them imagining their wives being ravished by better-looking men as they were forced to watch in humiliated agony. With my torturous thoughts, I realised I was inflicting a similar imaginary cuckolding on myself.

The fact of the matter was that I was never, ever going to look like a woman Sebastian could love. A conversation we'd had months ago now came to me. I'd been complaining about the roundness of my face, and wondering whether it was possible to have surgery to 'suck it out a bit'. It was the kind of remark that I would have recoiled from the moment I said it, and that Christos would have shot down as soon as it had left my lips. But Sebastian just smiled sympathetically as I contemplated whether surgery was a step too far.

Even Tim, my personal trainer, had noticed my malaise. 'Come on, Nichi, why are you so down on yourself all of a sudden? You're getting so strong now, so fit. You look great!'

I had been considering running a marathon but without eating properly I couldn't even think about running.

Gina called me every few days to check up on me. 'If I think you're not eating, Nichi, I'm coming over there to make you a packed lunch every day.'

'What's the point, Gina?' I would sob at her over the phone. 'I needed to lose half a stone anyway.'

'Nichi, don't even go there! This is not the way and you know it. Don't let this man make you ill and spoil all the good things you've worked so hard to create for yourself.'

During all the days and nights that suggested it might actually be very possible to die of a broken heart, it was thinking back to my split from Christos that reminded me that, however much of a cliché it was, in time, all things healed. If I'd recovered from losing the man who had loved me more deeply than I knew love could run, I could surely get over someone who seemed to have no idea what love was.

I had started to refer to Sebastian as the Tin Man, to myself and to anyone I discussed him with. I still found it impossible to believe that he could not love and wondered if it was just that he was too much of a coward to admit that he couldn't love me. I fantasised that if I'd only got to him before Lana had broken him down, the Sebastian I had thought I was getting to know would have been the one I ended up with. But I hadn't, and he wasn't. And I needed to move on.

So instead I planned a last-minute working holiday to Japan. A friend of a friend was organising the PR for the inaugural Rainbow Pride festival in Tokyo, and asked if I could help her find media outlets in Britain to cover the event. Finally, the journalist in me that had been sedated into miserable inaction stirred from her lovelorn stupor. Thank God nothing could kill my ambition. And so I decided to go and speculatively cover the festival myself, pitching to numerous magazines and papers in the hope that I might get a commission or two. If not, then I would at least have had a reviving trip. I asked Gina to come with me.

'Um, hell yes! This would be amazing! Look at you, all big-timing it. I've always wanted to go to Japan and I'd love to travel with you,' Gina gabbled at me excitedly.

'Well, I'm not exactly big-timing – no one's actually given me a commission yet,' I said. 'But I'm hopeful I can get a bit of work out of it. It's exciting to do it this way around. And there'll be time to do other things, too, although even the work will be fun – you're up for testing out some bars with me for a travel piece, aren't you? We should have a day or two at the end to go to some of the local temples.'

'I'm sold, Nichi. You know, I'm proud of you for deciding to do this. It's just what you need right now. Forget Sebastian. Fuck him! Or not any more, as the case may be!'

Just before we left, Sebastian sent me an email. A long email. A significant email.

Hello,

I don't want you to feel pestered, so please put me on ignore if you feel the need. There's a bit of a Catch-22 involved in giving you space yet caring, so I'll risk it.

I feel like things got very intense in a way that slipped into some painful territory for both of us. At the moment it feels like some kind of lingering dream that gets even less clear in the passing days. Some beauty, and some really raw, gut-level rending. Joy, lust, fear, and then a puff of smoke. There are pleasant memories, veiled threats. Some paranoia on both our parts. I don't really know what to make of it.

But that's not really what I wanted to say. I suppose the most important thing for me to express is that I feel my life would be less rich without you in it, in whatever capacity that is, and that I'm glad we met. For me, our connection has been very real, sometimes delirious and out of control, but always significant to me. I can't deal with you thinking I don't care about you.

Perhaps our expectations and emotions regarding each other are different, but that does not change the fact that it has all been very consequential to me, our meeting. I don't meet someone like you every day. You've touched my life.

I can understand your regrets, if you feel them towards having met me. I hope very much they change in time.

I'm happy to give you space, and quite frankly, I might need it, too. But not for too long, if it's at all up to me.

Sx

The first feeling I had when I read it was one of relief. So I wasn't crazy. So I hadn't imagined Sebastian had had feelings for me, after all. The second was anger. Why couldn't he have expressed any of this properly that last time we met? Or even before that? And then, the third feeling, of discontent, told me it wouldn't have made any difference anyway. There was still no advance on the no-love, no-monogamy offer. But it was a gesture. 'You've touched my life.' Wasn't that the best any of us could ever hope to do?

I told Sebastian that I was just about to go to Japan and that I'd reply on my return. 'But thank you for sending that.'

★   ★   ★

A few days later, as Gina and I waited for our flight to Tokyo, I told her about the email. She wasn't touched the way I had been, even though she recognised that it sounded as though Sebastian was genuinely contrite.

'Nichi, look, I've no doubt that the man has some good qualities, and probably a lot of good intentions. But he hasn't had to watch you tear yourself apart ever since you met him. He hasn't watched you come home after a date with him, morose until he texts you again. He hasn't heard you cry yourself to sleep for being born the way you are. He hasn't had to worry that you were going to start starving yourself again . . .' Gina broke off. There were actually tears in her eyes.

'Oh Gina, God, you're an incredible friend, there's nothing to cry over!' Her declaration of care made me feel like crying too. 'Please don't worry. I'm not going to start starving myself again; I can't go back there. And, I can't go back to Sebastian either. It's just, a tiny part of me can't help wondering whether this could be the start of something else. Maybe a genuine, platonic friendship could redeem some of the awfulness that has passed between us.'

Gina wiped her eyes and gave a laugh. 'Jesus, I'm getting sentimental in my old age. Let's just get on this plane to Tokyo, shall we? Go have some fun and see how you feel when you get back.'

'You're on.'

Thankfully, from the moment we got to Japan I had no time to dwell on any of this. Having bombarded every national news desk and features editor with email pitches, I secured three article commissions and did radio interviews in the early hours, staring out at the neon glitter of Tokyo's skyline as I shared my newly acquired cultural insights with listeners from Malvern to Macclesfield. I wrote late into the night to meet London teatime deadlines. Finally, my mind was free to focus on the one thing that could truly distract me from the complications of my own life – meeting other people and listening to their stories, then passing them on. No solace like someone else's story, I had once said to Sebastian, when, dismayed by losing funding for a major project, he had asked me to recommend some diverting reading material. It was time I took my own advice.

And Japan, especially Japan in Gina's company, really was the best place to soothe me back to strength. I didn't need time to dwell any more. I needed to be reminded that life was full of wonders. Tokyo, with its rainbow-painted taxis, Sunday dress-up rituals and relentless nightlife, was just the job, and Gina and I created a hundred more colourful anecdotes for ourselves. I worked as hard during the day as Gina and I partied at night, and our genial Japanese hosts were only too happy to show us around the city's carnivalesque nightspots. We drank delicious blackcurrant cocktails, danced to Japanese teeny-bopper pop and filmed one another singing the entire Abba back catalogue in private karaoke booth after private karaoke booth. Everywhere we went I had my English cleavage eyed up and my hair fondled. It was a full week before I saw another blonde. For once, I was 'exotic'.

On Rainbow Pride parade day I had to be up at the crack of dawn to decorate myself before I went off to report on the proceedings. Just because I was working didn't mean I couldn't look the part, too. In fact, dressing up might be a good ruse for getting a better story, I decided. Nobody likes a po-faced, khaki-clad journalist bounding up to report on his or her kooki-ness.

Before long, Gina and I were perfectly kitted out. We had spent far too much time in the Harajuku district, where the lissom manga-eyed sales assistants sold us all manner of over-the-top accoutrements, telling us 'No wig, no life!' in between high-pitched giggles. I wore the French-maid-style pinafore dress I had worn the night I met Sapphire, accessorised with fishnet polka-dot tights, lurid orange and blue nails and candy-coloured make-up to match my ice-cream sundae wig. Gina, meanwhile, had a romper suit, lace-trimmed ankle socks and a Disney princess-style brunette wig. She even very sweetly set her alarm so that she could attend to my false eyelashes for me before I left the hotel.

'I'm going to meet you at 12.00 by the press tent. Don't run off with any hot Japanese *akusas* without me, OK?' she warned me.

'*Akusas?*'

'You know, the Japanese mafia men with full-body tattoos. I know what you're like when you see men with tattoos.'

I shook my head and laughed. 'Dressed like this?'

'Definitely like that! You look like an anime dream!'

On the way to the park a handsome American tourist stopped me. '*Ohayo gozimas!* Picture?' He gestured to his camera.

'Oh sure,' I replied, slightly incredulous.

'You make such a good Harajuku girl!'

I laughed him off, hurrying on to begin my work. At the press tent I had been assigned a translator who would help me to ask the Japanese gay, bi, lesbian, trans and omnisexual revellers questions about their political beliefs and sex lives. In among the stories of prejudice, misery, love and joy, there were also some pretty hilarious lost-in-translation moments. As the day went on, I met bloggers and campaigners and even Japan's Minister for Equality. Overwhelmed by the proximity to such a dignitary, I barely managed a bow, caught as I was between not wanting to offend by not stooping low enough and not wanting to offend by my boobs escaping my bodice. I then committed the heinous social faux pas of not returning her business card with one of my own. Between the low-cut pinafore and the confectionary wig, the Swedish drag-ghoul I'd interviewed and a troop of gay Pokemon I'd posed for pictures with, there hadn't been much time to worry about how to carry business cards about my person.

Gina joined me an hour or two later, with some newly acquired Japanese friends in tow, and after the march, there were rousing political speeches and dancing in the decorated square. In a country without legal rights for gay couples, it was poignant to see so many people of all sexual orientations and genders celebrating the right to love.

One of Gina's new friends, Aiko, offered to take us for dinner in Shinjuku. Outside the station, a gaggle of Japanese people of all ages started to laugh and point at me, gasping as if they'd never seen a small white girl wearing an ice-cream sundae wig. 'I thought this was the land of costume?' I asked Aiko. 'It can't just be the ladder in my tights, surely?'

Aiko was laughing fit to burst. 'I think they think you're Lady Gaga!'

The one thing still weighing heavily on my mind was the matter of love, or rather Sebastian's inability to feel it. One day towards the end of my trip, I had sat in a deserted side-chamber of Tokyo's famous Senso-ji temple for twenty minutes in front of a statue of Buddha and contemplated what love might mean to Sebastian. Did Sebastian love his family? His friends? Did he merely not fall into it any more? Did he never experience pinpricks of it? And if he didn't love did that mean he didn't experience real connection with someone else? Or longing for them?

I wanted to know. I wanted to ask him. But what would I do with the answers? He couldn't love me and that's all that mattered. So instead I lit a candle for Sebastian, there in the temple, and prayed that one day his heart might thaw, that eventually he might find love with someone else.

And then I prayed for peace for the both of us.

On our last night in Tokyo, I was determined to revel in this newly recovered sense of what it felt like to be myself, and to feel good about it.

Gina and I had been invited by our hosts to an all-night end-of-season party at Tokyo's most notorious gay club, a resplendent theatre of decadent dreams built over three floors with drag queen go-go dancers and an outdoor rooftop swimming pool that sprayed water across the sweaty al fresco dancers. Gina and I were fast running out of money, with only one vodka and coke and two caffeine tablets between us. But I can't remember dancing a whole night away with more verve and enthusiasm than the way we did there.

As the evening wore on, I noticed a sexy mixed-race guy with a shaved head and the most incredible smile executing some inspired dance moves. I pointed him out to Gina. 'Classic! Hottest guy for ages, and he's gay!'

'Well, you must have known our chances of pulling were pretty low here, love!'

Gina and I carried on dancing, and as we danced, the man in question seemed to edge nearer to us, until quite suddenly he was unmistakably dancing with me.

'I'm Joel,' he said in a polite, Midwestern US accent, giving a mock bow as he doffed his cap with a deep flourish and flashed his perfect teeth at me, all without missing a beat.

We danced together for two hours, weaving in and out of one another's movements as we got to know one another. It turned out that Joel was actually a professional dancer, just finishing a tour of Tokyo and bound for New York the following morning, 'so I figured I'd stay up all night and sleep on the plane.'

'Likewise!' I laughed.

'Well then, we'd better make the most of it!' And with that he leaned towards me and had me whipped about in his arms before I could even pretend that I was about to venture off in the other direction. We danced like this for another hour or so, before Gina reappeared, exhausted and pointing to her wrist. We needed to catch the first train back to the hotel if we were to make our flight.

'What's your email address?' he asked me. I told him. But how the hell was he going to remember it? I know. I pulled out my fuschia lipstick and scrawled my email address down his arm.

He grinned and held his arm out from his body awkwardly. 'I'm not going to bend, I'm not going to dance, I'm not going to sweat, I'm just going to preserve your email address for as long as I possibly can on my arm here!'

It worked. He'd added me to Facebook by the time Gina and I had reached our hotel an hour later.

But before we left, Joel and I had kissed.

When I arrived back from Tokyo two days later I felt as though my internal circuit board had finally sparked back to life. I was reenergised, full of new ideas for similar travel-writing based ventures, and thinking seriously about taking the plunge to becoming a full-time freelance journalist.

Most importantly of all, finally, I felt free of Sebastian. What Japan had given me was the space to realise how toxic our relationship was, and always would be. For months he had made me feel as though I needed his affections and his attentions to feel whole, when really, I had been whole all along. It was he who had been lacking, taking advantage of my capacity to offer care and love, knowing full well he could never reciprocate.

Of course, none of this pain and heartbreak had anything to do with the BDSM aspect of our relationship. I thought about that conversation Christos and I had once had about it, my presumption and prejudice that all women who enjoyed submitting to men were damaged. I didn't regret the sex for one moment, well, except the scissor sex. But that was so toxic precisely because of the dynamic between Sebastian and me. Besides, once you'd crossed over to kinkdom there was no going back to straight vanilla sex. In time, perhaps not too long a period of time, I'd be ready to start over with someone who relished all the pleasures it could bring, but who also understood the meaning of love and respect. I had never met anybody who had me feel so disrespected, nor so emotionally depleted. And nor, inadvertently, so optimistic about the future, a future that did not contain him.

Sebastian and I were done.

Chapter 21

Tokyo had rewired me; now I needed to make sure there was no danger of slipping back into recently acquired bad habits. Finally, I snapped out of my self-obsessed narcissism. 'As the soul is far more worthy than the body, it deserves to be all the more cultivated and adorned.'

It was my favourite quote, ironically from the Renaissance courtier's manual I'd sat reading the night all those moons ago when Christos had commented on my red lips. Even a book advising men on the best way to seduce women several hundred years ago knew that real allure came from the inside. Ever since, I'd had it stuck to a small sliver of card above my desk at home, so that if I was letting petty, destructive thoughts about my appearance (or now, Sebastian) distract me from writing about rape, or the persecution of gay, bi or transgender people in Russia, or how the US government restricted safe access to abortion, I would remember what really mattered. I returned to it now. Work on your soul, I thought.

I went back to yoga. It was the practice that had taught me to appreciate my body for all it could do, not all that it couldn't or wasn't after I'd recovered from anorexia, and I knew it was the practice that would help me to heal now. It helped me foster a peace which permeated every other area of my life, allowed me to work under pressure more easily, reminded me to check up on my friends, to look out for the old man with the drinking problem who lived in my flat block, to ring my family and to be grateful for all my many blessings.

And then I got a cat. Ever since I'd moved to London I'd

been pining for a pet. In a rare twist of serendipity, Violet sent an email around saying that an escort friend of hers had had to bring her old cat to work because it didn't get on with her new dog. Did anyone know of someone who might re-home Brothel Kitty?

I went to meet him. He was rangily handsome, a too-white tabby with very pale green eyes, a brick-coloured nose and a striped brown chin that made him look as though he were sporting a goatee. Immediately he jumped into my lap. And so it was that I acquired Snap, the most wilful and demanding of cats.

Once re-homed with me, he was like the neediest of submissives, an expert in topping from the bottom, and would head-butt my fingers off the keyboard as I typed or scratch ferociously at the bedroom door in the middle of the night to be let in for a pet. If I'd been out all day, he would aggressively miaow when I opened the door and jump up at me, placing a white paw on my leg until he got the caresses he craved.

Gina came round to see him once he was installed. 'Trust you to acquire a cuddle-monster cat, Nichi!'

'I know, I know,' I laughed. 'He got too used to being petted by lots of nice naked ladies in the brothel. But it's a delight. Not the being woken up every night, but everything else. Although he did try to get down my top the other day . . .'

'Please, you are not being molested by your cat!' laughed Gina. 'Anyway, other VIP matters – how's the job-hunting going?'

Just as my personal life had been radically shaken up, so, on my return from Japan, was my professional one. I had come back to London to find out that, due to a lack of funds, I was being let go from my current job with immediate effect. And yet I had quickly begun to view it as a blessing in disguise. I had no money saved and only the smallest amount of writing work lined up, but my modest successes in Tokyo had convinced me that I could make it as a freelancer if I put my mind to it.

'I've only just really started properly looking, to be honest. I've decided I don't want another staff job. I want to free up time to write.'

'Hmm, sounds good. I'm wondering if there's anyone I know who might have some contacts for you,' Gina pondered aloud. 'You don't seem too stressed about it. Is that the yoga working?'

'Partly. . . But I think it's just more that after dealing with Sebastian, I reckon I can cope with anything.'

One wet Monday, I emailed round my friends to ask if anyone had any magazine contacts I could try to tap for work. A couple of them came back with suggestions. And then Gina called me. 'I'm putting you in touch with a friend of a friend, some guy who was looking for a copywriter for the design company he worked for. He's an absolute sweetheart. Called Jake. An all-round creative whizz and a really good egg. Drop him a line.'

As is often the case in London's incestuous medialand, it turned out that Jake and I had more than a few friends in common. But the Chinese whisper about looking for a copywriter turned out to be just that.

'Nichi, I'm so sorry, I wish I could help but there's no work going where I'm based!'

'Oh, no worries', I replied.

'I'm surprised you're job-hunting though. You write about sexual politics and things, don't you? I read all your stuff. I love your work!'

I love your work? I was just another one of the thousands of small-time journalists with odd bits in the nationals. I love your work? What a line! Who was this guy?

'Ha! Well, that's just the freelancer's lot. Always touting . . . Sorry to have bothered you, Jake.'

'Not at all! Why don't you add me on Facebook? That way if any of my friends have any work I can point them in your direction.'

Well, sure, no problem. This was how casual networking functioned.

I signed in a few days later and had a proper look at Jake's profile. My God, he was cute. Actually startlingly handsome with a wedge of playfully styled dark-blond hair, a wry smile, and the sexiest, hooded brown eyes. His profile page was filled with inspiring, unstaged shots of him out with his friends; at their picnics and parties, riding, skating, trekking, and painting. Painting? Oh God, no, please no more artists. But no, he was actually studying for a Masters in fine art in his own time. By day, he was a successful graphic designer with his own business. I liked the look of Jake.

The next day there was a message from him. 'Hey Nichi, I'm sorry I haven't been able to help workwise but I actually have a favour to ask you. I'm working on a portraiture module for my Masters and I was wondering if you might let me paint you? I'm asking lots of friends and contacts on Facebook so please don't worry if you can't. Jake.'

Oh God. No. No painting. I began to write him a note to decline. Snap jumped up on to the desk, demanding my hand, and promptly sat on the keyboard. The message disappeared. This cat needed some serious house-training. I sighed. Gina was calling, I'd sort it out later.

Later that evening, I saw Jake online. He instant-messaged me.

'Hey Nichi, how are you? Just checking if you got my email?'

Oh God, I'd completely forgotten to reply to it.

'Hi Jake, argh, so sorry, this will sound like a mad excuse but I did reply and then Snap deleted it before I could send.'

'Snap?'

'Sorry! My cat!'

'Oh! I was thinking you had some possessive, domineering bf who intercepted your communications with strange men, lol.'

'Ha. No. Alas not.'

'So would you be interested in the portrait?'

I took my fingers off the keyboard. I really should just have sent him an email. It was awful to get caught like this, having to explain yourself.

'Jake, I'm really sorry but I just don't have the time right now.'

'Oh but you don't need any time. You don't need to sit for me or anything. I was just wondering if I could use one of your profile pictures and make a drawing from that.'

Oh. Oh! Bloody hell, what was I going to say now? Now I was going to have to explain why I felt awkward about him doing it. Which would make me sound all uptight and narcissistic again. Which I might have been a few weeks ago but I really wasn't now. Well, no I was desperately trying not to be now. But I really didn't want to have to admit my silly insecurities to Jake. Anyway I didn't have to go in to detail. Just be firm. Invoke the domme! Say no!

'You have the most amazing eyes. And your face is such a unique shape.'

Ha ha. That was one way of describing the golden egg!

'Well, that's sweet!'

'Please?' typed Jake and sent a pleading emoticon.

I blushed hotly in front of my computer screen. No, Nichi, no! This was the stuff that didn't matter any more, I'd been telling myself for weeks. And yet it felt so nice to have someone pay me a compliment. I'd actually almost forgotten what it felt like.

Oh why not, what harm could it do.

Three days later Gina called me. 'Nichi! Have you been on Facebook? Get on Facebook now!'

I looked at the clock. It was 5.52 a.m. Even Snap, who generally functioned as my alarm clock, but had been curled up next to my head on the pillow, looked aggrieved at having been disturbed.

'Gina! Why are you up at this time?'

'I haven't been to bed yet, we had a lock-in at the restaurant. Anyway, did you check your FB page last night?'

Did I what? Oh, well, no. I'd been boxing with Tim, my trainer. And then I'd watched *Newsnight* and gone to bed.

'Well log in now. While I'm on the phone to you!'

'Gina, what the hell?'

'DO IT, bitch!' She affected a mock-uber-domme voice.

'OK, OK, hang on!'

'Can you see it yet?'

'Gina, I'm going to hang up in a minute, hang on! Right, OK, it's just loading now. OK I'm signed in . . . what am I looking . . .'

I answered my own question. There on the wall of my Facebook page was an exquisite painting of me. Jake had taken one of my better headshots and produced an impossibly flattering portrait colouring in my green eyes and my painted lips even more vividly. He hadn't altered the shape of my face, but somehow my cheeks didn't look quite so puffy painted so proficiently.

'I told you you needed to log in to Facebook!' Gina said in triumph, 'that's like the biggest come-on EVER! Has anyone ever drawn a picture of you before? This guy wants you.'

'We've never even met!'

'Yeah, well that's about to change. You're coming to this free art festival with me on Saturday. My friend Rebecca told me about it. Jake will be there. You're going to meet him.'

'Gina, what are you doing, I'm not ready to meet anyone else! I'm barely over Sebastian.'

'I'm not asking you to go out with the guy, just to hang around with someone who's nice for once! You might make some journo contacts. Anyway, you now need to say thank you to him for stroking your bruised ego back to full health!'

I was sceptical, but there was no resisting Gina when she'd formulated one of her dogged plans. On Sunday, I met her at Trafalgar Square where the event was being held. It was an alternative art fair, brimming with stalls displaying stunning, quirky textile pieces, sculptures and paintings by all kinds of artists working in mixed media. If I hadn't known better I might have worried that I would bump into Sebastian, but for months he'd been planning to go to Amsterdam to work on an expo out there.

'You look nice!' said Gina when she saw me. I'd taken the opportunity to pull on a bright shift dress, electric blue and orange, open at the back to reveal a flash of bright pink bra. I'd found an amazing necklace in a shop near my house that interwove all the exact same colours in a complementary rainbow. Plus some patent sherbet-orange heels I'd bought in Japan. They were utterly lurid but I loved them. And besides, it was an art fair after all.

Gina was dressed in her usual uniform of colour-pop jeans and flat boots, only this time she'd chosen an eye-grazing acid yellow. 'Well at least you're not going to lose me in a crowd, right?' she laughed. 'Anyway, colours are good. We like colours!'

Gina took out her phone and started tapping away at the screen.

'Who are you messaging?'

'Oh, just Jake. I got his number off Rebecca.'

'Gina!!'

'Come on, you have to say thank you for your picture! Aha, there he is now, over by that rubber jewellery stand. Manners, Nichi!'

I turned in the direction of the stall. Jake looked exactly like his pictures. Crazy blond hair, those sexy hooded eyes. He was slim but perfectly proportioned, leanly muscular, as befitting a man who spent so much of his time tearing up and down mountains, or whizzing about London on skates. He was wearing a red sleeveless tank and black jeans. I was instantly attracted to him.

Gina slid her hand behind me and covertly slapped me on the backside. 'Off we go!'

Jake clearly knew some of the guys at the stall and was

laughing and joking with them over the jewellery, some of which looked far more like bondage wear. Hang on a minute, I recognised these guys. Sapphire and I had once bought some special dildo gags off them from a stall at the London Fetish Fair. Did that mean . . .?

'Nichi, hi!' Jake came towards me and kissed me suavely on either cheek. I blushed a brighter pink than the colour of my bra. Thank God you couldn't see it to compare from the front. He smelled like fresh citrus and old leather. Mmm.

I turned round to Gina. Wasn't she going to greet him, too? They'd already met, hadn't they?

'Hey Gina, how are you doing?'

She gave him a quick smile but it seemed she had things to do.

'Look, you two, I need to go and meet Rebecca, she's going to help me select an original sculpture for the restaurant. I'll call you in an hour and we can have drinks or something. Have fun.'

Gina! She was leaving me? What the hell were Jake and I going to talk about for an hour? I looked back at the rubber jewellery stall. And then up at Jake. He was smiling at me with a slight hint of expectation on his face. The picture. I needed to say something about it.

'So, Jake, I saw the portrait you did of me, that was really something.'

He grinned and gave a funny little mock bow with his head. 'You're welcome. Did you like it?'

'Well, of course, it's gorgeous!' Uh oh. Did that sound as though I thought *I* was gorgeous? 'I mean, it's terribly overly flattering but the execution is really something. You'd have made a great Renaissance court artist, you know.' I said to him.

'Ha! Now that would have been a job and a half. Although I would probably have abused my position!'

Abused his position?

'Oh really?' I ventured. 'How so?'

'Oh, you know. Probably just enjoyed ordering my sitters into position too readily.'

I looked at him. He looked straight back at me, and gave a tight-lipped smile. Oh God, Nichi, you can't think about anything without it being related back to kink! He's probably a social anarchist who just means he'd have enjoyed bossing about his spoilt aristocratic patrons. Not commanding the beautiful ladies in waiting to bare more shoulder. Think about higher things for once! Think about art!

I cleared my throat and smiled demurely back. 'Shall we take a look at some of this art then? What's good? Care to educate me?'

For the next hour or so we wended our way around the fair, comparing the work here with that of our favourite artists. At every second stall, Jake stopped and greeted the holders, many of whom he knew, paying them thoughtful compliments about their work. I'd never watched someone be hugged so enthusiastically by so many friends. It touched me. There was clearly something very special about Jake, and it had nothing to do with his looks.

Suddenly my phone flashed up. It was Gina.

'How's it going with Jake?'

'Fine,' I replied cryptically. She must have known I couldn't possibly elucidate in front of him.

'He hasn't tied you up yet, then?'

'What are you talking about?'

I could hear giggling in the background and Gina muttering something to, well, I presumed it must be Rebecca.

'You know Jake is a kinkster, Nichi? That's how Rebecca met him. Her company was doing some PR for the kink club and he was one of the fetish models they used. A Master model, might I add . . .'

I turned and looked at Jake as Gina told me this, tightening my phone to my ear to prevent Jake from overhearing this.

'Why do you think he was looking at the rubber jewellery?'

'Gina, you have to save me. Get back here right now!'

'Save you? I'm throwing you at his feet, lady. This man is perfect for you!'

I looked at Jake's face again. But how could he be a Master? He was so sweet. But then again, those hooded eyes of his. That mouth . . .

Gina spoke again. 'Anyway, I can see the pair of you now. We're heading over. Time for drinks!'

'Everything OK?' asked Jake, placing his hand on the back of my shoulder in concern.

'Oh . . . yes . . . Gina's just coming.' I gestured up the path. Thank God. I couldn't get another sentence out.

I'd fired up underneath his fingers. *How*?

Gina and Rebecca arrived, full of excitement about the sculpture they had just purchased for the restaurant. In fact, they'd been toasting it in vodka and Ribena, and were already a little on the inebriated side. 'Do you want some, guys? We need another toast.'

'Where's the bottle?' Gina fiddled around in her bag.

'Here!' I laughed, and reached into her bag, pulling out the now half empty container sloshing with the makeshift purple cocktail. 'I can't believe you actually mixed Ribena with vodka. I didn't even do that when I was fifteen!'

'Well, then, you better make up for it now, Nichi!' Jake took the spirit bottle off Gina and gave me an order. 'Take the lid off, Nichi, while I pour the rest of the vodka in.'

'Jake, careful!' chastised Rebecca. 'The whole reason we were decanting it is because you aren't allowed glass in here.'

'It's not a real rule, it's just about profit-making. No one's going to try and take this bottle off me, anyway.' He looked up at me from underneath his hooded eyes and gave me a devilish grin. I felt the bottle in my hands shake. Oh God. I was actually trembling.

'Oh, how gloriously teenage!' he pronounced. 'Although I wouldn't be an inept teenager again for anything!'

There was a stage set up in a corner of the square. 'Let's go check that out,' suggested Gina. We headed over and discovered some kind of unpalatable ambient noise.

'It's this sonic art collective I've heard about,' Jake informed me. 'I'm not sure how good they are but it's worth a provisional listen.' Besides, we couldn't exactly just drink vodka and Ribena lingering over other people's paintings.

Jake came up and stood behind me, from time to time placing one hand on my waist as he passed the bottle around. Ten minutes and no lunch later I was already feeling the effects of the alcohol. I was also conscious that Jake had stopped removing his hands from about my waist when he took the bottle back. I could smell his citrus and leather scent even more richly now. Was I imagining it or could I also feel his hot breath on my neck?

Suddenly my phone started ringing. I left Jake, Gina and Rebecca and headed away from the stage to take the call. It was a big commercial radio station I'd never worked for before. Could I come on for a panel debate tonight? I said yes. And then immediately regretted it. If I was to sound even remotely sentient I had to go home right now and sober up. This was the freelance life. Pleasure had to be wound up whenever professional opportunities presented themselves. But why had they called me right now, damn it!

I went back over to the others. 'Hey guys, I'm so sorry but I'm going to have to go. I just got a radio call. I'm on tonight. I need to go home and prepare.'

'Nooooo!' Gina gave me a tipsy hug.

'Let me walk you to the tube then?' Jake offered.

It was 4 p.m. on a bright Saturday afternoon. Maybe this wasn't that kind of walk.

I began to pick my way through the crowds and Jake came up behind me, placing a smooth hand on the back of my neck. I gave the slightest of stumbles over a stack of free art catalogues. He took hold of my hand in a firm grip, then as we came to the edge of the square, entwined his fingers into mine, more sensually.

I didn't dare look at him. Instead we walked silently up Regent Street, until, waiting to cross over one of the smaller roads, we locked eyes in the reflection of the shop window ahead of us. We both began to laugh at the clichéd romance of it.

Jake turned to me. 'So, Nichi, that picture I did for you, you can have it if you like.'

'Oh!' I blushed. 'That would be lovely, thank you. But don't you need it for your portrait portfolio?' We were nearing the top of Oxford Circus now where I was to get on the tube. Jake hesitated with his reply. 'I lied. I'd already handed in my portfolio. I just wanted to paint you.'

I looked up at him. His hooded eyes had widened, and he licked his just-parted lips. His face was full of longing. Then he brought his mouth back into that delicious wry smile. I gasped and started to laugh softly, as Jake pulled me to him. I slid my hands up around his athletic back as he felt his fingers up underneath my hair, using the lightest grip on it to guide me in to him. Then finally he took my face in his hands, and as he brought my mouth up to his, the buses and the shoppers and the noise melted away until all I could sense was Jake's breath on my lips.

'Because how else could I have got you to sit for me?'

And then we kissed.

Acknowledgements

My family, who worried about the content but still pledged their support.

My friends, Kristi, Steph, Lynette, Clemence and Natalie, and the fabulous Agios.

Tom, who kept me on track during the days, and Aaron and Snap who soothed the nights.

All those lovers who didn't make the cut but still breathe between the pages.

My copyeditor Helen Coyle who stripped back the prose so skilfully, my agent Lisa Moylett, all at Hodder for their timely and tireless work, and special thanks to my superb editor Fenella Bates, whose indefatigable faith and support meant I could run the memoir marathon with no training.

And finally, he who can't be named, yet let me.